NEW PROFICIENCY ENGLISH

BOOK TWO

Reading Comprehension

W. S. Fowler

Nelson

Thomas Nelson and Sons Ltd
Nelson House Mayfield Road
Walton-on-Thames Surrey KT12 5PL

51 York Place
Edinburgh EH1 3JD

Thomas Nelson (Hong Kong) Ltd
Toppan Building 10/F
22A Westlands Road
Quarry Bay Hong Kong

Distributed in Australia by

Thomas Nelson Australia
480 La Trobe Street,
Melbourne Victoria 3000
and in Sydney, Brisbane, Adelaide and Perth

First published by Thomas Nelson and Sons Ltd
1985
ISBN 0-17-555606-7

NPN 9 8 7 6 5

Designed by The New Book Factory
Phototypeset by Parkway Illustrated Press Ltd
Printed in Hong Kong

Contents

CONTENTS

Introduction

New Proficiency English

New Proficiency English is planned as a replacement of *Proficiency English*, published in 1976–8, and as a logical continuation of *New First Certificate English*, published in 1984. In effect, it is the result of several years' experience of using the previous course and gradually adapting materials to the needs of students taught at earlier stages in the learning process by different methods from those current in the early 1970s. As in the case of *New First Certificate English*, my co-authors, John Pidcock and Robin Rycroft, and I have preferred to write a new course, taking this experience into account, rather than to revise the original. While some elements that have proved particularly successful have been retained – above all in *Book 3, Use of English*, where the revised Cambridge syllabus of 1984 for the paper shows no innovations – over 80% of the material in the course is new.

By this time, it will be evident that the examination as such has not changed to a noticeable extent either in level of difficulty or in form, except in the design of the aural/oral tests (covered in this course by *Book 4*). The main change in approach, especially in *Book 1*, has therefore been to shift the emphasis away from the formal presentation of grammar towards the acquisition of skills. At the same time, the overall coverage remains the same.

The main problem for teachers at advanced level and for students attempting the Proficiency examination is that the former are inclined to relax the pressure once students have passed First Certificate because the Proficiency examination is still a long way away, while the latter underestimate the difference in standard. This course has been written for students likely to attempt the examination two years after First Certificate if they attend classes five hours a week (300 hours) or three years afterwards if they attend three hours a week (270 hours). The material has been pretested and graded through use with students at each stage to allow for the time-span envisaged, but it is above all important to point out that the language learning process should be continuous. Our experience leads us to believe that it is necessary to develop skills methodically throughout the period and that it is unwise to imagine that students can be left largely to their own devices for a year or so before making a systematic approach to the examination.

The design of the course

The four books comprising the new course can be used independently in order to concentrate on a specific paper in the examination, but they have been written in such a way that they relate to each other. The 18 units of *Book 2, Reading Comprehension*, reflect the themes chosen as a basis for composition topics in *Book 1* to a considerable extent, offering an opportunity for the revision and expansion of vocabulary. However, they are in no sense a repetition. I have included a wide selection of modern writing in English, relating passages within a unit to a common theme, but wherever possible providing contrasts in terms of style and approach. If the book is used in conjunction with others in the course, it will be helpful for teachers to study the chart printed in the *Teacher's Guide* in order to gain maximum benefit from the planned interrelation of units.

Lexis and Comprehension

The Cambridge examination in Reading Comprehension at Proficiency level follows exactly the same format as in First Certificate, though there are some differences in emphasis in the choice of passages. I have therefore employed similar techniques to those used in *New First Certificate English Book 2*, so that this book forms a logical continuation to it. Two sections of the paper require related, but, to some extent, different areas of knowledge and technical skills; I have discussed them separately below but it is not my intention that they should be divided off. The texts of the book serve two purposes throughout: they exemplify lexis in context, the only way in which new vocabulary can be satisfactorily learned and subsequently used, and they also serve as passages for comprehension. I have used a wide variety of exercises in this connection, explained in more detail below. These exercises, preceding and following the passages, are presented in the order in which I habitually use them in the classroom.

Lexis

Students at advanced level, especially if they are already accustomed to the techniques suggested in *New First Certificate English Book 2*, should by this time realise that it is essential to learn new lexical items as far as possible by working out the meaning for themselves in context. Techniques to aid students are fully exemplified in connection with the lexical content of the first passage in Unit 1.

The lexical exercises have three main purposes:
1 to help students to decide on the meaning of new words in context;
2 to expand their vocabulary in general terms by associating words with appropriate contexts and differentiating between them;
3 to point out words that are commonly confused either because they are apparently similar in meaning in English (e.g. **raise, rise**), or because they are deceptively close to words with a rather different range of usage in their own language (e.g. **advertise, advise, announce,** etc. for speakers of Latin languages).

From the point of view of the examination, there is undoubtedly a shift of emphasis at Proficiency level towards words of the second category, and away from those of the third. Test items depend much more on the recognition of the appropriate word in the context of customary English usage. While taking this into account, I have nevertheless continued to include exercises to clarify lexical problems that persist in students' compositions at advanced level. The examination typically reflects usage rather than semantic distinctions, but it is still important for students in a course of long duration such as this to resolve their own difficulties with words like **travel** and **journey**, **work** and **job**, or **lay** and **lie**.

I have dealt with the problems listed above as follows. In the first case, I have considered whether the meaning of unfamiliar words in the text can reasonably be deduced from the context. If it can be, I have provided students with aids towards intelligent guesses; if not, or if a cultural item of information is involved, I have given an explanation alongside. Vocabulary expansion is handled at first in two ways; in the first place, I have frequently introduced the theme of the passage with warm-up exercises, primarily reminding students of words they already know, but also introducing some related words that may be less familiar; secondly, in the early stages of the book, I have asked them to find words in the passage similar in meaning to those provided in the exercise, thereby confirming their understanding of them. Exercises on words that are commonly confused are included to help students to distinguish clearly between them, and particularly in the case of verbs (e.g. **suggest, urge**) to draw attention to the structural differences in usage.

Where these exercises mark a departure from the types used in *New First Certificate English Book 2* is in the area that is most important for advanced students. True synonyms are rare in English and at this level it is no longer sufficient to know, for example, that words like **banish**, **evict** and **expel** have similar meaning, but to learn to associate them with specific contexts. To a native speaker it appears natural to speak of someone being evicted from his flat for not having paid the rent, or expelled from school for bad behaviour, but we would not use the words interchangeably or substitute **banish** in either case. A series of exercises throughout the book aims at helping students to identify the contexts associated with such words.

A further development in lexical terms in comparison with First Certificate level is the need for students to appreciate the nuances of language, particularly when it is used humorously or emotionally. Students have seldom been prepared by their previous reading for passages such as *It's a Hard Life for Commuters,* (Unit 2), where the writer makes an everyday situation amusing by the use of exaggeration and by employing phrases normally found in different contexts, such as comparing commuters to cowboys. Students are advised to study the advice given in connection with that passage very carefully.

Apart from the three test papers at the end of the book, there are six lexical progress tests, appearing at intervals of three units, which incorporate items that are all drawn from the lexis previously presented. These tests have been thoroughly pretested according to the guidelines laid down by Cambridge for the selection of items in their own syllabus and sample paper. I am very grateful for the collaboration of over 500 students who took part in the pretesting, which was carried out in two schools in Barcelona with an above average pass-rate in the examination. Full details of the pretesting appear in the *Teacher's Guide*.

Comprehension

In the Introduction to the book that preceded this one, *Proficiency English Book 2* (1977), I stated that multiple-choice questions, whatever their merits as testing instruments elsewhere, are unsuitable for testing comprehension because they give rise to ambiguity and very often test students' logical powers rather than their understanding of language. This is particularly true at advanced level, although it is to be hoped that the greater variety of passages proposed in the new Cambridge syllabus will make the problem less acute in future. I continue to believe, however, that teachers should ask direct questions in class in the first instance to discover whether students have understood a passage completely, and many of the exercises in this book therefore take that form. With regard to the multiple-choice questions, I have given students advice on how best to deal with them, depending on the type of passage they are confronted with.

The passages set in the examination, three in all, are expected to be of four main types; one in which students are required to gain a general impression of the content (reading for gist); one which depends on close attention to detail; a third that may either demand a recognition of stylistic elements, such as the humorous techniques referred to above, or may include two or more contrasting letters or advertisements from which information is to be derived. All of these types are exemplified throughout the book, together with the techniques recommended for handling them.

Reading

After nearly twenty years of preparing students for the Cambridge Proficiency examination, I am more than ever convinced that the students who read widely outside the classroom are those who are most likely to make progress at advanced level, not only in terms of their lexical knowledge but also in self-expression in speech and writing. English is a relatively simply language grammatically but it has an almost infinite range of expression that no course book can hope to cover fully. Reading a prescribed book may be of some use in helping students to develop their vocabulary, but they should not restrict themselves to one book written in an individual way. Wherever possible, class libraries should be formed, enabling everyone to read a variety of modern texts; quality newspapers and magazines, if the cost of them is not prohibitive, will also provide a valuable source of vocabulary to be learnt and recognised in context.

This book can of necessity only present students with an indication of what is available in terms of reading, but it is my hope that they will be interested in the texts they read and be stimulated to read more widely. The exercises contained here should at the same time make them better equipped to enjoy their reading.

Will Fowler,
Barcelona, August 1984

Acknowledgements

I am very grateful to Simon Clackson, English Language Officer, Barcelona, Sheila Hennessey, Assistant Director of Studies, The British Council Institute, Barcelona, and Peter Clements, Director, the CIC, Barcelona, for permission to pretest all the test materials in this book in their schools. I would also like to thank all the teachers and students who took part, and in particular Peter Goode and Peter Knowles for a number of useful suggestions.

The publishers wish to thank the following for permission to reproduce photographs:

Kobal Collection pp 8, 45; Barnaby's Picture Library pp 21, 32, 94; Sally Anne Thompson Animal Photography Ltd p 58; Rex Features Ltd p 65; Camerapix Hutchison Library p 110.

Photography (p 140) and photographic research, Terry Gross

Thanks are due to the following for permission to reproduce copyright material:

The *Daily Telegraph* for an article by Mary Kenny; The *Sunday Times* for the extract from 'A Modern Crossing of Australia' by Mark Ottaway, published in *The Sunday Times* Magazine of 6 January, 1980; The Bodley Head Ltd and Simon & Schuster, Inc. for the extracts from *A Sort of Life* by Graham Greene; Laurence Pollinger and the Estate of Alan Moorehead for the extract from *Cooper's Creek*; The *Guardian* for the article 'Picking up on dropping a line' by John Ezard; The *Sunday Express* for the article 'Ballooning for fun' by Lynn Barber; The *Observer* for articles by Janet Watts, Michael Braham, John Cannon, Rosamund Castle, Angela Levin, Ena Kendall, Sue Arnold, Michael John White, John Davis and Joanna Slaughter; William Collins & Sons Ltd for the extract from *Birds, Beasts and Relatives* by Gerald Durrell; Macmillan, London and Basingstoke for the extracts from *Habits* by John Nicholson; Punch Publications Ltd for the extracts from *Pick of Punch* by Basil Boothroyd; The National Trust for three publicity extracts; The *Daily Mail* for 'Dear Dad, to explain the phone bill' by Howard Foster; *Hollywood Greats* © Barry Norman, 1979. Reprinted by permission of Hodder and Stoughton Ltd and Curtis Brown Ltd; *Taking Sides* © Bernard Levin, 1979. Reproduced by permission of Jonathan Cape Ltd and Curtis Brown Ltd; *Encounters with Animals* © Gerald Durrell, 1958. Reproduced by permission of Granada Publishing Ltd and Curtis Brown Ltd; The Illustrated London News Picture Library for the extract from 'Deserving Prizewinner' by Michael Billington; *Double Takes: Notes and Afterthoughts on the Movies, 1956–76* by Alexander Walker (Elm Tree Books, 1977); Harrap Ltd for the extract from *The Boundaries of Science* by Magnus Pyke; *My Life and Hard Times* © The collection Hamish Hamilton, 1963. From *Vintage Thurber* by James Thurber, published by Hamish Hamilton Ltd; American Express Europe Ltd for an extract from publicity material; John Murray (Publishers) Ltd for *A Time of Gifts* by Patrick Leigh Fermor; Bass Holidays for their Holiday Club International advertisement; Gillon Aitken for the extract from a Paul Theroux review; *Mrs Parkinson's Law* © C. Northcote Parkinson, 1968. Reproduced with permission of Dr Northcote Parkinson; Mrs H. Hall for the extract from *Britain's Locust Years* by William McElwee; The Hogarth Press for the extract from *Cider with Rosie* by Laurie Lee; Hutchinson Publishing Group Ltd for *Invasion of the Space Invaders* by Martin Amis; John Johnson Ltd for extracts from *The Persuasion Industry* by John Pearson and Graham Turner; The Advertising Standards Authority for an extract from a leaflet; Times Newspapers Ltd for an article by Alan Hamilton published in *The Times* 9 March 1984; 'Politics and the English Language', © 1946 Sonia Brownell Orwell, renewed by Sonia Orwell 1974. Reprinted from *Shooting an Elephant and other Essays* by George Orwell reproduced by permission of the Estate of the late Sonia Brownell Orwell, Martin Secker & Warburg Ltd and Harcourt Brace Jovanovich, Inc.; *The Financial Times* for the extract from *Prospects for a National Economy* by Kevin Done; The extract from *The Murder of Roger Ackroyd* by Agatha Christie © 1954 Agatha Christie Mallowan reprinted by permission of Hughes Massie Ltd and Harold Ober Associates, Inc.; Helga Greene for the extract from *The Little Sister* by Raymond Chandler.

Every effort has been made to trace owners of copyright, but if any omissions can be rectified the publishers will be pleased to make the necessary arrangements.

People

Introductory exercise

One way of expanding your vocabulary in a logical way is to consider words in groups that are in some way related. In that way, it is easier, not only to remember their meaning, but to associate them with the contexts in which they are most likely to reappear.

1 **The face:** point to each of the features mentioned below, and then see if you can add anything else to the list.

a) forehead
b) chin
c) lips
d) cheeks
e) eyebrows

2 **Clothing:** find someone in the class who is wearing each of these items of clothing, and then add to the list anything else you can see people wearing.

a) shirt
b) skirt
c) dress
d) sweater
e) waistcoat

3 **Footwear:** when and where would you normally wear these?

a) boots
b) gymshoes
c) sandals
d) slippers
e) wellingtons

From East to West

Read the following passage to gain a general impression of its content before studying the vocabulary in detail.

Madhur Jaffrey in *Heat and Dust*, 1983

You might know Madhur Jaffrey as the lovely lady who teaches you Indian cookery on television and in books; but she is also a film star, about to be seen in James Ivory's latest Indian movie, *Heat and Dust.* Madhur Jaffrey played **Shashi Kapoor's** mistress in Ivory's first film, *Shakespeare Wallah* (1964); in this new film she plays Shashi Kapoor's mother, the wicked old **Begum**, who watches her son the **Nawab** make a dishonest woman of a ravishing English rose (played by Greta Scacchi).

Off the screen, Madhur Jaffrey looks almost uncannily young and beautiful for her 49 years. But in *Heat and Dust,* without any of the gunk the make-up men thought she would need, Madhur Jaffrey presents the betel-chewing face of ancient Indian **dowagerhood**: powerful, devious, veiled in jewelled silk, menace and tobacco smoke.

She knew this face: she had met it plenty of times in her own family. But Madhur Jaffrey is herself elegant and eloquent, full of smiles and stories. On a drab winter morning she sat in a London hotel, radiating colour and warmth. The lustrous silk of her sari shone against a worn armchair; and she talked of an Indian past that is at the heart of her American present.

Madhur Jaffrey seems a Western woman in all the best ways – resourceful, enterprising, courageous – yet she is also deeply Indian. She sees her daughters growing up in a free society, and admits – reluctantly – to certain regrets about this.

'I was brought up in a very formal way. Girls never swore; we were escorted everywhere; and sometimes I think how nice it was, when I was growing up, to spend my time in the garden, and think the parrots and the flowers were lovely, and not to have to face the ugliness of life. At times that protection by the men – which I resented – seems charming, and I almost want it for my daughters. On the other hand, I fought it. So it can't have been that charming.'

Heat and Dust is a film about the relationship between East and West, and it is an affair in which the West seems the loser. Madhur Jaffrey feels sympathy, rather than resentment, for India's Western invaders – **the British Raj** that has gone, the tourists who are still coming. 'India can suck out all your starch, your crisp European consciousness: and everything you hold dear can seem to slip out into this Indian vastness.'

Not for her, of course. In India's complexity and contradictions Madhur Jaffrey finds her energy and strength. 'I'm part of the vastness – I'm its product. It's taking nothing away from me: because I *am* it.' In Indians, for all their submission to invaders and their technological backwardness, she sees little of an inferiority complex. 'They may have doubts like "Can I land a job?" – but they don't question their existence in the nice way Westerners do. Indians know who they are. On the whole they're a **cocky bunch**.'

From an article in the *Observer Magazine* by Janet Watts

Shashi Kapoor: actor who has played alongside Madhur Jaffrey in films
Begum: Muslim princess or lady of high rank
Nawab: Indian Muslim title similar to the European 'Duke'
dowagerhood: state of possessing a title derived from a former husband, usually used when the son has succeeded to the title
the British Raj: the British government of India (used especially of the period 1858–1947)
cocky bunch: (slang) self-confident bunch of people

A

Reading for gist

In many cases we read to gain a general impression of a text, rather than to study every detail. From an initial reading of this text, you might have noticed that it is constructed out of a series of contrasts.

1 Find phrases and sentences beginning with **but**, **yet** or **on the other hand** to note what these contrasts are.
2 Relate the following statements to the paragraphs they summarise, noting down an appropriate paragraph number for each.
   a) Madhur Jaffrey gives the impression of having a Western attitude to life, but remains closely identified with her Indian upbringing.
   b) Indians appear to be inferior to Westerners in some ways but, in fact, are more sure of themselves.
   c) Madhur Jaffrey sometimes feels nostalgic about her sheltered upbringing, but recognises that it must have had defects.
   d) Although she is extremely good-looking for her age, she had no difficulty in taking the part of a much older woman in the film.
   e) *Heat and Dust* seems to suggest that there was a struggle between East and West, but Madhur Jaffrey feels that it does not symbolise a Western defeat as much as the change that can take place in Europeans in India.
   f) In real life Madhur Jaffrey is very different from the character she portrayed in the film.

B

Unfamiliar words

When you come across a word for the first time in a reading passage, you may be tempted to stop reading and look it up in a dictionary. Before you do so, you should always try to work out the meaning from the context. This is important for two reasons:

a) because dictionaries do not necessarily give an equivalent in your own language or else give several, only one of which is appropriate to the passage you are reading;
b) because if you learn the meaning for yourself in the context without the help of a dictionary, you are much more likely to remember it and know when to use it.

One way to help decide the meaning of a word is to look at the form of the word and its position in the sentence to see what part of speech it is. Look at the second paragraph of the passage you have just read. The following words may be new to you: **uncannily, gunk, betel-chewing, devious, veiled, jewelled.**

Gunk is evidently a noun. It is something that the make-up men thought the actress might need. In fact, it is the heavy make-up required to make someone look different.

Betel is also a noun, and the character in the film 'chewed' it. The dictionary will tell you that it is a form of nut, but a reasonable guess would be close to the truth.

Devious is an adjective, which in context goes with 'powerful', 'menace' and 'veiled'. You might not guess its meaning exactly, but it implies from its context someone who is dangerous and not straightforward.

Veiled and **jewelled** are alike in form, but their position indicates that 'veiled' is a participle used in apposition, while 'jewelled' is an adjective. The words are derived from **veil** and **jewel**. The first is associated with a woman wearing a veil, but also implies that her personality is hidden behind the veil, the threat of her actions and the smoke from her cigarette. The second clearly means that she wore silk and that jewels were sewn into her clothes.

Uncannily is an adverb. There is a contrast between the actress's age and her youth and beauty. It means 'inexplicably' here, since it seems strange that a woman of 49 could look as she does.

Decide from the context what part of speech the following are and what their probable meaning is. Do not attempt to find a synonym, but make suggestions. e.g. It describes. . ., It is a thing that. . ., It means that she. . ., etc.

a) sari (line 42)   b) reluctantly (line 54)
c) resentment (line 79)   d) land (line 102)

A second way of making intelligent guesses about the meaning of words is to consider the way in which they fit in with those around them. Adjectives accompanying nouns are presumably appropriate. **Ravishing** (line 17) is applied to an 'English rose', and this is clearly not a flower but a young woman, 'played by Greta Scacchi'. In the context, it obviously means 'very attractive'.

Other adjectives in the passage are chosen so as to highlight the contrasts on which the passage depends. What do you think is the meaning of the following, taken from paragraph 3 of the passage?

1 **Elegant and eloquent** describe Madhur Jaffrey's real personality, as distinct from the character of the Begum, who was 'betel-chewing' and 'devious'.
2 **Drab**, describing a winter morning, contrasts with 'radiating colour and warmth'.
3 **Lustrous**, describing silk, contrasts with 'a worn armchair'.

C

Words often confused

1 The words which present the greatest problems to students are not new vocabulary, but those which *seem* familiar and yet are easily confused with another in their meaning or usage. Compare the use of the following in the passage: **plenty of** (line 34) and **full of** (line 37), **grow up** (line 52) and **bring up** (line 56).

Now complete the following sentences, and then make sentences of your own, using these words. Change the verb forms where necessary.

a) She has __________ money. Her house is __________ valuable objects.
She is __________ indignation because __________ young men ask her out and she knows they are only interested in her money.
b) She __________ in India. Her parents __________ her __________ in a formal way and so she __________ sheltered from society. Her daughters have been __________ differently in the West and have __________ in a different atmosphere.

2 Now compare the two sentences written below.

Heat and Dust is a film about the **relationship** between East and West.
A distant **relation** of mine was brought up in India.

Make sentences of your own, using **relationship** and **relation**.

3 A word in English may resemble another in the student's own language, and yet have a different, or more restricted meaning. In order to avoid making false assumptions about the meaning of words which *look* familiar, you should concentrate on the context to make sure the assumed meaning is, in fact, appropriate. Consider this sentence.

Madhur Jaffrey feels **sympathy**, rather than **resentment**, for India's Western invaders.

This means that she feels sorry for them in an understanding way, and does not carry hate for them inside her because they invaded her country. In what circumstances would you expect a person to be **sympathetic**, or **resentful**?

4 In the case of verbs, it is important to note the structures that can be used with them and the prepositions that may follow them. (If you are using Book 3 of this course, you can consult the appendix in that book for reference.) Study the examples indicating the different meanings and structures possible with the verb **admit**, and then make sentences of your own.

Only ticket-holders **are admitted to** the theatre. (allow to enter)
He **admitted** his responsibility/**that** he was responsible. (acknowledge)
She **admits to** having certain regrets about her daughter's upbringing. (confess to)

Now make sentences with these phrases.

a) the price of admission
b) an admission of guilt
c) no admittance except on business (**Admittance** is used when permission is required.)

First meeting with Sven

Read the following passage carefully, paying attention to detail, and noting down words you do not understand.

It was at this time, when I was deeply involved with the water spiders, that Sven Olson at last turned up. Larry had, to Mother's consternation, developed the habit of inviting hordes of painters, poets and authors to stay without any reference to her. Sven Olson was a sculptor and we had had some warning of his impending arrival, for he had been bombarding us for weeks with contradictory telegrams about his movements. These had driven Mother to distraction, because she kept having to make and unmake his bed. Mother and I were having a quiet cup of tea on the veranda when a cab made its appearance, wound its way up the drive and came to a stop in front of the house. In the back was seated an enormous man who bore a remarkable facial resemblance to the reconstructions of **Neanderthal Man**. He was clad in a white singlet, a pair of voluminous brightly checked **plus fours** and sandals. On his massive head was a broad-brimmed straw hat. The two holes situated one each side of the crown argued that this hat had been designed for the use of a horse. He got ponderously out of the cab carrying a very large and battered **Gladstone bag** and an accordion. Mother and I went down to greet him. As he saw us approaching, he swept off his hat and bowed, revealing that his enormous cranium was completely devoid of hair except for a strange, grey, tattered duck's tail on the nape of his neck.

'Mrs Durrell?' he enquired, fixing Mother with large and child-like blue eyes. 'I am enchanted to meet you. My name is Sven.'

His English was impeccable with scarcely any trace of an accent, but his voice was quite extraordinary for it wavered between a deep, rich baritone and a quavering falsetto, as though, in spite of his age, his voice was only just breaking. He extended a very large, white, spade-shaped hand to Mother and bowed once again.

'Well, I am glad you have managed to get here at last,' said Mother, brightly and untruthfully. 'Do come in and have some tea.'

I carried his accordion and his Gladstone bag and we all went and sat on the balcony and drank tea and stared at each other. There was a long, long silence while Sven munched a piece of toast and occasionally smiled lovingly at Mother, while she smiled back and desperately searched her mind for suitable intellectual topics of conversation. Sven swallowed a piece of toast and coughed violently. His eyes filled with tears.

'I love toast,' he gasped. 'I simply love it. But it always does this to me.'

From *Birds, Beasts and Relatives* by Gerald Durrell

Neanderthal Man: primitive form of man from the Stone Age
plus fours: wide, loose type of trousers not reaching to the ankles
Gladstone bag: light travelling bag, named after W E Gladstone (1809–98), British Prime Minister

Unfamiliar words

Before attempting the comprehension questions, make up your mind about the meaning of the following words, using the clues given.

1	**voluminous** (line 20) refers to	a) age	b) size
2	**checked** (line 21) refers to	a) the pattern	b) the shape
3	**devoid of** (line 31) means	a) full of	b) lacking in
4	**tattered** (line 32) means	a) neat	b) untidy
5	**wavered** (line 39) means	a) fluctuated	b) paused
6	**quavering** (line 40) means	a) firm	b) unsteady
7	**munched** (line 51) refers to	a) drinking	b) eating
8	**gasped** (line 58) indicates that Sven was	a) hungry	b) out of breath

Reading for detail

Passages of this kind demand close attention to detail. The questions asked about them depend on an understanding of precisely what is being said, though they seldom depend entirely on the meaning of unusual words.

Answer the following questions about the passage in your own words, indicating the phrases that help you to make up your mind.

1 Did Sven arrive on his visit according to plan?
2 What was the writer's first impression of Sven's appearance?
3 Why did Sven's hat seem to have been designed for a horse?
4 Why did Sven's greeting sound odd at first?
5 Why did the writer's mother and Sven have little to say to each other at first?

Such questions are usually asked in examinations in a multiple-choice format to make it easier for the examiners to assess the answers. In that case, it is wise to test every statement by comparing it with the text and deciding whether it is *true* or *false*. In many cases, it is possible to demonstrate that it is false by quoting a line from the passage; in others, where there is no mention of it, you must assume it is irrelevant and therefore false.

Answer the following multiple-choice questions, choosing the answer that expresses most accurately what is stated in the passage. Only one answer is correct. Test each statement against the passage and explain why the incorrect ones are wrong, as in the examples.

6 Sven Olson arrived
A at Mrs Durrell's invitation. (*False.* Larry had invited him 'without reference to her' (line 6).)
B at the time stated in his telegram.
C later than expected.
D quite by chance.

7 The writer's first impression of Sven's appearance was that he looked rather like
A a lunatic. (*False.* There is no mention of this.)
B a typical artist.
C a well-dressed gentleman.
D an enormous caveman.

You must be particularly careful in dealing with questions of this kind to read the introduction to the question and not allow your imagination to mislead you. For example, you may think that artists typically look like Sven, but that was not 'the writer's first impression'.

8 Sven's hat seemed to have been designed for a horse because
A he wore it to disguise his baldness.
B his head was so large.
C it looked like a crown with holes in.
D there were apparently spaces for the ears.

9 Sven's greeting sounded odd because
A he spoke English correctly, but had an unusual accent.
B he spoke such strange English.
C his tone of voice varied so much.
D his voice had only just broken.

10 At first, Mrs Durrell and Sven said very little because
A he was too hungry to speak.
B he was waiting for an invitation to play his accordion.
C she could not think of anything appropriate to talk about.
D she wanted to make it plain that he was not welcome.

F

Synonyms

Although true synonyms are rare in English, it is frequently possible to find words that mean approximately the same thing in the context of the passage as those the writer has chosen. The form of the word given below should help you to identify its equivalent in the passage. Find words or phrases that mean the same thing as the following.

1	horror	6	heavily
2	large numbers	7	delighted
3	similarity	8	faultless
4	dressed	9	hardly
5	huge	10	held out

G

Use of language

Many expressions depend on the association of verbs, nouns and adjectives in a standard manner, and you can only recognise them by having heard or read them. Throughout the book there are practice exercises aimed at reminding you of the normal usage.

bear, come, drive, fill, make, search, wind
Without referring to the text, complete the sentences below, using the above verbs *once only* in the correct form.

1 Sven's contradictory telegrams had ________ Mother mad.
2 We were having tea when a cab ________ its appearance, ________ its way up the drive and ________ to a stop in front of the house.
3 Sven ________ a remarkable resemblance to a caveman.
4 Mother ________ her mind for suitable topics of conversation.
5 Sven coughed and his eyes ________ with tears.

H

Words often confused

advice (uncountable), **forecast, promise, threat, warning**
Words used precisely can usually be distinguished from others similar to them in meaning by reference to the context. In line 8, **warning** means 'advance notice'; the context helps us understand that problems or difficulties are expected, too. We thus have a fuller understanding of the meaning of **warning**.
Decide which of the five sentences below typifies each of the words listed above.

1 The weather tomorrow will be bright and sunny.
2 If you don't give me the money, I'll kill you.
3 On your birthday, I'll buy you a bicycle if you're a good girl.
4 Cigarettes can seriously damage your health.
5 I should ring him up if I were you. He may be able to help you.

In line 44, Sven **bowed** to Mrs Durrell, which means he 'bent his head towards his chest in a formal greeting'. In what circumtances might he have **knelt**, **nodded**, or **stooped**?

2

Work

Introductory exercise

1 **Company organisation**. Study the diagram below indicating the executive structure of XYZ Ltd, and explain what you consider to be the responsibilities of all the people listed there.

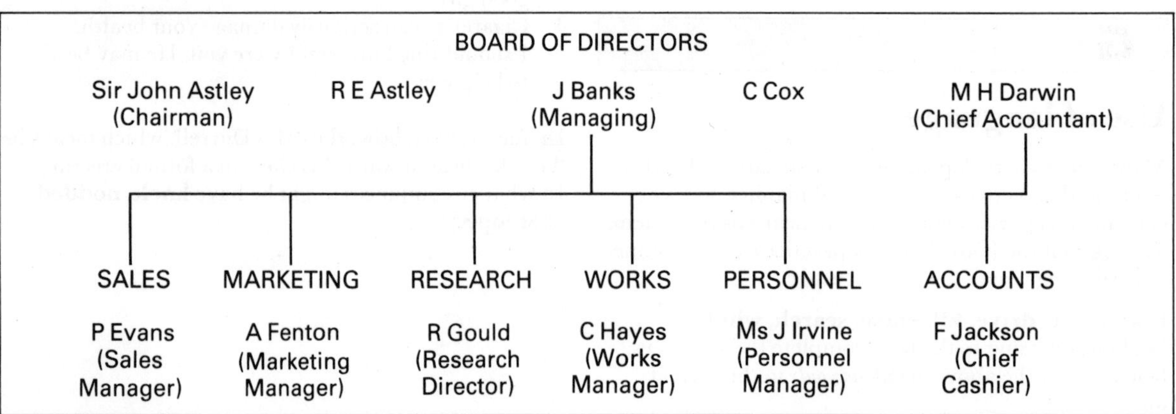

Now answer these questions.

1 James Keeler is the foreman in the factory. Who is he directly responsible to?
2 Paula Lane has just been appointed Research Assistant. Which two people interviewed her?
3 A company must decide what people want, make it and sell it. Which three of the six managers listed above are primarily responsible at each stage?

2 **The balance sheet**. It is Mr Darwin's responsibility to prepare the company's balance sheet at the end of the financial year. The **turnover**, or the total value of the products sold, was £40 million. The following must be deducted from this to establish the company's **profit**. Define what they mean.

a) wages and salaries
b) raw materials
c) depreciation of equipment
d) investment in new plant
e) overheads

This year, the company has made a profit, but has a problem with **cash flow**. What do you suppose this means?

Why Do We Work?

Read the following passage to gain a general impression of its content before studying the vocabulary in detail.

The strange fact is that the last hundred years have seen not only the dehumanising of manual work, with the introduction of mass-production methods and 'scientific management', and a consequent reduction in the satisfaction which an individual can derive from the performance of a skilled craft, but also universal acceptance of the idea that everyone ought to work, even though they may have no absolute economic necessity to do so. Even those fortunate enough to inherit great wealth have been unable to resist the prevailing climate of opinion and a large proportion of those who suddenly find that they no longer have to work, after winning a lottery or the football pools, now choose to continue working, finding it too difficult to sustain a lifestyle which is not built around some form of work.

I don't think that we should be unduly impressed by surveys which claim to show that the vast majority of workers, even in what appear to be the most soul-destroying jobs, actually enjoy their work: the workers' response may just indicate that they are happy to be doing any job at all, rather than a positive feeling about their particular work. But we do seem to have reached a position where people prefer to work rather than not to work, and the reasons for this are complicated by the fact that different people look for different sorts of rewards, while different people look for different types of satisfaction in their work. A basic tenet of the scientific management pioneered by Frederick Winslow Taylor at the end of the last century was that man the worker was a rational, economic creature, motivated only by his pay-packet. As the original Henry Ford put it, 'The average worker wants a job into which he does not have to put much physical effort. Above all, he wants a job in which he does not have to think.' What Ford thought the average worker *did* want can be deduced from the fact that he paid his workers a minimum wage which was more than twice the national average.

Money is certainly an effective motivator, but it is not the only reason why we work. There is no doubt that the economic motive can be overridden by other considerations: for example, even when they are being paid according to individual productivity, people tend to work at the same pace as those around them, and a number of studies have shown that the output of a team may actually fall when it gains a new member who refuses to accept the group norm and works at a faster rate. Being accepted as a member of a stable working group brings its own social reward, which may explain why many workers have mixed feelings about technological advances that remove them from the noise and dirt of the shop floor and leave them in splendid isolation, in charge of a machine which can carry out the tedious work they formerly did. It may also account for the behaviour of people who choose to work even though there is no economic necessity for them to do so – after all, it is not easy to be a playboy when there are so few people to play with!

From *Habits* by John Nicholson

A

Reading for gist

Decide in each case which of the statements contains the meaning conveyed in the passage. Then read the six statements together as a summary of the passage as a whole.

1 It is curious that
- A everyone now thinks work is necessary, even though mass production methods offer less job satisfaction.
- B the introduction of mass production methods has made it necessary for everyone to work.

2 People who can afford not to work do so, nevertheless, because
- A they find it difficult to organise their lives if they don't.
- B they feel guilty about having so much money.

3 Men like Taylor and Ford believed that the vast majority of workers
A enjoy their work. B work only for money.

4 In fact, people working with others
A try to work faster to earn more.
B adapt to the speed of their workmates.

5 Most workers in factories are more interested in
A better conditions that may separate them from others.
B the companionship of those around them.

6 The rich may therefore choose to work because they
A are afraid of leading lonely lives.
B believe that work is good for them.

Synonyms

Find words or phrases in the passage approximately equivalent in meaning to the following.

1 need (n.)	5 really	9 worked out
2 lucky	6 show	10 speed
3 go on	7 principle	11 production
4 excessively	8 being (n.)	12 boring

Use of language

Without referring to the text, complete the following sentences.

1 It would be unwise to introduce the new system at present because of the prevailing ______ of opinion in the works.

2 The introduction of mass-production methods has resulted in many people having to do soul-______ jobs.

3 The ______ majority of people work because they have to.

4 I'm not altogether happy about the proposal. I regard it with ______ feelings.

5 Come and join us! Don't sit there by yourself in splendid ______!

Words often confused

1 particular, private, special

Use each of the words listed above *at least once* to complete the paragraph below.

In a ______ company like this, with no shareholders to worry about, we must nevertheless be very ______ about the people we employ. This does not mean that we should concern ourselves with their ______ lives, or give them ______ treatment because they work for us, but in this ______ case we have in front of us, the case of Joan Smith, I think we must take her personal problems into account and make a ______ recommendation to the Managing Director. Mark the letter '______' of course.

2 craft, employment, job, work

Use each of the words listed *at least once* to complete the paragraph below.

It is fashionable to talk of the decline in ______ satisfaction for the majority of workers, who no longer need to learn a skilled ______ to obtain ______ (or ______). But while most people prefer to do a ______ that interests them, the evidence gained from those who are out of ______ suggests that the worst thing about un______ is that people do not know how to organise their lives. For that reason, some workers are learning ______s like pottery or carpentry as a hobby.

3 award, benefit, profit, reward

Use each of the words listed *at least once* to complete the paragraph below.

The firm was given one of the Queen's ______s for industry as a ______ for their efforts in the export trade. Of course, as far as we are concerned, it does not make much difference, because we had already made our ______ from our customers, but I think these ______s are really made for the ______ of other firms that have not yet seen the importance of selling abroad.

4 economic, economical, economics, economy

Use each of the words listed *at least once* to complete the sentences below.

1 Taylor thought workers were ______ creatures, who only worked for money.

2 The new machine is very ______. It has already saved us a great deal of money.

3 He is studying ______ at the university.

4 The Chancellor of the Exchequer made a speech about the state of the national ______.

5 Bank managers always advise us to practise ______ before they will lend us money. The opposite seems to be true when they are dealing with countries. The less ______ they are in running their affairs, the more they can borrow. That is why ______ is such a difficult subject for the layman to understand.

Starting Your Own Business

Read the following passage carefully, paying attention to detail, and noting down words you do not understand.

Marks & Spencer, now one of Europe's biggest businesses, started life as a market stall in Leeds. Clive Sinclair, whose personal wealth is well over £100 million, set up his first electronics firm when he was only 22. Retailing and high technology remain among the most promising fields for fledgling entrepreneurs. But you don't need to create a Marks & Spencer or a Sinclair Research to get satisfaction from minding your own business.

Every year, thousands of people start businesses of their own because they want more independence and job satisfaction. Subsequent wealth, if it materialises, is almost incidental. The go-it-alone route is now being taken by many victims of redundancy and has been strongly recommended by the politicians. The Conservatives, for instance, devoted a section of their election manifesto to the subject, stressing helpful measures such as their loan guarantee scheme for projects the banks consider too risky for normal lending. The 1983 Budget raised the ceiling for total lending to £600 million. The last Budget also lifted the limit on the Business Start-Up Scheme, now renamed the Business Expansion Scheme. Individuals willing to put up risk capital can now get tax relief on up to £40,000 a year invested in new companies.

Do the various schemes and incentives have any effect? The Department of Industry has produced provisional figures for 1982, based on **VAT** registrations, which suggest that 125,000 new firms were born last year – about 500 every working day. However, the same statistics indicate that some 118,000 traders went out of business in the same period. In round figures, one in three of all new businesses fails in the first 12 months, and four out of five collapse within five years..

Even the survivors cannot always be judged successes. As the owner of such a business, you may well find yourself working harder, for longer hours, with less security and for smaller financial rewards than when you were in somebody else's employment. On the other hand, thanks to the recession, you stand a better chance these days of getting your hands on the capital, labour and raw materials you need at a reasonable price. The missing ingredient – in the short term anyway – is strong demand.

From an article by Michael Braham in the *Observer Magazine*

VAT: Value Added Tax, charged on a wide variety of goods and services in Common Market countries

Unfamiliar words

Some words may be familiar to you, but not in the context you find them in here, where they may have a different meaning. Use the clues below to differentiate between their common meaning and their meaning here.

1 **A stall** (line 3) is
  a) an open-air shop.
  b) a seat in a theatre.

2 **A fledgling** (line 7) is
  a) a person without business experience.
  b) a bird too young to leave the nest.

3 **Minding your own business**(line 9) means
  a) not interfering in others' affairs.
  b) becoming your own boss.

4 **Capital**(line 26) refers to
  a) the seat of a country's government.
  b) (uncountable) money to be invested.

5 **Round figures**(line 36) are
  a) noughts.
  b) approximate numbers ending in 0.

F

Reading for detail

Answer the following questions about the passage in your own words, indicating phrases that help you make up your mind. Be careful to take the content of the whole passage into account when answering.

1 What is the essential requirement for success in establishing your own business in the early stages?
2 What is the attraction of going into business on their own for the majority of people who attempt it?
3 In what ways does the Government encourage small businesses?
4 What is the fate of most new businesses?
5 What are the advantages of starting a new business at a time of recession?

Now use your answers as a means of choosing the correct answer from the four choices offered below, only one of which is correct, and indicate why you are not satisfied with the alternatives.

6 In the early stages of establishing your own business, it is essential to
  A begin in a small way.
  B concentrate on technology.
  C sell a product for which there is a clear need.
  D start young.
7 Most people who go into business on their own account do so
  A to avoid redundancy.
  B to become rich quickly.
  C to get loans from the Government.
  D to obtain more job satisfaction.
8 The Government encourages small businesses by
  A allowing them to operate tax-free in the first year.
  B guaranteeing money lent by banks.
  C offering loans without interest.
  D recommending that redundant workers should 'go it alone'.
9 Most new businesses
  A fail in the first year of operation.
  B fail within five years.
  C are set up on the premises of others that have gone bankrupt.
  D survive whether they are a success or not.
10 One of the advantages of starting a new business at a time of recession is that
  A it is easier to obtain good workers.
  B people are more willing to lend you money.
  C profits are greater.
  D it is not necessary to work such long hours.

G

Synonyms

Find words or phrases in the passage approximately equivalent in meaning to the following.

1 firms
2 established
3 selling direct to customers
4 inexperienced businessmen
5 is produced
6 emphasising
7 considered
8 obtaining
9 work-force
10 in the early stages

Words often confused

be dismissed/sacked, be made redundant, resign, retire

Use each of these verbs *at least once* in the correct form to complete the paragraph below.

The conditions of work have changed considerably in Britain over the past fifty years. In those days, it was quite common for workers to __________ for small infringements of company regulations, which would be very unusual now. Executives expected to spend most of their lives in the same firm, and unless they __________ for incompetence, to __________ at the age of 65, usually without a pension. Now, when the company loses business, it is normal for workers to __________, and be paid compensation, while executives __________ from one post and take up another at regular intervals.

It's a Hard Life for Commuters

Commuters live at considerable distances from the city where they work – in London, at places like Chipping Ongar or Aylesbury – and travel to the termini, London Bridge, Victoria, etc., by train or underground every day. On arrival, they probably have to catch a bus to their offices.

AFTER THE WEEKEND, the week. Not too bad, I daresay, if you live over the shop, like grocers or **Chancellors of the Exchequer**; just a matter of remembering it's time for a collar and tie again after two days of informality. But these happily placed breadwinners are considerably outnumbered by you and me, for whom Monday means saddling up once more for the hard trail from Chipping Ongar, Aylesbury, Haywards Heath. We don't mind the work. No, honestly. It's getting to it that kills. It may be just as tough for the toil-bound of Liverpool, Glasgow, Birmingham, but I can only speak as I find, and what I find is travel sickness. Also no bus shelters at London Bridge.

I've been meaning to mention this for some time.

It's a thing that worries me less as the week wears on. Even as early as Wednesday the end is in sight: two days, faintly showing at the end of the tunnel, when you won't have to be at London Bridge. But Monday, as the east wind scythes in, or the soft, refreshing rain cascades out of my hat, I feel the deprivation keenly. They tell me it's the same at Victoria, which means it also goes, very probably for Liverpool Street, Marylebone and Waterloo. I don't know. My working glide-path is restricted. I don't see these outposts in the ordinary course of business.

If it's true, where are the responsible authorities? Not waiting for a bus, with the next man's umbrella in their eye, that's for sure. If they're whispering in from **Chequers** in their weatherproof limousine, agonising over the productivity shortfall, it might pay them to make a detour and have a look at us, stooped and disconsolate, waiting to be splashed up to the ears by a No. 13 (marked Very Rare in the timetables). I'm not arguing for the soft life – just the state of the nation. Any rural bus stop, with a daily turnover of eight customers and an inspector, has its stout cabin against the elements. You and me and the rest of the commuting millions, no. Let the responsible authorities ask themselves, 'What sort of a day's work do you get out of workers who start the day – and more particularly the week – like this?' By the time they've steamed for an hour on the office radiators, and collapsed into the old **tilt-and-swivel** for another half-hour's scarifying exchange of journey stories, all they're good for is – I was going to say the journey back . . . but they'll need a couple of gins and a long restoring lunch before they begin to feel equal to that.

There's nothing to be done about the railways, of course. We've grown up with the points breakdown, broken rail, power failure, signal collapse, defective stock, missing guard and the rest of the familiar apology-fodder. It's our own fault, for being so many, and having to get to work. But I still don't see that we have to be wet. Can't someone prop a bit of roof on a few tin poles outside London Bridge? It's not much to ask in return for a zestful grin over a million Monday morning **white collars**.

Well, I said I'd been meaning to mention it.

From *Pick of Punch* by Basil Boothroyd

Chancellor of the Exchequer: Minister responsible for finance, who lives at 11 Downing St, next to the Prime Minister

Chequers: the Prime Minister's country residence, often used at the weekend for conferences, etc

tilt-and-swivel: office chair that can be adjusted for height and turned round on its base

white collars: indicating the dress worn by office workers

I

Use of language

The appreciation of humorous writing depends considerably on the ability to recognise that words and phrases are being used out of their normal contexts. There are many examples of words or phrases being used in unusual contexts in this passage. Sometimes, the result is an exaggeration of reality; at other times, the author uses metaphors we normally associate with one context in another, or else he puts words next to each other which we do not normally associate together.

1 The expressions below, taken from the passage, are all exaggerations of reality. In each case, decide what the exaggeration consists of, and then replace each phrase with one that reflects what really happens.
   a) the toil-bound (line 12)
   b) as the east wind scythes in (line 22)
   c) with the next man's umbrella in their eye (line 31)
   d) whispering in (line 33)
   e) agonising (line 34)
   f) splashed up to the ears (line 37)
   g) steamed for an hour (line 47)

2 To understand the humour of the following, you must consider the contexts in which the phrases are normally used and compare it with the context here. Name the usual context, and say whether you think the picture created is funny because of the contrast.
   a) saddling up once more for the hard trail (line 8)
   b) faintly showing at the end of the tunnel (line 20)
   c) I don't see these outposts (line 28)
   d) a daily turnover of eight customers and an inspector (line 40)
   e) stout cabin (line 41)
   f) scarifying exchange of journey stories (line 49)
   g) a long restoring lunch (line 52)
   h) apology-fodder (line 58)

3 Part of the humour depends on juxtaposition. What is funny about the following?
   a) grocers and Chancellors of the Exchequer 'living over the shop'.
   b) the soft, refreshing rain 'cascading' out of his hat.

J

General understanding

While most of the interest in the passage lies in the way things are written, not what is said, it does make certain points clearly. Answer the following questions.

1 What makes the commuter's life so hard?
2 Which station does the writer normally travel to, and what does he dislike most about it?
3 Why is he happier on Wednesdays than Mondays?
4 Why does he think it is important for the authorities to take commuters into consideration? Why, apparently, do they do nothing, and why are people who live in the country much better off?
5 How would the nation benefit if the authorities took his advice, and how would he benefit personally?

K

Interpretation of text

Answer the following questions on the text.

1 Why does a commuter's week contrast more strongly with his weekend than a grocer's does?
2 What criticism is the writer anticipating by saying 'No, honestly.' (line 10)?
3 Why do you suppose the writer has no personal experience of what happens at Victoria and is ignorant about the state of affairs at Waterloo? (All these stations are on the same side of London.)
4 Why is the need to catch a 13 bus particularly unfortunate for the writer?
5 When does the writer customarily hear such phrases as 'points breakdown', 'broken rail', etc., (line 55) and why do they have no effect on him?
6 What is it that he had 'been meaning to mention' (line 16 and line 65)? What particular experience, do you imagine, caused him to write the article?

3

Country Houses

Introductory exercise

1 **Fields:** the following words can be grouped together under this general heading. Can you describe the appearance of each so as to distinguish between them?

a) a common
b) a heath
c) a meadow
d) a moor
e) a park

2 **Boundaries:** the following are all types of boundaries that separate one field or piece of land from another. What is the difference between them?

a) walls
b) hedges
c) fences

Where would you find a ditch or a moat? What is the difference between them?

3 **Farm buildings:** what are the following commonly used for?

a) a barn
b) a dairy
c) a shed
d) a stable
e) a sty

Georgian Houses

Beningborough Hall, Yorkshire. Built in 1716

Read the following passage to gain a general impression of its content before studying the vocabulary in detail.

When we lived in Bristol a visitor from Denmark, who had driven across southern England from Dover, remarked that it was 'just like driving through a series of parks'. The contrast she was registering was between the landscape she was familiar with in Denmark, based on peasant- and small-holdings, and that created in England in the 18th century by **enclosures and 'emparkments'**. That pattern is still with us today, though submerged in many places by the growth of the great 19th century towns and their 20th century suburbs.

In the middle of the parks, usually behind stout stone walls, stand the surviving houses of **Georgian** England. In the early years of the 18th century they were often no more than jumped-up farmsteads, sitting in a clutter of barns and sheds and cottages, surrounded by fields. But as the century wore on some were totally rebuilt, others given a face-lift, the squalor removed, pieces of land fenced in to round off corners and add depth and privacy, and the fields drained, planted out and embellished. In shire after shire, the old common lands with their great open fields and vast horizons gave way to private estates.

The fashionable mode of rebuilding was classical, and it is the overwhelming dominance of one architectural style that gives Georgian England so clear a definition for us today. True, in the earlier years, there was a survival of boisterous baroque influence; the middle years of the century saw the tentative emergence of Gothick in its **Strawberry Hill** variety, and in the 1760s there was even a little Chinese influence, of which Sir William Chambers' pagoda at **Kew** is the best-known example. But, by and large, the whole century was under the thrall of Greece and Rome.

The classical tradition blends in so well, has become so familiar a part of the English landscape, that it requires an effort of imagination to remember how strange it all is. Eighteenth century schoolboys spent almost the whole of their time learning the two dead languages, Latin and Greek: Members of Parliament spattered their speeches with Latin quotations and quips; statues of plump **Hanoverian** kings were decked out in togas as Roman senators. The most famous of Georgian literary assassins wrote under the name of 'Junius', and when he and the printer wanted to insert private codes in the *Public Advertiser* to contact each other, it was agreed to use Latin **tags**. Never has one civilisation paid such intellectual homage to another.

From *The Ages of Britain – VIII: The Georgians* by John Cannon in the *Observer Magazine*.

enclosures and emparkments: from 16th century onwards, rich men 'enclosed' the common land previously belonging to the people and turned it into estates and parks. This process reached its height in the 18th century.
Georgian: period of history during the reigns of first four King Georges (1714–1830)
Strawberry Hill: house built in romantic style partly imitating Gothic architecture at Twickenham in Middlesex
Kew: district in west London which houses Royal Botanical Gardens
Hanoverian: the Georgian Kings came originally from Hanover, in Germany
tags: well-known quotations

A

Unfamiliar words

From the context, decide on the more probable meaning of the following.

1 **jumped-up** (line 26)
a) raised off the ground b) aspiring to social elevation (without much justification)
2 **clutter** (line 27) a) a neat line b) an untidy collection
3 **given a face-lift** (line 30) a) made superficially more attractive b) raised off the ground in the front
4 **planted out** (line 35) a) replaced b) filled with plants and trees in an ordered manner
5 **boisterous** (line 47) a) noisy b) lively
6 **spattered** (line 69) a) included occasional quotations from Latin and Greek b) made their speeches incomprehensible by including quotations

Reading for gist

Decide in each case which of the statements contains the meaning conveyed in the passage. Then read the five statements together to produce a summary of the passage as a whole.

1 A Danish visitor to the south of England said that the countryside reminded her of a series of parks because
  A it had grown out of peasants' farms.
  B the natural landscape had been carefully modified.
  C it was familiar to her.
2 The reason for the change was that
  A the common lands were enclosed in private estates.
  B the countryside disappeared as towns and suburbs grew.
  C farms were rebuilt.
3 The Georgian houses that survive today were
  A constructed from the ruins of farmhouses and cottages.
  B rebuilt in a more imposing style.
  C surrounded by fields.
4 The architecture of the Georgian period is easily recognisable because it
  A fits in so well with the countryside.
  B imitates all kinds of foreign models.
  C is almost all classical in style.
5 This preference
  A indicates the respect people had for ancient Greek and Roman civilisation.
  B resulted from people learning Latin and Greek at school.
  C shows that the architects had no originality.

C

Synonyms

Find words or phrases in the passage approximately equivalent in meaning to the following.

1 buried
2 dirty conditions
3 made beautiful
4 county
5 style
6 in general
7 domination
8 jokes
9 fat
10 dressed elaborately

Use of language

Decide on the meaning of the following phrases in the context of the passage, and then make sentences of your own, using them.

1 based on (line 10)
2 wore on (line 29)
3 round off (line 32)
4 gave way to (line 38)
5 were decked out in (line 72)

The National Trust

Read the three passages that follow one after another before answering any questions. Decide what their purpose is and why they were written, and explain what features of style and content lead you to your conclusions. Then give each passage a heading.

A

The National Trust protects historic buildings and gardens, countryside and coastline for you forever. It is a charity and it needs your support.

Join, and you will get a great deal of pleasure out of it. You'll get in free to all the Trust's great houses and gardens.

You'll have a complete information pack on all our properties and activities, and our colour magazine every spring and autumn.

But more than that, you'll get the satisfaction of doing something to save the Britain that's disappearing all too fast.

The Trust owns and opens to the public more than 200 buildings of architectural or historical importance, almost all the houses complete with their contents – paintings and furniture, books and porcelain, tapestries and armour.

They embrace every period of Britain's history, from Roman villas to Victorian mansions. Many have fascinating associations with famous people as diverse as Sir Winston Churchill and **Beatrix Potter**. We care for simple cottages, for magnificent **Palladian** houses, for windmills, for mediaeval castles; for monuments to our industrial past, sometimes even for whole villages. We even own a pub or two.

The Trust's work is truly nationwide. With properties to be found all over England, Wales and Northern Ireland, there is much to see. (There is a separate National Trust for Scotland, to whose properties you are also admitted free.)

The word 'national' does not mean we are government funded. We rely entirely on private individuals like yourself – people who think their heritage is worth a few pounds to save – if only for the pleasure they get from looking round it.

Beatrix Potter: authoress of several popular books for children
Palladian: in the style of the Italian Renaissance architect, Palladio

B

The National Trust for Places of Historic Interest or Natural Beauty is a charity which holds countryside and buildings in England, Wales and Northern Ireland for the benefit of the public. Although its name might suggest that it is run by the State, the Trust is jealously independent of Government: it depends on the generosity of those who give it properties and the money to maintain them, on well over a million subscribing members and on its friends and supporters everywhere. The Trust does of course accept grants from statutory bodies, in the same way that other owners of historic properties and other charities may accept them when eligible; and it is 'national' in the sense that it works on behalf of the nation with the supportive recognition of successive Governments.

The Trust was founded in 1895. Three imaginative people foresaw an increasing threat to the countryside and ancient buildings of England, Wales and Northern Ireland: Miss Octavia Hill, a social worker of vision known also for her pioneering work in housing reform; Sir Robert Hunter, a solicitor whose special concern was for open countryside in Surrey; and Canon Hardwicke Rawnsley, a parson who lived in and loved **the Lake District**. They formed the National Trust as a public company not trading for profit, with powers to acquire and preserve beautiful and historic places. The Trust's first property was the gift of 4½ acres of cliffland in North Wales; its second the purchase – for a mere £10 – of the fourteenth-century timber-framed Clergy House at Alfriston (East Sussex).

The Lake District: an area of mountains and lakes in Cumbria

C

Obviously the sort of things you can do very much depends on the individual house — some are more suitable than others for a particular activity, some are too confined and crowded to allow you to do much more than shuffle round in the queue, though possibilities widen if you can bring your pupils at a quite time — but discuss this with the Administrator.

When exploring a house with children it is wiser to concentrate on a particular aspect of the place, perhaps on the art and craftwork and how it was done, or the lives of the people, above and below stairs, or the costume and hairstyles in the portraits, than to expect the children to comprehend everything in a single visit. A growing number of school parties now arrive at our properties armed with paper, boards and pencils, and drawing is an excellent way to help children to become observant. Some of our Administrators would also be happy to discuss the possibility of the class coming in home-made costumes with the intention of re-creating the life of the house through drama, or bringing musical instruments with them to play period music in an appropriate setting.

From a selection of National Trust publicity leaflets.

E

Comparison of texts

Answer the following questions in your own words.

1 Why might someone be interested in becoming a member of the National Trust, and what advantages would he or she obtain?
2 In what sense is the word 'National' used here, and what mistaken impression is the writer anxious to correct about it?
3 How can the buildings of the National Trust be used most effectively for educational purposes?
4 How does the National Trust obtain property, and how does it raise the funds to maintain it?
5 In view of the eventual aims of the Trust, what do you imagine was the particular interest of Miss Octavia Hill, compared to those of her co-founders?

Synonyms

Find the words or phrases approximately equivalent in meaning to the following. The letter in brackets indicates the passage to refer to.

1 different (A)
2 look after (A)
3 depend (A)
4 appropriate (C)
5 feature (C)
6 understand (C)
7 increasing (C)
8 fiercely (B)
9 for the benefit of (B)
10 menace (B)

Use of language

Answer the questions below, looking carefully at the context of each phrase in the passage.

1 Why do you think the writer wrote 'all too fast' (A, line 11) and not 'quickly'?
2 What sort of thing, do you imagine, is meant by 'monuments to our industrial past' (A, line 18)? Why are they 'monuments'?
3 Who do you imagine lived 'above and below stairs' (C, line 11)?
4 What is 'period music' and how would it help children to understand the house better?
5 What do you suppose is meant by 'statutory bodies' (B, line 11) and why is the writer at pains to explain the conditions on which their help is accepted?
6 Miss Octavia Hill is described as a social worker 'of vision' (B, line 22). Does this refer to her sight, or foresight, and what is the difference?
7 What is the significance of saying 'a mere £10', instead of £10 (B, line 32)?

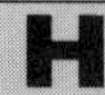

Words often confused

Consider the following pairs of words in the context, decide what the difference is between them, and then make sentences of your own, using them in a way that shows this difference.

1 **historic** (A, line 1 and B, line 1) and **historical** (A, line 11)
All events in history are 'historical', but not all of them are 'historic'. What do you think makes the difference?
2 **rely** (A, line 25) and **depend** (C, line 2)
We could substitute 'depend' for 'rely' in the first context, but not 'depend' for 'rely' in the second. Can you see why?
3 **discuss** (C, line 7) and **argue**
Why would the second word be inappropriate? What is the difference between a **discussion** and an **argument**?
4 **heritage** (A, line 26) and **inheritance**
In what sense does our national heritage belong to us? How could we get an inheritance?
5 **foresee** (B, line 19), **forecast**, **look forward to**, **predict**
Why would 'look forward to' be an inappropriate expression in the context?
In considering the future, which verb would be most appropriate to describe the following?
a) a general impression of what is likely to happen
b) someone telling fortunes with cards
c) a scientific estimate of events

Lexical Progress Test 1

You must choose the word or phrase which best completes each sentence. For each question, 1 to 25, indicate the correct answer, A, B, C or D. The time for the test is 20 minutes.

NOTE: A few words of advice. Do not try to answer the questions by translating into your own language. This will almost certainly produce a wrong answer. If you are in doubt, read the sentence to yourself, including each possibility in turn, until you think you recognise the form of the phrase. Do not hurry. You have more time than you imagine. But do not spend a long time over one question. Go on to the next, and then come back to any that you have not answered at the end.

1 She was __________ in India but now lives in New York.
A brought up B developed C grown up D prepared

2 The weather __________ for tomorrow is 'fine, with occasional showers.'
A anticipation B advice C forecast D warning

3 He wasn't able to find a suitable class at the Institute so he has employed a __________ teacher.
A particular B private C proper D singular

4 They had not cleaned the house for weeks and the health visitor found them living in the utmost __________.
A contamination B decay C pollution D squalor

5 The police have offered a large __________ for information leading to the robbers' arrest.
A award B benefit C prize D reward

6 Will you __________ the children for me while I go shopping?
A care B look after C look over D take care

7 It's much more __________ to buy a season ticket if you travel every day.
A cheap B economic C economical D saving

8 I'm __________ to meet you.
A bewildered B delighted C grateful D pleasant

9 When the firm closed down, several hundred people were made __________.
A obsolete B redundant C resigned D unemployed

10 There are still many problems ahead of us, but by this time we can see light at the end of the __________.
A battle B day C road D tunnel

11 That noise is __________ me mad.
A driving B putting C setting D running

12 I was so late arriving at the airport that I __________ had time to board the plane.
A justly B nearly C scarcely D seldom

13 As they reached the edge of the town, the houses gave __________ to fields and woods.
A place B position C up D way

14 He's so __________ in running his business that he never has time to relax.
A complicated B implied C involved D mixed

15 Can you rely on him to __________ a secret?
A guard B hold C keep D maintain

16 Don't __________ your hopes too high! I wouldn't like you to be disappointed.
A arise B arouse C raise D rise

17 I'm sorry. No one called Jones lives here. You must have __________ the wrong number.
A dialled B fingered C pressed D pushed

18 He __________ out his hand to me in greeting.
A gave B held C laid D took

19 These people still __________ the years of colonial domination bitterly.
A disregard B grudge C object D resent

20 The horses have returned to their __________ after the morning exercise.
A barns B kennels C stables D sheds

21 We realised that he was under great __________ because of his wife's illness, so we took no notice of his bad temper.
A excitement B crisis C nervousness D stress

22 At the end of last night's __________ on the Mining Bill, the Government obtained a majority of 30 in the House of Commons.
A act B debate C discussion D referendum

23 The room was so __________ with furniture that it was impossible to move.
A assembled B burdened C cluttered D overrun

24 I caught a __________ of them as they went past the window.
A glance B glimpse C look D sight

25 He received a __________ from the university in order to continue his research.
A credit B grant C prize D reward

Health

Introductory exercise

What do you imagine are the main causes of people worrying? Which of them do you consider to be natural, and which of them would you regard as abnormal, e.g., people who are so terrified of being shut in that they refuse to use lifts?

Worrying

Read the following passage to gain a general impression of its content before studying the vocabulary in detail.

There are at least two precipitating causes of anxiety, conflict and stress. As an example of the former, we can rarely predict the precise consequences of what we do, but we are blessed (or cursed) with the intellectual capacity to anticipate the advantages and disadvantages which may accrue from any action we may be contemplating. Very commonly we are faced with a choice between several courses of action, all of which have pros and cons. This state of affairs – in psychological jargon, multiple approach-avoidance conflict – accounts for a great deal of our worrying, that is, about what to do.

The other major source of worry is the dreadful things which may happen or have happened to us or to those we care for. Among the most stressful of these are death, illness, loss of work, money problems, marital problems and retirement. Such worries have a rational basis, but we are curiously irrational in the way we pursue them. For example, fear of death is as strong among young adults as among the elderly and it does not seem to be reduced by any sort of religious faith, including the belief that there is life after death. It is equally surprising that objective measures of anxiety suggest that we are as worried the hour before having a tooth filled as when we face major surgery.

It is difficult to decide at what point worrying ceases to be 'normal', but it is clearly reasonable to worry. People get seriously ill, plans go awry, tube trains sometimes crash. In practice, anxiety is judged to be pathological when it curtails our ability to lead a normal existence. We can manage perfectly well without travelling in planes or lifts, and an evening out isn't spoiled by the fact that we are unable to leave the house without triple-checking the front-door lock. Such quirks are widespread in the general population and can easily be distinguished from the behaviour of someone unable ever to leave their house or people who can't go shopping for fear of trembling when they handle money in front of another person.

In its extreme form, anxiety may be experienced either as a generalised, 'free-floating' state (the sufferer becomes tense and frightened for no apparent reason), or it may be more specifically focused – for example on open spaces, enclosed situations or certain insects or animals. Many people will have experienced the former – taut muscles, dry mouth and the feeling of agitation, dread or even panic – while mild phobias are also very common.

But at less intense levels, anxiety and worrying have great value. They help us to avoid trouble, or to cope with it when it cannot be avoided. Worrying may be an internal monologue, allowing us to solve problems at times of crisis; by worrying, we may understand better the origins of the worry and thereby stave off a possible breakdown. It may also play a significant part in the recovery from bereavement by helping us to come to terms with reality (in these circumstances tranquillising drugs may be counterproductive). In everyday life, anxiety energises us and improves performance of a wide variety of tasks (including IQ tests); it also galvanises us to achieve more. Without it, it is difficult to see how there could be either social or intellectual progress. So worrying is not after all an unproductive activity. Perhaps the time to be worried is when you're not worrying.

From an article by John Nicholson in *New Society*

Reading for gist

Answer the following questions on the passage.

1 What are the main causes of people worrying?
2 Define in general terms the difference between conflict and stress, and the kind of circumstances in which each occurs.
3 Is worrying 'normal'? At what point does it require medical help?
4 What are the symptoms of extreme anxiety, and what are their likely causes?
5 Is worry always negative, or can it be a good thing? If so, in what circumstances?

Now link your answers together to provide a summary of the passage, limiting the examples you give, e.g., of conflict or stress, to one example only.

Now answer the following multiple-choice questions, choosing the answer that expresses most accurately what is stated in the passage. Compare the answers you have already given to the alternatives here, and find one that seems to you more or less the same.

6 Conflict causes people to worry because they
A are aware of different possible consequences resulting from their actions.
B are incapable of analysis of their actions.
C cannot imagine what the results of their actions will be.
D want to avoid their problems.

7 According to research on worry caused by stress, the fear of death apparently
A decreases as we get older.
B depends on our religious beliefs.
C exists, irrespective of age or beliefs.
D has no logical foundation.

8 The writer describes people who refuse to get into lifts as
A a little unusual, but not enough to cause concern.
B likely to become pathological cases.
C perfectly normal.
D so common that society considers their behaviour reasonable.

9 A state of anxiety that is sufficiently serious for it to require medical attention
A is always one that is fixed on a specific object.
B displays physical symptoms normal people never experience.
C is evident when it prevents a person from leading a normal life.
D shows itself when people become tense for no apparent reason.

10 The writer's main conclusion about worry is that it
A is more useful to us than we imagine.
B is the main reason for progress.
C makes us more energetic.
D prevents us from ever getting into trouble.

Unfamiliar words

In Unit 1, we have already looked at some techniques for guessing the meaning of unfamiliar words. Once you have decided whether the word is a noun, verb or adjective, etc. consider its relationship to other words in the sentence and in the context surrounding it.

1 Look for synonyms or phrases of similar meaning close to the word. Consider the following in relation to the words surrounding them on this basis and decide on their meaning:
awry (line 34), **taut** (line 55), **galvanises** (line 74).
2 Look for opposites, noting the punctuation, such as brackets, or clues like the use of 'but'. Consider the following in this way:
cursed (line 5), **pathological** (line 35), **counterproductive** (line 71).
3 Note words that form part of a logical context, linking the sense of what has gone before with what follows, and use the context to decide on their meaning:
accrue (line 7), **stave off** (line 66).
4 Some words clearly refer to the content of the previous sentence or phrase, and from that you can derive their meaning:
quirks (line 41).
5 Others are explained by the content of the sentence that follows:
curtails (line 36).

Synonyms

Find words or phrases in the passage approximately equivalent in meaning to the following.

1 worry
2 seldom
3 exact
4 thinking of
5 terrible
6 are fond of
7 foundation
8 strangely
9 common
10 deal with

Use of language

Study the words and phrases referred to in context and answer the questions on them.

1 **blessed** (or **cursed**) (line 5). What is the writer's intention in linking these opposites together?
2 **pros and cons** (line 11). Find an equivalent expression for this phrase elsewhere in the same paragraph.
3 **that is** (line 14). What is the purpose of this phrase and what is the writer drawing our attention to by using it?
4 **in practice** (line 34). What is the opposite of this, and why is there a difference in this context?
5 **agitation, dread, or even panic** (line 56). Why are these placed in this particular order?

Words often confused

1 a cliché, jargon, slang, a slogan
Which of these words would you use to describe the phrases or sentences printed below? There are two examples of each.

1 I've always thought he was *a bit round the bend.*
2 I'm prepared to *take up the cudgels for* freedom.
3 *Make love, not war.*
4 *Multiple approach-avoidance conflict.*
5 *Persil washes whiter.*
6 *The teacher-student interface.*
7 *Get lost, creep.*
8 It looks as if this performance will be her *swan song.*

2 reasonable, unreasonable, rational, irrational
Use each word *once only* to complete the following sentences.

1 Be __________! You can't expect me to give you a rise of 100%.
2 Worries about death have a __________ basis, even if we do not relate them to age or religious beliefs.
3 What an __________ argument! There's no connection between one point and the other.
4 It's __________ to expect students to remember everything you say.

3 antique, elderly, senile, senior
Use each word *once only* to complete the following sentences.

1 Although he is __________, he goes to work every day. He is the __________ partner in a firm that sells __________ furniture.
2 It is a tragedy when old people become __________ and cannot look after themselves.

4 assignment, chores, errand, task
Use each word *once only* to complete the following.

While I was busy with the household __________, I sent Johnny on an __________. It was a really difficult __________ to persuade him to go. He said he had to complete an __________ for his English teacher, and he hadn't got time.

Introductory exercise

What do you do when you catch cold? Have you tried any remedies from the chemist's? Did they work? Are there any traditional remedies used in your family, recommended by grandparents, for example?

The Cold War

Read the following passage carefully, paying attention to detail and noting down words you do not understand.

MEN HAVE WALKED on the moon, transplanted hearts and invented machines to think for them. But they cannot cure the common cold. A spokesman at the world-famous cold research centre in Salisbury sounded understandably bad tempered when I spoke to him about it. They've been working on the problem for years but the most optimistic he could be was to hope that they would find a cure within the next 10 years. So what was their advice on coping with a cold meanwhile? 'Ignore it,' he sniffed.

In urban areas we average about three colds a year and they are caused not by wet feet or sitting in a draught, but by a virus, or rather many viruses which are always changing, so that a vaccine prepared from one is useless against the next. But every year the pharmaceutical companies spend millions of pounds trying to persuade us that their products will banish the miseries of sneezing, runny noses, sore throats, headaches and coughs. They admit they can't cure the cold, but they do promise to relieve the symptoms.

We looked at 10 well-known brands of cold remedies and asked a doctor to explain, in layman's terms, exactly what they contain, each ingredient is for, and his opinion on their effectiveness. Although none of the preparations had exactly the same ingredients, they fell into certain categories.

Nearly all contained a painkiller, either aspirin or paracetamol. These help to reduce temperature and relieve general aches and pains. Aspirin can irritate the stomach, so paracetamol is generally preferred. Many also contain decongestants, which constrict the blood vessels in the nose and relieve congestion. But they can raise blood pressure and should be avoided by people with hypertension or any heart complaint. The decongestant in Vicks Medinite is known to cause wakefulness, so it is strange to find it in a night-time remedy. But maybe it is counterbalanced by the antihistamine which it also contains, like the other night-time preparations. Antihistamines are used to treat hay fever and other complaints caused by allergies, but for a common cold all they will provide is sedation. They shouldn't be mixed with alcohol.

None of the preparations was harmful, as long as you observed the warnings on the packets and didn't take them if you were suffering from certain conditions, were under other medication or were pregnant. But the worst thing about them was the cost. Advertising and packaging had grossly inflated the price of relatively cheap ingredients, and in many cases you could get the same relief from straightforward paracetamol taken with a soothing warm drink of lemon and honey.

Maybe the **old wives** had it right all along with their remedy of 'hanging your hat on the bed-post, drinking from a bottle of whisky until two hats appear, then going to bed and staying here.' That's probably what the researches will come up with in 10 years' time.

From an article by Rosamond Castle in the *Observer Magazine*

old wives: traditionally associated with folk wisdom

F

Unfamiliar words

Use the techniques suggested in Exercise B to decide on the meaning in context of the following.

1 **draught** (line 22)
2 **layman** (line 41)
3 **congestion** (line 59)
4 **sedation** (line 77)
5 **soothing** (line 94)

Reading for detail

Read the following statements, comparing them with the passage, and decide which one is correct in each case. Say why you reject the alternatives.

1 You are likely to catch cold if you
  A fall into a river.
  B meet someone who is affected by a virus.
  C sit near an open window.
  D travel with other people who have colds.
2 Paracetamol is preferable to aspirin because it
  A does not affect your stomach.
  B kills pain.
  C reduces temperature.
  D relieves congestion in the nose.
3 If you suffer from heart trouble it is unwise to take
  A aspirin.
  B antihistamines.
  C decongestants.
  D paracetamol.
4 Antihistamines are dangerous for people who
  A are allergic to pollen.
  B suffer from hypertension.
  C suffer from sleeplessness.
  D take them with the 'old wives' remedy'.
5 The writer's main criticism of the pharmaceutical industry is that it
  A charges too much for its products.
  B claims its products cure colds.
  C claims its products relieve cold symptoms.
  D does not warn people of the medical risks involved.

Words often confused

1 **banish, discharge, dismiss, evict, expel, extradite, relegate**
Banish (line 31) means 'drive away' or 'get rid of' in this context, but it is traditionally associated with people being sent away from court or forced to live in another country and forbidden to return. Words with a similar meaning can often be dissociated only by referring to the context in which they most frequently appear. Use each of the verbs given above, apart from **banish**, *once only* in the correct form to complete the sentences below.

1 He was ________ from school for setting fire to the language laboratory.
2 At the end of the season, they were ________ to the Second Division of the league.
3 How soon do you expect to be ________ from hospital?
4 If they don't pay the rent, they will be ________.
5 He has been arrested in South America, and we are trying to get him ________ to face trial here for the crimes he has committed in this country.
6 He was ________ from the firm for calling the boss a senile old fool.

2 **adhere to, acknowledge, conform to, comply with, observe**
Observe (line 81) means 'pay attention to' in this context, though in others it can mean 'watch carefully'. In each of the sentences below, replace the phrases shown with one of the verbs above, in the correct form. Pay attention to the contexts in which these verbs are customarily found.

1 The party has always *remained faithful to* its programme.
2 While we *recognise* the truth of what many members have said, and sympathise with their attitude, we must at all times *respect* the law, and *act in accordance with* it.
3 I *admit* that I failed to *pay attention to* the traffic regulations.
4 If you are not prepared to *act in accordance with* the rules of the club, and do not *recognise* the authority of the committee, we must ask you to resign. If, however, you are prepared to sign this statement and promise to *keep to* it in future, we will overlook the matter.

3 **observer, onlooker, sightseer, spectator, viewer, watchman**
Which of these words would you use to describe the following people?

a) someone who is watching a TV programme
b) someone who is invited to an international conference to represent his government but cannot take an active part
c) someone who is watching a football match
d) someone who stops to see something in the street that catches his attention
e) someone who looks after a factory at night to prevent thieves entering
f) someone who visits the principal places of interest in a town

4 **discount, ignore, neglect, omit, overlook**
The doctor's advice (line 17) was to **ignore** a cold, or 'take no notice of' it. We **ignore** facts or people by pretending we are not aware of their existence. Use each of the verbs in the list *once only* in the correct form to complete the sentences below. Then make sentences of your own, using each of them appropriately.

1 Newspapers always exaggerate, so we can ______ most of what it says as journalistic invention.
2 I'm afraid that this page was ______ when the book was printed. We'll have to put it in the second edition.
3 I'm afraid I ______ those mistakes when I corrected your homework.
4 I said 'hello' to her, but she just ______ me.
5 You must not ______ your studies, even though you have so much else to do.

5 **avoid, escape, evade, hinder, prevent**
Use each of these verbs *at least once*, in the correct form to complete the sentences below. Then make sentences of your own, illustrating the use and structure of each of them.

1 We were lucky to ______ an accident. Fortunately, your prompt action in wrenching the wheel to the right ______ us from going into the tree.
2 Britain's most wanted criminal, Dick Turpin, ______ from Albany Jail yesterday; he ______ capture by stealing a car. Police road-blocks were set up to ______ him from leaving the area.
3 He's always ______ me in my work by coming for a chat. I can't ______ talking to him without being rude because he is in the next office.

Giving Blood

Read the passage to gain a general impression of its meaning, and also note down any phrases you do not fully understand.

It was a crisp, clean, clear October morning. A **Salvation Army** band was playing in the square, pigeons scratched around the fountain and two scarlet-coated **Chelsea Pensioners** were **selling flags** outside the station. It was the sort of morning on which young men pack in their insurance jobs and go off to join the Army, a morning for doing something different, something selfless, something good. There was a large grey van parked outside a modern office block with National Blood Transfusion Service written on the side. Of course. I would become a Blood Donor.

As I pushed through the swing doors humming **Lilli Marlene**, I almost collided with a man who was coming out carrying a bucket and mop. Before I could change my mind a young woman in a crisp white shirt came up to me and said, 'Hello, are you a regular donor? No? Well, thank you very much for coming, this way please,' and I was shown into a large room with a row of temporary beds covered with scarlet blankets at one end and a lot of rather pale-looking people drinking tea at the other.

Don't worry. I'm not going into gory details about the injections and the tubes and the sight of my blood draining quite slowly into a sort of hot water bottle that the nurse kept shaking gently up and down or the row of little test tubes filling up with scarlet, because I know some people are squeamish about these things. As I lay there feeling woozy but worthy, a charming Indian doctor with a **goatee** beard told me in a soothing bed-time-story voice all the things they might do with my generous contribution.

'If you're interested,' he added pleasantly, 'why not come down to the laboratories at Tooting and see all the products for yourself?'

'Excuse me, doctor, a woman has just fainted,' murmured a nurse. The doctor went off to administer, leaving me to the State-registered vampire who was still shaking the hot water bottle like a set of **maracas**. And then I suddenly remembered (I suppose it was the equivalent of the drowning man having his life flash before him) that I had given my blood once before. It was years ago when I was a student hitch-hiking abroad. We ran out of money in one town and two Americans in the youth hostel told us we could get good money for our blood. They had done it several times. One of them had funded his entire European holiday by selling his body for spare-part surgery to a **Midwest** hospital. I think he'd got $500 for it which, he said, was a better financial proposition than selling off the parts separately. He had a serial number stamped on to his heel like a laundry mark indicating that he was hospital property, and he spent a few minutes every day scrubbing at it hopefully with a **pumice stone**.

'There, that's it, I think,' said the nurse, unplugging me. 'Go and have a lie down for 15 minutes and then help yourself to tea.'

From an article by Sue Arnold in the *Observer Magazine*

Salvation Army: a religious group who usually march with a band playing hymns
Chelsea Pensioners: retired soldiers who live at a home in Chelsea, and are dressed in bright red coats
selling flags: it is usual to sell small paper flags when collecting for charity
Lilli Marlene: German ballad also adopted by the Allied forces in the Second World War
goatee: small tuft of hair on the chin like a goat's beard
maracas: hollow, club-shaped instrument filled with beans, which rattle when shaken
Midwest: middle west cf the United States
pumice stone: porous stone from volcanic lava used for cleaning

I

Unfamiliar words

Use the techniques suggested in Exercise B to decide on the meaning in context of the following.

1 **pack in** (line 10)
2 **gory** (line 39)
3 **squeamish** (line 47)
4 **woozy** (line 49)
5 **soothing** (line 52)

J

General understanding

Answer the following questions on the passage.

1 What put the writer in the frame of mind where she was willing to give blood?
2 How did the efficiency of the young woman who welcomed the writer contrast with the behaviour of the doctor?
3 What caused the writer's state of mind to change when the doctor left her?
4 What was the nature of the bargain the writer's American friend had concluded with the hospital in the Midwest?
5 Why do you suppose he scrubbed his heel with a pumice stone?

Use of language

The humour of this passage depends primarily on the contrast between the writer's good intentions in giving blood, and the choice of expressions emphasising the more unpleasant aspects of the process and the fears of the donor. Answer the following questions.

1 The writer uses the word 'scarlet' in three different contexts in the first three paragraphs. Why do you think the word is repeated in this way?
2 Why did the sight of a man carrying 'a bucket and mop' (line 25) almost make the writer change her mind?
3 Why did she imagine that the people drinking tea were 'rather pale-looking' (line 35)?
4 What is ironically funny about the writer's saying 'Don't worry' at the beginning of the third paragraph, and its juxtaposition with the sentence that follows?
5 What is the normal context in which we would find the expressions 'bed-time-story' (line 52) and 'generous contribution' (line 54), and why are they ironically appropriate here?
6 Explain the exaggeration of 'the State-registered vampire' (line 64), 'like a set of maracas' (line 66) and the reference to 'a drowning man' (line 69).
7 What is the usual context of the words 'spare part' (line 82) and why is their use grotesque here?
8 What is ironic about referring to the American as 'hospital property'?

L

Words often confused

1 **drain, drip, leak, spill**
Use each of the verbs above *at least once* in the correct form to complete the sentences, paying attention to the context. Note that **drain** and **spill** can take an object, **leak** cannot in these examples, and **drip** never takes one.

1 By the time he finished work, sweat was ________ from his face.
2 The water was ________ slowly from the ceiling, drop by drop.
3 The explosion was caused by gas ________ from the pipes.
4 Take this soup to your father and don't ________ it.
5 They have ________ the land near the harbour and built some flats on it.
6 We'll have to wait for the water to ________ off the court before we can play tennis.
7 The ship was ________ badly, so we decided to abandon it and take to the lifeboats.
8 I wish I'd brought an umbrella. The rain is ________ down my neck.
9 When you are giving blood you can convince yourself that your life is ________ away.
10 It is time we talked about making peace. Too much blood has been ________ in this quarrel already.

2 **worthy, worthwhile, invaluable, valuable, precious, priceless**
Study the following examples.

The writer felt **worthy** because she was giving her blood.
The doctor was trying to convince her that she had made a **worthwhile** contribution (or that her contribution had been **worth while**).

Valuable and **precious** mean more or less the same, but note the typical expressions – a **valuable** discovery, **precious** stones.
Priceless and **invaluable** mean 'too precious or valuable to be measured', but note the typical expressions – **invaluable** assistance, **priceless** works of art.
Now make as many sentences as you can, using these words.

Vocabulary expansion

1 **chant, hum, sing, whistle**
The writer **hummed** 'Lilli Marlene'. What would have been the difference if she had **sung** it or **whistled** it? Where would you expect to hear people **chanting**? What is the difference between **chanting** and **singing**?

2 **file, queue, row**
Which of these words would you use to refer to the following?

1 people waiting to go into a cinema
2 beds in a hospital
3 people walking behind one another, one by one – in single __________
4 shops or houses side by side
5 seats in a theatre

3 **murmur, mutter, whisper**
All mean to 'speak softly', but which would you apply to the following?

1 a person speaking so that only one person can hear
2 a person grumbling in a low voice to himself
3 a person speaking quietly so as not to disturb others

4 **brush, rinse, scrub, sweep, wipe**
All are connected with cleaning, but which would you use in the following contexts? Complete the sentences below with an appropriate verb in the correct form, using each verb *at least once*.

1 After I have washed the clothes, I must __________ them to get the soap out, then hang them up to dry.
2 Your jacket needs __________. You have some chalk on it.
3 – I have __________ the floors, Mum, but there's this stain here on the carpet.
– Well, you'll have to get down on your hands and knees with soap and water and __________ it till it comes out.
4 'I feel better now,' she said, __________ the tears from her eyes.
5 __________ your hair before you go out.
6 I've washed up, and __________ the cups and saucers. Would you like me to __________ them and put them away, or shall I leave them on the draining-board to dry?

The Press

Introductory exercise

A large number of people are engaged in producing and selling newspapers every day. Can you describe the part played in this process by the following?

1 a cartoonist
2 the City Editor
3 a compositor
4 our own correspondent
5 the Editor
6 the Features Editor
7 a freelance journalist
8 a gossip columnist
9 a newsagent
10 a news-vendor
11 the proprietor
12 a reporter
13 a reviewer
14 a sub-editor
15 the Sports Editor
16 a typist

Sub-Editor on *The Times*

Read the passage below carefully to gain an idea of the overall meaning, and also note points of detail.

I can think of no better career for a young novelist than to be for some years a sub-editor on a rather conservative newspaper. The hours, from four till around midnight, give him plenty of time to do his own work in the morning when he is still fresh from sleep – let the office employ him during his hours of fatigue. He has the company of intelligent and agreeable men of greater experience than his own: he is not enclosed by himself in a small room tormented by the problems of expression; and, except for rare periods of rush, even his working hours leave him time for books and conversation (most of us brought a book to read between one piece of copy and another). Nor is the work monotonous. Rather as in the game of **Scrabble** the same letters are continually producing different words; no one knows at four o'clock what the evening may produce, and death does not keep a conventional hour.

And while the young writer is spending these amusing and unexacting hours, he is learning lessons valuable to his own craft. He is removing the clichés of reporters; he is compressing a story to the minimum length possible without ruining its effect. A writer with a sprawling style is unlikely to emerge from such an apprenticeship. It is the opposite training to the **penny-a-liner**.

The man who was of chief importance to me in those days was the chief sub-editor, George Anderson. I hated him in my first week, but I grew almost to love him before three years had passed. A small elderly Scotsman with a flushed face and a laconic humour,* he drove a new sub-editor hard with his sarcasm. Sometimes I almost fancied myself back at school again, and I was always glad when five-thirty came, for immediately the clock marked the hour when the pubs opened, he would take his bowler hat from the coat-rack and disappear for thirty minutes to his favourite bar. His place would be taken by the gentle and courteous Colonel Maude. Maude was careful to see that the new recruit was given no story which could possibly stretch his powers, and if he had been chief sub-editor I doubt if I would ever have got further than a **News in Brief** paragraph. At the stroke of six, when Anderson returned and hung up his bowler, his face would have turned a deeper shade of red, to match the rose he carried always in his buttonhole, and his shafts of criticism, as he scanned my copy with perhaps a too flagrant headline, would have acquired a tang of friendliness. More than two years went by, and my novel *The Man Within* had been accepted by a publisher, before I discovered one slack evening, when there was hardly enough news to fill the Home pages for the ten o'clock edition, that a **poet manqué** had dug those defences of disappointed sarcasm. When a young man, Anderson had published a volume of translations from **Verlaine**; he had sent it to **Swinburne** at The Pines and he had been entertained there for tea and kind words by **Watts-Dunton**, though I don't think he was allowed to see the poet. He never referred to the episode again, but I began to detect in him a harsh but paternal apprehension for another young man, flushed with pride in a first book, who might suffer the same disappointment. When I came to resign he spent a long time arguing with me, and I think his real reason for trying to prevent my departure was that he foresaw a time might come when novel-writing would fail me and I would need, like himself, a quiet and secure life with the pubs opening at half-past five and the coal settling in the grate.

* I am grateful to Mr Arthur Crook, the editor of *The Times Literary Supplement*, for this characteristic example. 'E Colston Shepherd, the former aeronautical correspondent of *The Times*, once told me that he was infuriated by a very truncated version of a story he had written with great care. He complained bitterly to Anderson, saying that his story had been very badly cut. "Heavily, my dear Shep, heavily. Not badly. I cut it myself."'

From *A Sort of Life* by Graham Greene

Scrabble: word game played with pieces of plastic carrying letters
penny-a-liner: someone paid by the number of lines he writes, and so anxious to write as much as possible
a poet manqué: someone who would have been a poet if he had had the chance
News in Brief: a series of short news items in a single paragraph or under the same headline
Verlaine: Paul Verlaine (1844–96), the French lyric poet
Swinburne: A C Swinburne (1837–1909), the English poet
Watts-Dunton: W T Watts-Dunton (1832–1914), an English literary critic, who looked after Swinburne during the last thirty years of his life

Unfamiliar words

Decide on the most probable meaning of the following words in the context of the passage.

1 **unexacting** (line 13)
2 **sprawling** (line 16)
3 **flushed** (line 21)
4 **laconic** (line 21)
5 **sarcasm** (line 22)
6 **shafts** (line 31)
7 **flagrant** (line 32)
8 **tang** (line 32)
9 **slack** (line 34)
10 **harsh** (line 41)

B

Reading for gist

Answer the following questions on the passage.

1 Why does the writer think it is valuable experience for a novelist to work as a sub-editor on a newspaper?
2 What makes the work of a sub-editor interesting?
3 What is the most useful advantage a writer can gain from editing other people's work?
4 Why did the writer gradually gain an affection for George Anderson, and why would he not have made so much progress with Colonel Maude?
5 Why did Anderson try to persuade him not to resign?

Link your answers together to provide a summary of the passage.

Now answer the following multiple-choice questions, choosing the answer that expresses most accurately what is stated in the passage. Compare the answers you have already given to the alternatives here, and find one that seems to you more or less the same.

6 The main advantage for a young novelist working as a sub-editor is that
A he can combine his creative work with instructive experience.
B he doesn't need to worry about how he expresses himself.
C he only has to work for the newspaper when he is tired.
D there is never very much to do.

7 The work of a sub-editor is not dull because
A everyone has time to read books.
B he is using different words all the time.
C news may come in at any time.
D the employees can play word games together.

8 The most useful lesson a young writer can derive from his work as a sub-editor is that of
A learning how to get the maximum amount of money out of what he writes.
B learning to write clearly and concisely.
C listening to good conversation.
D watching professionals at work.

9 The writer preferred George Anderson to Colonel Maude because
A he was kind and understood writers' problems.
B he used to go out for a drink and leave him alone.
C he had such a good sense of humour.
D he gave him more opportunity to develop his skill.

10 Anderson tried to persuade the writer to stay on because he
A thought the writer was too pleased with himself.
B was afraid of losing such a valuable employee.
C was afraid that he would find creative writing unrewarding.
D felt that the writer was ungrateful to him.

Use of language

A number of phrases that may be unfamiliar to you are important to a good understanding of this text. Study these phrases and use the information given below to decide on their meaning.

1 **drove. . .hard** (line 21). What is the normal context for these words? How could Anderson 'drive' the writer by sarcasm?
2 **stretch his powers** (line 27). What context do you usually associate the word 'stretch' with? How could a story 'stretch' the writer's 'powers'?
3 **turned a deeper shade of red** (line 30). Why is this associated with Anderson's visit to the bar?
4 **Heavily . . . not badly** (lines 50–51). What is the difference between cutting a story or speech 'heavily' and cutting it 'badly'?
5 **dug those defences** (line 36). In what context would 'defence' normally be associated with 'digging'? What was Anderson trying to defend himself against?

Reading for detail

Read the following statements, comparing them with the passage, and decide which one is correct in each case. Say why you reject the alternatives.

1 George Anderson's technique in training his assistants was to
A go out for a drink and let them solve their own problems.
B provoke them into disliking him.
C stand over them while they worked and make unpleasant remarks.
D use bitter humour to draw their attention to their mistakes.

2 The point of the story quoted in the footnote is that
A Shepherd thought Anderson did not take him seriously.
B Shepherd thought Anderson was incompetent.

C Shepherd was upset that Anderson had cut the story so much.
D the word 'badly' could have referred to the quality or the quantity of the cutting.

3 When Anderson returned from the pub he was usually
A a little careless in reading the writer's copy.
B more conscious of the writer's mistakes.
C more good-humoured towards him.
D red in the face from heavy drinking.

4 The reason for Anderson's sarcastic humour was that he
A envied the writer for having published a novel.
B had had a volume of poetry rejected by a publisher.
C had not been able to fulfil his early ambitions.
D was bored when there was not enough news to fill the paper.

5 The poet Swinburne had apparently
A given Anderson's translations to his assistant to read.
B ignored them.
C sent them back without reading them.
D told his assistant to deal with Anderson.

E

Words often confused

1 fit, match, suit, take after

Use each of these verbs *at least once*, in the correct form, to complete the sentences, paying attention to the context.

1 When he returned from the bar, Anderson's face __________ the rose he wore in his buttonhole.
2 – It's the right size, isn't it?
– Yes, it __________ me, but I don't think this colour __________ me.
3 I have chosen the wallpaper to __________ the carpet.
4 The room is such a strange shape that we shall have to __________ new carpets.
5 You can see that he __________ his father. They have the same eyes and the same expression.
6 I'm not surprised they've broken off their engagement. I never thought it would __________ her to be told what to do all the time.

2 deceived, disappointed, discontented, disillusioned, frustrated

Use each of the above *at least once* in the correct form, to complete the sentences, paying attention to the context.

1 I have never been so __________ in a person. I thought he was honest and he turned out to be a crook.
2 We had been planning to go to the beach today but as it's raining we've had to stay at home. The children were very __________ that we could not go.
3 – You can't expect to achieve good results in the factory if the workers are __________. The only answer is to pay them what they demand. Our efforts to reach a settlement last month were __________ by the management refusing to listen to reason. I don't blame the workers. They feel that they were __________ by the promise of an open discussion of their claims.
– Naturally, as Personnel Officer, you're __________ at the outcome.
– It's much more than that! I'm totally __________. When I took this job I was promised co-operation, but I feel completely __________ when I can't even speak to the Managing Director. His attitude is that if workers are __________, they should leave. Well, that applies to me, too.

F

Vocabulary expansion

Look carefully at the way the words below are used *in the context of the passage*, and decide which of the three alternatives, a), b), or c) is closest in meaning. Then work out whether either of the remaining choices could ever be correct, and if so, in what context.

1 **career** (line 1) a) course of study b) profession c) vocation
2 **conservative** (line 2) a) opposed to change b) out of date c) right-wing
3 **enclosed** (line 6) a) locked up b) restricted c) shut up
4 **expression** (line 7) a) idiom b) meaning c) phrasing
5 **fancied** (line 22) a) desired b) guessed c) imagined
6 **courteous** (line 26) a) kind b) polished c) polite
7 **episode** (line 40) a) chapter b) incident c) period
8 **apprehension** (line 41) a) anxiety b) arrest c) dread
9 **resign** (line 42) a) abdicate b) leave c) retire
10 **arguing** (line 43) a) discussing b) quarrelling c) reasoning

Writing Letters Becomes Popular Again

The following three articles were all published on the same day. Read all three and compare their approach to the same subject before answering the questions.

A

Art of letter-writing flourishes against all the odds

By Alan Hamilton

Despite the explosion of electronic communication, declining standards of literacy and the difficulty of buying a stamp on Sunday the British have not entirely lost the art of writing letters to each other, according to a survey published yesterday by the fibre-tip pen and pink writing paper trade.

Research by the Letter Writing Bureau, a front organization of the stationery industry which has the backing of the Post Office, indicates that in 1983 we sent each other 679 million personal letters, an increase of 37 million on the previous year. The figure excludes all greetings cards, business letters, bank statements, junk mail and **final demands from the Inland Revenue**.

But there is no concealing the fact that, compared with previous decades, personal letter-writing has tended to go the way of tramcars and the wind-up gramaphone. The golden age of written communication between individuals was the 1940s and 1950s; in 1950 the Post Office handled 8,500 million letters and estimates that half of them were personal, sent from one private address to another.

We are barely even back to the levels of 1900, when the Post Office delivered 2,323 million letters, which by its rough rule of thumb would indicate that about 1,100 million of them were items of congratulation, condolence or mere conversation between individuals.

The survey largely confirms the expected: that the letter is a better vehicle for self-expression than the telephone, that the telephone has lost its novelty and relative cheapness, that women write more than twice as many letters as men and that the most ardent writers are the over 65s, who pen 45 missives a year compared with the national average per author of 37.

Among the less expected findings of the survey is that the second most prolific age group are the 16 to 24s, who write an average of 36 letters a year each.

As their principal category of communication is the love letter, and as they follow the overall trend of many more female than male authors, it must be concluded that many an expression of undying affection remains disappointingly unanswered. Or else the youthful Romeo prefers to express his feeling down the relative anonymity of the telephone.

The survey also found that the most ardent letter-writers of all age groups lived in the south-west of England and in Scotland. The north-easterners and the Welsh are the least prolific.

Details were compiled from the Post Office's own statistics, together with the replies to 75,000 questionnaires.

From an article by Alan Hamilton in *The Times*

final demands from the Inland Revenue: The Inland Revenue is the Government tax office, and final demands are the last of a series of warnings it sends to people who have not paid their taxes.

B

Picking up on dropping a line

By John Ezard

Hopes of a reverse – or at least a pause – in the decline of personal letter-writing, the cherished art of **Jane Austen** and **Queen Victoria**, were held out yesterday.

A market research survey found that 37 million more personal letters were posted in 1982–3 than in the previous year, the first known increase for nearly 30 years. This rise of 6 per cent was put down in particular to a return by 16–24-year-olds to the habit of writing love letters.

This age group is now writing more personal letters than its parents and not many fewer than its surviving grandparents. Yet the survey's sponsors, the Letter-Writing Bureau, note that this generation has grown up during a doubling of telephone ownership and a 50 per cent expansion of the greeting card market.

Twenty-nine per cent of the teenage letters are love letters, the research finds. Twenty-two per cent are thank-you letters, 19 per cent letters sent abroad, 12 per cent penfriend letters, and 7 per cent fan letters. Women in general write twice as often as men. With teenage love letters the pattern appears to be that the girl writes to the boy and he replies – if at all – by telephone.

The research is based on a survey of 75,000 people by the Post Office Letter Information System and an attitudes survey of 5,000 people by **Gallup**. Some 659 million personal letters – defined as those written from one private address to another – were sent in 1980–1. In 1981–2 the total fell to 642 million. But in 1982–3 it rose to 679 million accounting for about 7 per cent of all mail.

One euphoric bureau release claimed that teenagers were 'fast catching up on the golden age of correspondence of their grandparents' time' and beginning to emulate 'the marvellously prosy Victorians'. However, a study of historical figures suggests that they are still far from doing this.

In 1930 an estimated 3,000 million personal letters were sent in Britain, despite the lower literacy rates and relatively higher postal charges of the time. In 1900 – when a modern teenager's great-grandparents or great-great-grandparents were young – an estimated 1,000 million personal letters were sent. The 1982–3 total is still more than 300 million below this.

From an article by John Ezard in the *Guardian*

Jane Austen (1775–1817): great English novelist, famous for her clear, ironic style, and also a prolific letter-writer, as was **Queen Victoria** (1819–1901)

Gallup: an organisation that conducts opinion polls

zany: mad, but attractive

C

Dear Dad, to explain the phone bill

By Howard Foster

It may come as a surprise to fathers shuddering at mountainous phone bills clocked up by teenagers chattering night after night about everything and nothing.

But young people, it is said, are turning to old-fashioned letters as a way of keeping in touch with their friends.

Part of the answer to the apparent contradiction is, it seems, the allure of new-fashioned writing paper, often with romantic or **zany** motifs.

And love, too, helps the mail go round. The most popular type of letter sent by the under-18s is the love letter – and twice as many girls as boys pen these.

Another part of the explanation could be that the revelation comes from the Letter-Writing Bureau, a consortium including the Post Office and stationery and pen manufacturers.

The bureau attached questionnaires in post offices to mail that looked personal and then questioned another 4,000 people about letter-writing habits.

The research, monitoring almost 80,000 people altogether, revealed a 37 million increase in private letters last year, says the Bureau – up from 642 million to 679 million.

Top of the letter-writing league, predictably, were the over 65s, with an average of 45 personal letters sent in a year, it says. But 16 to 24-year-olds notched up an average of 36 each.

Teenagers, despite a doubling in the number of telephone calls made over the past ten years, send vast quantities of letters abroad to pen-friends and as thank-you notes, says the bureau. And 7 per cent of their correspondence is fan-mail to pop idols.

The 35 to 44 age group are less keen on letter writing, says the Bureau, sending only an average of 29 letters each last year.

The Bureau's boss, Jonathan Wootliffe, said: 'Over the past 20 or 30 years there has been a long-term decline in social correspondence and during the Fifties we were attuning ourselves to the telephone.

'But in the past year there has been an upward turn. The most important factor in this is the availability of new products – fashion writing papers and pens.

From an article by Howard Foster in the *Daily Mail*

G

Unfamiliar words

Decide on the most probable meaning of the following words and phrases in the context.

1 **condolence** (A, line 44)
2 **ardent** (A, line 54)
3 **prolific** (A, line 61)
4 **the overall trend** (A, line 67)
5 **undying affection** (A, line 71)
6 **cherished** (B, line 4)
7 **put down** (B, line 13)
8 **euphoric** (B, line 56)
9 **catching up on** (B, line 58)
10 **emulate** (B, line 61)
11 **clocked up** (C, line 4)
12 **allure** (C, line 14
13 **consortium** (C, line 26)
14 **notched up** (C, line 48)
15 **attuning ourselves** (C, line 70)

Comparison of texts

Having gained an overall impression of the content of the three articles, answer the following general questions.

1 The three journalists regard the report presented by the Letter Writing Bureau as
   a) an important indication of the return of literacy through self-expression.
   b) a boring, unreliable publicity trick.
   c) an amusing, but not very serious, source of information.
2 Which of the articles pays most attention to the phenomenon of letter-writing increasing among young people?
3 Which seems to take this phenomenon least seriously?
4 There is some confusion about when the 'golden age of letter writing' was in Britain. When were the greatest number of personal letters written, and what argument is advanced to explain this?
5 There is also apparent disagreement about the literacy rates in Britain (A, lines 1–10, B, lines 67–72). Both statements are, in fact, believed to be true. How is this possible, and why is it likely that a right-of-centre newspaper would emphasise the first and a left-of-centre newspaper the second?

I

Use of language

Answer the following questions.

1 Look at the three headlines. What does 'dropping a line' mean in the context, and how does the report show that people are 'picking up on it'? Rephrase the headline in simple language. Study passage C, paragraph 1, and explain what the headline is meant to suggest. Why does it begin 'Dear Dad'? What are 'the odds' referred to in the third headline?
2 What distinction is being made between 'a reverse' and 'a pause' (B, lines 1 and 2)?
3 Explain the circumstances in which people write 'thank-you letters, pen-friend letters' and 'fan letters'.
4 'Prosy' (B, line 62) really means 'dull and long-winded', but the bureau press release obviously meant something else by referring to 'the marvellously prosy Victorians'. What impression was the writer intending to create?
5 Why should fathers 'shudder at mountainous phone bills' (C, line 2) and in what way can it be said that teenagers talk about 'everything and nothing' (C, line 7)?
6 'Love. . .helps the mail go round' (C, line 17) is a transformation of a popular phrase. What is the phrase, and why is the transformation appropriate here?
7 In what context is the phrase 'top of the. . .league' (C, line 43) normally used, and why is it being used here?
8 'Junk food' refers to pre-packaged, pre-cooked food like hamburgers, which are not thought to be nourishing. What, then, do you understand by 'junk mail' (A, line 21)?
9 Who is 'the youthful Romeo' referred to in passage A, line 73, why is it an appropriate expression, and why does the writer conclude that he prefers to express his feelings by telephone?

Words often confused

cope with, deal with, handle, manipulate, regulate, see to, supervise
The meanings of most of these words overlap, depending on the context. In the exercise below, *either* complete the sentence with the one word that appears

most suitable in the correct form, *or* substitute the most suitable other word that could be used appropriately instead of the word or words from the list that already appear.

1 These days television provides politicians with an ideal means of __________ public opinion.
2 It is wise to wear sterilised gloves when __________ chemicals.
3 The traffic lights have fused, so they have sent for a policeman to __________ the traffic.
4 Don't worry, Sir. I'll *deal with* the customer immediately.
5 The Post Office *deals with* millions of letters every year.
6 Managers in factories tend to talk about __________ the work that goes on there, while army officers speak of __________ their men.
7 I have so much work to do that I don't see how I could *deal with/handle* any more.
8 The machine is so carefully designed that it can *handle* scientific instruments with great precision and can also __________ the flow of production through the factory.

Cinema

Introductory exercise

See how many of the questions you can answer in the quiz that follows, in each case naming the actor or actress concerned.

1 Who was The Godfather?
2 Who was The Graduate?
3 Who was M. Hulot?
4 Who was Harry Lime in *The Third Man*?
5 Who was Philip Marlowe in *The Big Sleep*?
6 Who were Bonnie and Clyde?
7 Who were Butch Cassidy and The Sundance Kid?
8 Who sang in the rain in *Singin' in the Rain*?
9 Who danced in the cabaret in *Cabaret*?
10 Who killed whom in a shower in *Psycho*?
11 Who was Zorba the Greek?
12 Who met whom in *Casablanca*?
13 Who took the Road to Morocco?
14 Who built a bridge on the River Kwai?
15 Who broke up the French Connection?
16 What was The General and who drove it?
17 What was The African Queen and who owned it?
18 What was Rosebud and who lost it?
19 What was Jaws and who killed it?
20 What climbed the Empire State Building and was shot down by planes?

How many of these films have you seen? Would you describe them as crime films, comedies, Westerns, musicals, adventure films, war films, social films, fantasies, horror films?

The Birth of a Star

Read the following passage to gain a general impression of its content before studying the vocabulary in detail.

He was now twenty-three years old, a long, lean fellow, well over six feet tall, not aimless exactly but with no clear idea of what he wanted to do with his life. He tried to find work as a newspaper cartoonist and failed. He also failed as a door-to-door salesman, trying to hustle young mothers into having their babies photographed.

So he was simply drifting from one unsatisfactory job to another when he bumped into a couple of old friends from Montana who convinced him that there was money to be made from working as an extra in the movies. They took him to Poverty Row, a ramshackle stretch of old Hollywood which, in those comparatively early days of the silent pictures, was where the makers of **quickie westerns** maintained their headquarters.

By virtue of the fact that the years on the family ranch had made him an excellent horseman, Cooper was rapidly hired and through 1925 and into 1926 galloped across the screen in countless westerns, sometimes falling off his horse as a mortally wounded cowboy in the morning and then falling off a different, or even the same, horse as a mortally-wounded redskin in the afternoon.

Not surprisingly, however, this somewhat

painful way of life had lost much of its magic after six months or so and Cooper decided that if he were to stay in the movies it would be sensible to seek larger, more lucrative and more sedentary roles. So with the aid of an agent and a demonstration reel of film showing highlights of his work as an extra, he began to hawk himself round the studios. By now, Hollywood being for some reason tolerably well stocked with aspiring young actors named Frank Cooper, he had changed his first name to Gary after the birthplace of his agent, Gary, Indiana. As a name it seemed as good as any other and was certainly more suitable than that of **his own birthplace** and it appeared on screen for the first time in a film called *Lightnin' Wins*, a **two-reeler** in which the newly-dubbed Gary Cooper provided modest support to a wonder dog.

Soon afterwards, however, a far better opportunity presented itself. The actor who was to play second male lead in *The Winning of Barbara Worth*, which starred Ronald Colman and Vilma Banky, was delayed on another film and Cooper was standing in for him in the long-shots. Eventually the director, Henry King, decided he could wait no longer for his second lead to report for duty and handed the role to Cooper. Even though he had had no formal dramatic training of any kind, he turned in a useful enough performance to impress **Paramount** who offered him a contract. Cooper accepted and thus embarked on a career that was to last for thirty-five years.

From *The Hollywood Greats* by Barry Norman

quickie westerns: Western films made cheaply in a very short period of time

his own birthplace: Gary Cooper was born at Helena, Montana

a two-reeler: a short film lasting only two reels of film.

Paramount: one of the major Hollywood studios

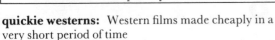

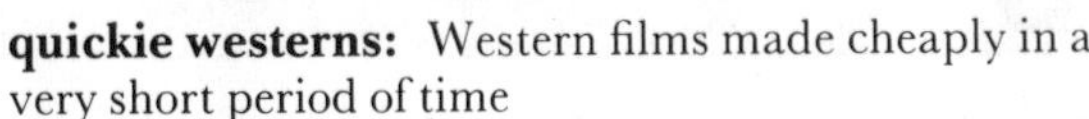

Reading for gist

Answer the following questions on the passage.

1 What ideas did Gary Cooper have about his future career at the age of 23?
2 How did he get into the film industry?
3 Why was he accepted as an extra?
4 How did he obtain his first parts in films?
5 What gave him the chance of becoming a star?

Now link your answers together to provide a summary of the passage.

Answer the following multiple-choice questions, choosing the answer that expresses most accurately what is stated in the passage. Compare the answers you have already given to the alternatives here, and find one that seems to you more or less the same.

6 At the age of 23, Gary Cooper
  A had not made up his mind about his future career.
  B was keen to become a film actor.
  C was lazy and not interested in a steady job.
  D wanted to be a photographer.
7 He was attracted to Hollywood because he
  A had heard they needed cowboys there.
  B realised that he would become a success.
  C thought it was an easy way of making friends.
  D was offered a job by friends of his in the industry.

8 The studios accepted him as an extra because he
  A had had previous acting experience.
  B had worked as a cowboy.
  C looked like the typical Western hero.
  D was so good-looking.

9 He was given his first real part in a film because he
  A changed his name.
  B had advertised his ability.
  C had impressed the studios as an extra.
  D was used to handling animals.

10 He eventually gained a contract because
  A he acted well as a substitute for another actor.
  B he looked more appropriate for the part than the actor who had originally been chosen.
  C he was a great success in *Lightnin' Wins*.
  D Ronald Colman was unable to play his part in *The Winning of Barbara Worth*.

Unfamiliar words

Decide on the most probable meaning of the following words in context, from the choices offered below.

1 **aimless** (line 2)
  a) lacking in purpose
  b) lazy
  c) indirect

2 **hustle . . . into having** (line 6)
  a) persuade someone to have
  b) push someone into having
  c) threaten someone to have

3 **drifting** (line 9)
  a) moving aimlessly
  b) moving determinedly
  c) moving hurriedly

4 **ramshackle** (line 14)
  a) broken-down
  b) delightful
  c) rich

5 **galloped** (line 22)
  a) rode professionally
  b) rode quickly
  c) rode slowly

6 **mortally-wounded** (line 24)
  a) badly wounded
  b) dead
  c) dying

7 **lucrative** (line 32)
  a) financially rewarding
  b) professionally rewarding
  c) spiritually rewarding

8 **more sedentary** (line 32)
  a) less active
  b) less demanding
  c) less monotonous

9 **hawk himself** (line 35)
  a) offer himself for sale
  b) promote himself aggressively
  c) publicise himself

10 **standing in for** (line 52)
  a) keeping still for
  b) speaking the lines for
  c) substituting for

Interpretation of text

Answer the following questions.

1 How had Cooper become such a good horseman?
2 Why does the writer refer to Cooper's work as an extra as 'this somewhat painful way of life' (line 28)?
3 Why did Frank Cooper decide to change his name to Gary?
4 Who was the star of *Lightnin' Wins*?
5 Why was Cooper's participation in *The Winning of Barbara Worth* at first limited to the 'long-shots'?

Words often confused

1 sensational, sensible, sensitive, sensual, sensuous

Use each of these words *once only* in the sentences below.

1 I never take any notice of the __________ headlines in the popular newspapers. They are always a gross exaggeration.
2 Puritans and priests are wrong to spend too much time attacking the pursuit of __________ pleasure.
3 If I were __________ to the criticisms of envious people, I would have given up writing long ago.
4 It was very __________ of him to call the doctor as soon as he realised that she was not well.
5 The last movement of the symphony is full of __________ melody, creating a perfect image of romantic love.

2 adaptable, adequate, qualified, suitable
Substitute one of these adjectives for each of the phrases below, changing the word order where necessary.

1. We do not believe that *sufficient* provision has been made in the budget for the additional expenses that are bound to occur.
2. He may be *an appropriate person* for the job but in the advertisement we have specifically stated that the person appointed must be a doctor *who has passed his examinations*.
3. The greatest quality he has as an actor is that he is *capable of playing a variety of parts*.

3 by chance, casually, eventually, occasionally
Substitute one of these words or phrases in each case for the phrases below, changing the word order where necessary.

1. He dropped his cigarette ash on the floor *without showing any concern about what he was doing*.
2. I met him in the street the other day *without expecting to*.
3. *From time to time* he comes to visit us.
4. At first it was difficult for Gary Cooper to establish himself in films, but *after a time* he became a great star.

Good and Bad Reviews

Read the following two reviews before answering the questions that follow.

A

Francis Ford Coppola's *The Conversation*, which won the Grand Prix at this year's Cannes Festival, is a remarkable film in that it works so well on so many different levels: as an ambiguous, **Hitchcockian** thriller, as an indictment of modern surveillance techniques, as a psychological study of profound loneliness and as a **Kafkaesque** vision of the world of giant corporations. But in the end, as Coppola himself has said, it is a film about responsibility. Harry Gaul, the wire-tapping protagonist of Coppola's immaculate screenplay, regards himself at the outset as a pro doing a skilled, technical job. 'I don't care what they're talking about,' he says as the tape spools on, recording the conversation of two young lovers in San Francisco's Union Square. 'All I want is a nice fat recording.' And his job is supposed to end when he hands over the tape to a mysterious Director, head of some giant, faceless corporation, for $15,000. But Gaul is also a devout Roman Catholic and when he realizes the tape might be used to bring about someone's death, he is plagued with guilt and remorse about his own involvement.

Some critics have complained that the thriller element is a bit obscure: that you never quite know who has been killed and that you are not even sure at the end whether you have been watching reality or fantasy. But all good thrillers leave you with an element of doubt; and finally Coppola is simply presenting you with a metaphor of a security-obsessed individual whose whole world is falling apart.

But, apart from the thriller aspect, the film is also a brilliant study of the sterility and emptiness of one man's life style. This stems partly from Gene Hackman's portrait of Harry Gaul, which never lapses into twitchy mannerism or show-off demonstrations of loneliness; everything about the man is meticulous, orderly and a little grey, right down to the plastic mac that he never bothers to take off, even when he is on the sofa with his girl friend. But the accuracy also stems from Coppola's vision of a man who gets upset when an unsolicited birthday present finds its way into his apartment, who spends his leisure hours accompanying jazz records on the saxophone and who can truthfully remark, 'I have nothing personal except my keys.'

From *Deserving Prizewinner* by Michael Billington in the *Illustrated London News*

Hitchcockian: in the style of Alfred Hitchcock, the famous Anglo-American director renowned for his use of suspense

Kafkaesque: mysteriously claustrophobic, in the style of the writer Franz Kafka

B

You know all's not well with Faye Dunaway when she turns up at this uninhabited palace outside Venice and flops down on the best four-poster after simply dropping her valises on the front doorstep, where they remain for the next forty-eight hours. Dying, that's what she is – so why unpack? What seems like half an hour of screen-time later, just when you're wondering if the makers have forgotten **the credit titles**, she revives slightly to send for Marcello Mastroianni to come and keep her company. After that, the only thing left to wonder at is, have the people also forgotten the movie?

A Place for Lovers is one of those costly, empty films that look as if they've been made with someone's **blank chic**. It's filled with **Beautiful People**. People like Miss Dunaway, who may be on her way to death's door from some nameless cinema disease that doesn't interfere with her looks but en route has scooped the wardrobe empty of Theodore Van Runkle's **jet-set creations**. Each crisis she passes through, on goes a new gown. Mastroianni can only look at her in that quizzical Italian way which may denote love, amazement or just envy. The luxury of how the rich die! And, oh, the lethargy of it, too! Five scriptwriters have laboured – collectively or consecutively, it's not stated – to do as little as possible in the way of providing a story, and after eighty-eight minutes have merely managed to move things from the marchese's Venetian palace to a millionaire's Alpine chalet. There Miss Dunaway, who's taken to posing to show how her spirits are sinking, decides at least to die generously and gives away all her pretty things to the local pig-keeper's daughter and then, when she changes her mind about dying, is caught above the snow-line in an above-the-knee-line number while every other sensible person is in woollies.

From *Double Takes* by Alexander Walker.

the credit titles: list of people involved in the making of a film usually given at the beginning of the film

blank chic: a 'blank cheque' is one where the recipient can fill in the amount, so it means, metaphorically, an opportunity to do whatever one likes; here, the phrase means 'empty sophistication'

Beautiful People: well-dressed people from high society

jet-set creations: clothes specially created for people rich enough to be able to fly from one place to another in jet planes in search of pleasure and amusement

E

Unfamiliar words

Using the aid given, decide on the most probable meaning of the following words, taken from passage A.

1 **surveillance** (line 8): has to do with recording, or keeping people under close observation?
2 **wire-tapping** (line 16): refers to what sort of wire?
3 **spools** (line 21): a noun or a verb in this context?
4 **faceless** (line 29): 'without a face', but in what sense?
5 **lapses** (line 56): 'deteriorates', but in what context?
6 **twitchy** (line 57): refers to bad acting, but of what kind?
7 **meticulous** (line 60): describes Gaul's professionalism.
8 **unsolicited** (line 67): why would a man like that be upset?

The context in itself should be sufficient to tell you the meaning of the following, taken from passage B.

9 **flops down** (line 4)
10 **four-poster** (line 5)
11 **valises** (line 6)
12 **en route** (line 30)
13 **gown** (line 35)
14 **quizzical** (line 37)
15 **lethargy** (line 40)
16 **above the snow-line** (line 58)

F

General understanding

Answer the following questions on the passage, and then use your answers to complete the multiple-choice questions beneath, looking for choices that seem to you more or less the same.

1 What sort of film-goer would be most likely to enjoy *The Conversation*?
2 In what way is the theme of responsibility emphasised in the film?
3 What is particularly good about Gene Hackman's performance?
4 While *A Place for Lovers* might not appeal to film-goers as such, it might attract people interested in something else. What, and what sort of people?
5 What is the main defect of *A Place for Lovers*?
6 *The Conversation* would appeal particularly to those who
A admire intelligently written films.
B are interested in films of social protest.
C enjoy murder mysteries.
D like romantic films.
7 The theme of responsibility in *The Conversation* is emphasised by Harry Gaul's
A professionalism.
B determination to find out the truth.
C realisation that his work can be manipulated.
D religion.
8 Gene Hackman's performance is outstanding because he
A gives a convincing picture of a dedicated professional.
B has created a character with no personality.
C has developed a series of characteristic gestures.
D is so careful in attending to details.
9 The main defect of *A Place for Lovers* is that
A the actors are inconsistent.
B the credit titles are too long.
C the setting is inappropriate.
D there is very little plot.
10 The writer suggests that *A Place for Lovers* would appeal to people who
A admire good acting.
B are interested in Italy.
C go to fashion-shows.
D like romantic films.

Interpretation of text

Answer the following questions about *A Place for Lovers*, passage B.

1 Why does it seem as if half an hour of screen time has passed before Faye Dunaway sends for Marcello Mastroianni?
2 Why may Marcello Mastroianni feel envy while Faye Dunaway is dying?
3 What is the point of the critic's remark that it is not clear whether the scriptwriters worked 'collectively or consecutively' (line 42)?
4 In what way does Faye Dunaway decide to 'die generously' and why is it absurd that she 'changes her mind' (lines 53–57)?
5 What is absurd about the way she is dressed at the end of the film? How does the critic's reference to 'an above-the-knee-line number', in contrast to 'woollies' (lines 58–61), point to one of the most absurd features of the film throughout?

Use of language

Sometimes a writer will deliberately use one word rather than another, similar in meaning to it. Compare the following words used in passage A, with the rough equivalents, and try to define what the difference is.

1 **ambiguous** (line 6) unclear
2 **indictment** (line 8) criticism
3 **immaculate** (line 17) excellent
4 **devout** (line 31) convinced
5 **plagued** (line 34) troubled
6 **remorse** (line 35) regret

Words often confused

1 add, allege, comment, notice, remark (verbs)
Use each of the above *once only* in the correct form to complete the following paragraph.

Asked whether he had ________ the editorial in yesterday's *Daily News*, blaming the Government for the increase in violent crime, the Home Secretary, ________ on the article, said that he could not be responsible for what newspapers printed but ________ that it was indeed irresponsible to ________ that any government encouraged crime. 'Attacks of this kind,' he ________ to me afterwards, 'can only give comfort to lawbreakers'.

2 addition, allegation, comment, notice, remark (nouns)
Use each of the above *once only* to complete the following paragraph.

'No doubt the editor concerned would argue that what was printed', he continued, 'was fair ________ on a matter of public interest, but we must distinguish between the kind of ________ made casually among friends and a serious ________ with no substance in fact printed in a newspaper. I do not normally take any __________ of such attacks, but this one seems to me a needless __________ to the problems of the police.'

3 appearance, aspect, complexion, outline
Use each of the above *once only* to complete the sentences, noting the context.

1 She always takes great pride in her __________. Of course, she has a lovely __________ – if it's genuine!
2 I can give you an __________ of the article I propose to submit to the review, but I still need further data in order to handle the most serious __________ of the problem satisfactorily.

4 characteristic, gesture, mannerism, trait
Use each of the above, *once only*, in the singular or plural, to complete the following sentences.

1 'Leave me alone', he said, brushing me aside with an angry __________.
2 An interesting __________ of the development of the cinema industry in recent years has been the success of a number of low-budget films like *Chariots of Fire*.
3 He has a number of strange personality __________, but what irritates me about him are the peculiar __________ he has developed, such as stroking his ear while he is talking to you.

5 recover, repair, restore, revive, survive (verbs)
Use each of the above *at least once* in the correct form to complete the sentences below.

1 I'm glad to find you completely __________ to health.
Yes, I've __________ completely from my illness.
2 The season of Buster Keaton films on television has __________ interest in his work. It is fortunate that prints of his masterpieces __________ during the time when he was forgotten in Hollywood, and a French admirer painstakingly __________ them so that we can see them today.
3 My brother and I work in similar professions, but I __________ television sets while he __________ pictures!

6 recovery, repair(s), restoration, revival, survival (nouns)
Use each of the above *once only* in the correct form to complete the sentences.

1 He has made a complete __________, I'm glad to say, after six weeks in hospital.
2 There is a __________ of a Bernard Shaw play at the Palace.
3 It is one of the few countries in the world where there has been a successful __________ of the monarchy.
4 How much did they charge you for the __________ they made to the fence?
5 Darwin's theory of evolution was based on 'the __________ of the fittest'.

Vocabulary expansion

audience, costume, cue, dress, first night, footlights, hero, heroine, lines, make-up, performance, producer, rehearsals, scene, speech, stage

Look at these words which are all associated with the world of theatre, and then use each, *once only*, to complete the passage below.

The only important part I ever played on the [1] __________ was that of a Shakespearean [2] __________, Othello. A group of teachers at the British Institute got together to act the play on the 400th anniversary of Shakespeare's birth. After months of [3] __________, we all knew our [4] __________ and the only problem was whether we would remember them on the [5] __________. The [6] __________ rehearsal the night before, however, caused added complications. In making my dying [7] __________ and falling dead, the black wig I was wearing fell off. The [8] __________, who also took the role of the villain, Iago, insisted that I should have my hair dyed, in case the same thing happened at the first [9] __________. In the end, everything went off very well. I had a magnificent [10] __________ for the part and although I was nervous when I first went on stage, I soon found that I remembered the lines and did not miss a [11] __________. Even so, technical problems persisted. By the last [12] __________, the heat of the [13] __________ was beginning to worry me. I was terrified that my chocolate face would melt, and this caused another problem when I had to strangle the [14] __________, Desdemona. I was sure that the [15] __________ on my hands would come off on her neck, and she would be lying in full view of the [16] __________ until the end of the play with chocolate finger marks around her neck. But she cleverly put her hands close to her neck to defend herself, and we gave the impression of strangling without my having to touch her neck at all.

Lexical Progress Test 2

You must choose the word or phrase which best completes each sentence.
For each question, 1 to 25, indicate the correct answer, A, B, C, or D.
The time for the test is 20 minutes.

1 You should not make serious accusations like that unless they have a sound __________ in fact.
A basis B foothold C precept D principle

2 Worrying serves the purpose of enabling us to come to __________ with our problems.
A bearings B pass C reason D terms

3 I just have a few household __________ to cope with, and then I'll be ready to go out.
A charges B chores C errands D works

4 I couldn't sleep because the tap in the bathroom was __________.
A draining B dripping C dropping
D spilling

5 The book gives a brief __________ of the course of his research so far.
A outline B outlook C reference D aspect

6 The newspaper defended the report by saying it was fair __________ on a matter of public interest.
A allegation B comment C remark
D statement

7 He was standing outside in the snow, __________ with cold.
A shivering B shuffling C staggering
D stuttering

8 There's your seat – in the fifth __________.
A file B line C rank D row

9 It's obvious that he __________ his father. He looks just like him.
A copies B impersonates C matches
D takes after

10 All the rooms have __________ carpets, which are included in the price of the house.
A adapted B equipped C fitted D suited

11 He earns his living by __________ works of art.
A recovering B renewing C restoring
D reviving

12 Once the picture was proved to be a forgery, it became quite __________.
A invaluable B unpriced C unworthy
D worthless

13 He hopes to be __________ from hospital next week.
A discharged B dismissed C expelled
D resigned

14 She __________ the stranger by leaving by the back door.
A avoided B missed C neglected
D prevented

15 The party the ambassador gave was intended as a goodwill __________.
A attitude B gesture C mannerism
D image

16 Competitors who do not __________ with the regulations will be disqualified.
A assent B comply C consent D perform

17 From the __________ of the negotiations, it was clear that it would be hard for the two sides to reach agreement.
A onset B outbreak C outcome D outset

18 He was __________ from school because of his bad behaviour.
A evicted B expelled C relegated
D resigned

19 I came across him quite __________ as I was walking to the station.
A by chance B by the way C carelessly
D occasionally

20 These articles are __________ from customs duty.
A acquitted B dispensed C exempt
D unaccountable

21 'I'm happy to see you've made such a swift __________ from your illness.'
A recovery B renewal C restoration
D revival

22 They __________ him as their leader.
A acknowledged B complied C conformed
D observed

23 The official term for old people nowadays is '__________ citizens'.
A archaic B elderly C senile D senior

24 'It's hot, isn't it?' he said, __________ his brow with a handkerchief.
A rinsing B scrubbing C sweeping
D wiping

25 He's in trouble because he hasn't paid his National Insurance __________.
A contribution B subscription C subsidy
D tribute

Animals

Introductory exercise

Link the animal or bird named in the left-hand column to the word you associate with it in the right.

A			B			C			D		
	1 bee	a) den		1 bird	a) fur		1 cat	a) hoof		1 bird	a) snout
	2 bird	b) lair		2 cat	b) hide		2 eagle	b) paw		2 elephant	b) beak
	3 fox	c) hive		3 cow	c) skin		3 horse	c) talon		3 pig	c) trunk
	4 lion	d) warren		4 pig	d) wool						
	5 rabbit	e) nest		5 sheep	e) feathers						

Intelligence in Animals

Read the passage to gain a general impression of its meaning. Note down the differences between the creatures referred to.

Before considering this question it is interesting to review briefly the evolution of the mind as an instrument. The commonest way that has been used to find out the relative intellectual levels of creatures at different stages of evolutionary complexity has been to study the way they behave when set different kinds of puzzles. For example, an ant possesses a complex routine of behaviour, but can it think? The answer is that if an ant is forced to go through a maze of passages, many of which are dead ends, on its way to its nest, it starts by making a lot of mistakes and taking a great many wrong turnings. In the end, however, after it has had to worry its way through often enough, it does learn to get to its nest without going into any of the blind alleys. As one moves up the evolutionary scale the test of brain-power exemplified by solving the problem of getting through a maze becomes too simple. Among mammals, for example, the maze is an inadequate test. The learning problem does not tax enough attributes of the mind. In this sort of learning, as a matter of fact, rats can beat university undergraduates and have, in fact, repeatedly done so.

The next, more subtle test of mental ability is to see at what level an animal can think about something when it is not there. The usual test is to train the animal to go through one of several doors when a light is turned on at that particular door. When the preliminary lesson has been learnt – that is, that food can be obtained by going through the door with the light – the more subtle trial is imposed. The light is shone as before at one or other of the different doors and is then extinguished. After an interval the animal is released. When posed with this test rats and dogs can remember which was the lighted door only if they are allowed to keep their heads steadily pointing at where the light was. On the other hand, a raccoon, possessing a more highly evolved brain, can pace up and down until it is released and then go straight to the correct door. But it can only remember for about twenty-five seconds which is the right door for any particular test.

Monkeys and chimpanzees, although they are weaker and less fierce than many other animals, possess brains which are as far along the evolutionary road as any creature other than man. Birds can perform marvels of aerobatics, they can catch insects on the wing with unparalleled skill, they can navigate in a remarkable manner half round the world and back – but they cannot think and reason. In technical terms it can be said that they are lacking in insight. The abilities which they do possess are built-in instincts derived from their genetic inheritance. Monkeys, on the other hand, can reason. They can easily remember a lighted door indicating the presence of food. They can remember what kind of food they are looking for. A monkey set the problem of reaching a banana, say, hung high up in its cage, can work out a system for getting it even if it involves piling up boxes to stand on and then knocking down the banana with a stick. A charming story is told about the psychologist Wolfgang Köhler, who had provided various boxes and other gear by which he proposed to test a chimpanzee's ability to think out a method of reaching a fruit hung nine feet in the air. The animal looked about it and sized up the probem. Then it took Köhler by the hand, led him to a position immediately under the banana, jumped up on to his shoulder and reached it down from there.

But evolution, although it has brought monkeys to a remarkable degree of cleverness, has stopped short at a crucial ability, the possession of which places man at a clearly superior level. Their minds cannot cope with abstract ideas. For example, an ape can be taught to fill a can with water from a barrel and take the can of water to extinguish a fire so that it can reach into a box and get food. But if the whole set-up is arranged on a raft the animal will continue to draw its water only from the barrel. It cannot grasp that any water, taken more conveniently, say, from the pond on which the raft is floating, will put out the fire just as well. The abstract idea that water quenches fire is beyond it.

From *The Boundaries of Science* by Magnus Pyke

A

Reading for gist

Answer the following questions on the passage.

1 What is the commonest method of measuring the intelligence of different creatures?
2 Why is it an inadequate test for human beings? What is the proof of this?
3 How does a raccoon demonstrate that it is more intelligent than a rat or a dog?
4 What demonstrates the superior intelligence of monkeys, compared with other creatures, apart from man?
5 What shows the limitations of monkeys' development, compared to that of man?

Link your answers together to provide a summary of the passage, and use the information to answer the multiple-choice questions that follow, finding answers that mean more or less the same as what you have written.

6 The commonest way by which scientists have evaluated the intelligence of different creatures has been by
A comparing the complexity of their behaviour.
B leading them into blind alleys to see what they will do.
C giving them problems to solve.
D measuring the size of their brains.

7 The maze test is inadequate for human beings because
A it is too difficult.
B it has a limited application, compared with the range of human abilities.
C it is too easy.
D they are so much better at it than other species that it proves nothing.

8 Birds owe their remarkable abilities to
A inheritance.
B insight.
C intelligence.
D navigation.

9 Monkeys demonstrate their superiority in intelligence over other creatures apart from man by
A being less fierce.
B piling up boxes
C remembering lighted doors.
D working out their own methods for solving problems.

10 Monkeys are differentiated from man because they lack our ability to
A comprehend abstract ideas.

B draw water from a pond.
C stop short and consider difficult problems.
D use water to put out fires.

Unfamiliar words

Decide which of the choices offered below is the most probable meaning of the following words and phrases in the context.

1 **maze** (line 16) a) labyrinth
b) puzzle c) wilderness
2 **dead end** (line 17) a) blind alley
b) by-pass c) one-way street
3 **on the wing** (line 80) a) by their wings
b) while flying c) with their wings
4 **insight** (line 87) a) instinct
b) intuition c) perception
5 **built-in** (line 88) a) developed
b) innate c) interior
6 **say** (line 98) a) for example
b) in other words c) so to speak
7 **sized up** (line 112) a) appreciated
b) evaluated c) measured
8 **crucial** (line 122) a) decisive
b) important c) primary
9 **grasp** (line 135) a) grip
b) take hold of c) understand
10 **beyond it** (line 140)
a) on the other side of the raft
b) outside its normal range of experience
c) too complex for its level of intelligence

Reading for detail

Read the following statements, comparing them with the passage, and decide which one is correct in each case. Say why you reject the alternatives.

1 The maze test applied to ants proves that they
A cannot think.
B eventually learn from experience.
C find the way to their nests without making many mistakes.
D worry too much when given problems.
2 The second trial imposed (line 40) is 'more subtle' because
A lights are never shone at the same door as before.
B lights are shone at more than one door at the same time.
C the animal has only one opportunity of associating the light with the correct door.
D the animal must remember at which door the light was shone.
3 Tests on raccoons show they are more intelligent than dogs or rats because they
A can remember where something was when they can no longer see it.
B keep their heads pointing in the direction of the light.
C never forget where a light was once they have seen it.
D pace up and down while waiting for the test to begin.
4 A monkey in the experiment quoted (lines 96–103) piles up boxes
A as a kind of game.
B to charm spectators.
C to reach food.
D to reach its stick.
5 The story about Köhler's monkey is 'charming' because the monkey
A chose Köhler himself as the quickest route.
B successfully completed the experiment.
C took Köhler by the hand.
D used all the gear provided.

Words often confused

1 instrument, equipment, gadget, tool
Use each of these words *at least once* in the correct form, singular or plural, to complete the sentences below.

1 We manufacture everything for the medical profession, from the finest surgical __________ to the most complex laboratory __________.
2 It is not the practice in this company for workmen to be compensated for the loss of their __________.
3 This is a neat little __________. It can open tins and also chop onions.
4 In the old days some musicians mastered a variety of __________ but modern pop musicians take so much electronic __________ around with them that you would think they were electrical engineers rather than entertainers.

2 beat, earn, gain, win

Use each of these verbs *at least once* in the correct form to complete the sentences below.

John McEnroe [1] __________ the Chicago tournament last night, [2] __________ Ivan Lendl by two sets to one and [3] __________ 50,000 dollars in the process. Lendl [4] __________ the first set, but once McEnroe levelled the score, he quickly [5] __________ an overwhelming advantage in the third set and from then on Lendl seemed certain to be [6] __________. This victory enabled McEnroe to [7] __________ ground on Lendl in the prize-winners' list, but Lendl, who has [8] __________ several major prizes this season and has already [9] __________ the record set up last year when he [10] __________ more than a million dollars, still leads.

3 analyse, experiment on, prove, sample, test, try, try on, try out

Use each of these verbs *at least once* in the correct form to complete the sentences below. Where more than one verb is possible, this is indicated, but you should note whether there is any change in meaning and say what it is.

1 That's a lovely dress. Can I __________ it __________?

2 He has been __________ rats to __________ their resistance to certain viruses. He has not yet __________ the results completely but he seems to have __________ that they are immune to the effects of the majority of them. Mind you, I wouldn't let him __________ them __________ on human beings.

3 I've been __________ a new recipe. Would you like to __________ my cooking?

4 The forensic experts __________ the blood on the defendant's clothes, and found it was indeed the victim's. This __________ him guilty beyond reasonable doubt to my mind. However, as a last resort, he began shouting and hurling insults at everyone in court, pretending he was mad. After a while this really began to __________ the patience of the judge. I can't say I blame him for __________ it __________ (or __________) though.

E

Vocabulary expansion

crawl, march, pace, shuffle, stagger, stride, stroll, wade

All of these verbs are associated with movement. Which of them would you associate with each of the people mentioned below? When you have decided, make a sentence for each, using the word in an appropriate context.

a) a soldier
b) a baby
c) a couple out for a walk on a Sunday morning
d) a very old man wearing slippers
e) a boxer who has just received a blow
f) an anxious father waiting for a baby to be born
g) a trout fisherman in a stream
h) a man anxious not to miss a train, walking to the station

Which of these words could you use as nouns in the following common expressions? Complete the sentences below.

1 Jones set the __________ with a first lap of 57 seconds.

2 You won't have any difficulty with the exam. You'll take it in your __________.

3 They were mending the road ahead of us and the traffic had slowed to a __________.

4 He hoped to steal a __________ on his rivals by publishing his book before them.

Wild Animals: The Raccoon

Read the following passage carefully, paying attention to detail and noting down words you do not understand.

In the evening, a crab-eating raccoon would come down to drink. They are strange-looking animals, about the size of a small dog, with bushy tails ringed in black and white, large, flat, pink paws, the grey of their body-fur relieved only by a mask of black across the eyes, which gives the creature a rather ludicrous appearance. These animals walk in a curious hump-backed manner with their feet turned out, shuffling along in this awkward fashion like someone afflicted with chilblains. The raccoon came down to the water's edge and, having stared at his reflection dismally for a minute or so, drank a little and then with a pessimistic air shuffled slowly round the outer rim of the valley in search of food. In patches of shallow water he would wade in a little way and, squatting on his haunches, feel about in the dark water with the long fingers of his front paws, patting and touching and running them through the mud, and he would suddenly extract something with a look of pleased surprise and carry it to the bank to be eaten. The trophy was always carried clasped delicately between his front paws and dealt with when he arrived on dry land. If it was a frog, he would hold it down and with one quick snap decapitate it. If, however, as was often the case, it was one of the large freshwater crabs, he would hurry shorewards as quickly as possible, and on reaching land flick the crab away from him. The crab would recover its poise and menace him with open pincers, and the raccoon would then deal with it in a very novel and practical way. A crab is very easily discomfited, and if you keep tapping at it and it finds that every grab it makes at you with its pincers misses the mark, it will eventually fold itself up and sulk, refusing to participate any more in such a one-sided contest. So the raccoon simply followed the crab around, tapping him on his carapace with his long fingers and whipping them out of the way every time the pincers came within a grabbing distance. After five minutes or so of this the frustrated crab would fold up and just squat. The raccoon, who till then had resembled a dear old lady playing with a Pekinese, would straighten up and become businesslike, and, leaning forward, with one quick snap would cut the unfortunate crab almost in two.

From *Encounters with Animals* by Gerald Durrell

F

Unfamiliar words

Decide on the most probable meaning of the following, in the context of the passage.

1 **ludicrous** (line 6)
2 **afflicted with** (line 8)
3 **wade** (line 13)
4 **patting** (line 15)
5 **clasped** (line 18)
6 **decapitate** (line 20)
7 **flick** (line 23)
8 **poise** (line 24)
9 **pincers** (line 25)
10 **discomfited** (line 26)

G

Reading for detail

Read the following statements, comparing them with the passage, and decide which one is correct in each case. Say why you reject the alternatives.

1 When it began hunting, the raccoon gave the writer the impression that it
A didn't expect to catch anything.
B was not familiar with the surroundings.

C was thirsty, but not hungry.
D was very hungry and eager to eat.

2 If the raccoon caught a frog, it
A bit off its head and carried it to the shore to eat it.
B carried it to the shore before killing it.
C killed it and ate it immediately.
D killed it by crushing it between its paws.

3 The raccoon's technique with crabs was different from its technique with frogs because it
A didn't bite them to death.
B killed crabs on shore.
C killed them in the water.
D was more patient.

4 The crab's downfall resulted because it
A became frustrated.
B lost its balance.
C struck out wildly.
D was too terrified to fight.

5 The raccoon broke the crab's resistance by
A grabbing its pincers.
B hitting its shell.
C jumping up and down in front of it.
D pretending to sit down and play with it.

Use of language

In the following phrases, the writer humanises the animals he is talking about by using words to describe actions that are normally associated with human beings. Explain the usual context in which they are used and why they create an amusing picture here.

1 like someone afflicted with chilblains (line 8)
2 stared at his reflection dismally (line 9)
3 with a pessimistic air (line 11)
4 with a look of pleased surprise (line 16)
5 recover its poise (line 24)
6 . . . sulk, refusing to participate any more in such a one-sided contest (line 29)
7 . . . had resembled a dear old lady playing with a Pekinese (line 35)
8 become businesslike (line 36)

Words often confused

attack, intimidate, menace, threaten, warn
Use each of these verbs *at least once* in the correct form to complete the sentences below.

1 My father had __________ me not to go too close to the beehive, but I was very curious and not in the least __________, so I overturned one of the hives to see what would happen. A swarm of angry bees __________ me and I was lucky to escape with only about a dozen stings.

2 One of our neighbours once __________ to call the police because I climbed into his garden to get a ball. I was not __________ by that, but when he bought a large, fierce dog I kept out of trouble. It used to stand inside the gate, __________ (or __________) the passers-by and would have __________ them if it could have got out. Our neighbour put up a notice __________ people of what would happen if they went near it. Eventually, it bit the postman and he __________ the neighbour with a court action.

Vocabulary expansion

1 border, edge, frame, fringe, rim
These words are similar in their general meaning, but which would you associate with the following contexts?

1 a cliff	7 a knife
2 a cup	8 leaves round a window
3 two countries	9 spectacles (two possibilities)
4 flowers in a garden	10 a picture
5 a handkerchief	11 a window
6 hair	12 a volcano

2 bite, gnaw, peck, snap, sting
The raccoon **bit** the frog's head off with a quick, sharp bite. In other words, he **snapped** it off. What sort of creatures **gnaw, peck** and **sting**?

Domestic Animals: The Dog that Bit People

Read the passage to gain a general impression of its meaning.

The Airedale was the worst of all my dogs. He really wasn't my dog, as a matter of fact: I came home from a **vacation** one summer to find that my brother Roy had bought him while I was away. A big, burly, choleric dog, he always acted as if he thought I wasn't one of the family. There was a slight advantage in being one of the family, for he didn't bite the family as often as he bit strangers. Still, in the years that we had him he bit everybody but mother and he made a pass at her once but missed. That was during the month when we suddenly had mice, and Muggs refused to do anything about them. Mother slipped out into the pantry once to see how everything was going. Everything was going fine. It made her so mad to see Muggs lying there, oblivious of the mice – they came running up to her – that she slapped him and he slashed at her, but didn't make it. He was sorry immediately, mother said. He was always sorry, she said, after he bit someone, but we could not understand how she **figured this out**. He didn't **act sorry**.

Mother used to send a box of candy every Christmas to the people the Airedale bit. The list finally contained forty or more names. Nobody could understand why we didn't get rid of the dog. I didn't understand it very well myself, but we didn't get rid of him. I think that one or two people tried to poison Muggs – he **acted poisoned** once in a while but Muggs lived to be almost eleven years old and even when he could hardly get around he bit a Congressman who had called to see my father on business. My mother had never liked the Congressman – she said the signs of his horoscope showed he couldn't be trusted (he was Saturn with the moon in Virgo) – but she sent him a box of candy that Christmas. He sent it right back, probably because he suspected it was trick candy. Mother persuaded herself it was all for the best that the dog had bitten him, even though father lost an important business association because of it. 'I wouldn't be associated with such a man,' mother said, 'Muggs could read him like a book.'

We used to take turns feeding Muggs to be **on his good side**, but that didn't always work. He was never in a very good humour, even after a meal. Nobody knew exactly what was the matter with him, but whatever it was it made him irascible, especially in the mornings. Roy never felt very well in the morning, either, especially before breakfast, and once when he came downstairs and found that Muggs had moodily chewed up the morning paper he hit him in the face with a grapefruit and then jumped up on the dining room table, scattering dishes and silverware and spilling the coffee. Muggs' first free leap carried him all the way across the table and into a brass fire screen in front of the gas grate but he was back on his feet in a moment and in the end he got Roy and gave him a pretty vicious bite in the leg. Then he was all over it; he never bit anyone more than once at a time. Mother always mentioned that as an argument in his favour; she said he had a quick temper but that he didn't **hold a grudge**. She was forever defending him. I think she liked him because he wasn't well. 'He's not strong,' she would say, pityingly, but that was inaccurate; he may not have been well but he was terribly strong.

From *My Life and Hard Times* by James Thurber

vacation (USA): a holiday
mad (USA): angry, in this context
figured this out (USA): worked this out
act sorry, acted poisoned (USA): act as if he were sorry, poisoned
candy (USA): sweets
right back (USA): straight back
on his good side (USA): on the right side of him
hold a grudge (USA): bear a grudge

Unfamiliar words

Decide on the meaning of the following words in the context.

1 **burly** (line 4)
2 **choleric** (line 4)
3 **pantry** (line 12)
4 **oblivious** (line 14)
5 **slashed** (line 15)
6 **irascible** (line 43)
7 **moodily** (line 46)
8 **grudge** (line 56)

Interpretation of text

The humour of this passage is based on a sustained comparison between the facts and the writer's mother's interpretation of them. First, find four examples of her attempts to deceive herself. Now answer these questions.

1 Why was there 'a slight advantage in being a member of the family', and why didn't the writer benefit from this?
2 What is amusing in the context about the fact that the mice 'came running up to her' (line 14)?
3 What was the writer's mother's reason for disliking the Congressman, and how did it justify Muggs biting him?
4 Why did the Congressman refuse to accept the Christmas present the family sent him?
5 What provoked Roy into attacking the dog, and how did the writer's mother excuse the dog's revenge?
6 Why did the writer's mother feel sorry for the dog, and why didn't the writer share her sympathy for it?

Words often confused

1 deny, neglect, refuse, reject, resist
Use each of these verbs *at least once* in the correct form to complete the following sentences.

1 I'm sorry I __________ to answer your letter. I just didn't find the time.
2 They wanted to get married but her father __________ to give his permission.
3 He is very depressed and __________ his work because the manuscript of his novel was __________.
4 When the police caught him he __________ having had anything to do with the robbery at first and tried to escape, so he has also been charged with attempting to __________ arrest.
5 Of course there are cases of mothers __________ their children at birth for psychological reasons. That cannot be __________. But it is quite a different matter when they __________ them systematically over a period of years and __________ to allow the local authority to do anything to help. When I saw the condition the children were in, I couldn't __________ asking the woman what she thought she was doing.

2 distribute, space, scatter, spray, spread
Use each of these verbs *at least once* in the correct form to complete the following sentences.

1 The dog jumped on the table and __________ the cups and saucers in all directions. I was in the kitchen, __________ fish paste on the sandwiches for tea. Apparently, it had all started when a mosquito bit John and he got so angry that he started __________ the whole room with fly-killer. Unfortunately, some of it got in the dog's eyes.
2 I want you to __________ out the plants about a foot or so apart. While you're doing that Henry can __________ the roses to get rid of the greenfly and Caroline can __________ these breadcrumbs for the birds.
3 As soon as he was dead the rumour __________ that he had left all his money to the cats' home, but in fact he __________ it fairly among his relatives. Of course the family is so widely __________ all over the world that it will be some time before the solicitors have traced them all.

Travel

Introductory exercise

There are many ways of travelling from one place to another. How many can you think of? Which method do you prefer? Why?

Look at the drawings below. Work with a partner, and see if you can complete the diagrams by labelling the parts indicated.

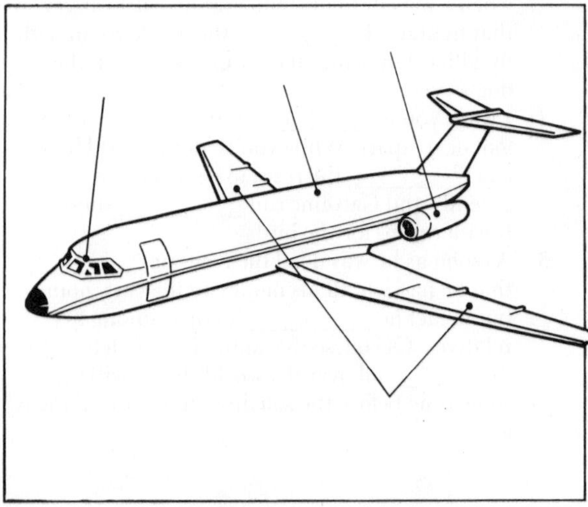

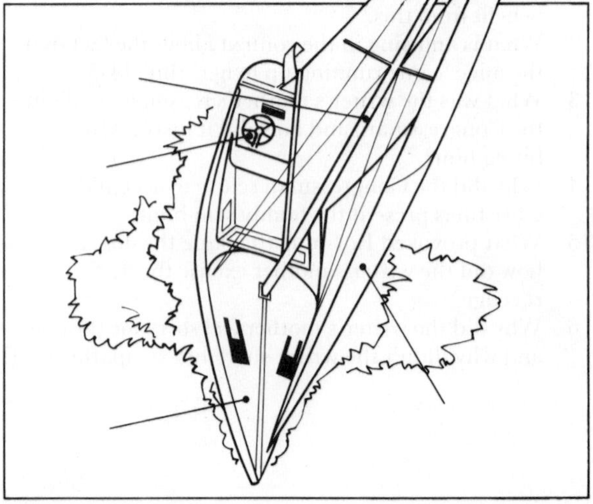

A Wanderer in Europe

Read the following passage to gain a general impression of its meaning.

The day was dark and threatening. Why didn't I stay on a bit? How I would have liked to! But I was entangled in a fiction that no one believed and there was no way out. We were talking in the library, snugly surrounded by books, when the man in green announced that the car was waiting. No good saying, now, that I would rather walk to the station: I would have missed my unwanted train and been late for my phantom rendezvous . . . But when we said goodbye, they looked truly worried, as though I were not quite safe on my own.

I sailed away, half-cocooned in a fur rug, in the back of an enormous car that swished its way, under an ever-darkening sky, to a little country station on the St Polten-Vienna line. A few warning flakes were falling when we arrived and the chauffeur jumped out, carrying my rucksack and stick. He wanted to help at the ticket office, put me into a corner seat and see me off.

Here was a new panic. Even had I wanted to go by train, I hadn't enough money for the ticket. All this brought on a recrudescence of last night's folly: someone had told me – who, and where? – that one tipped chauffeurs in Central Europe. Taking my stick and shouldering the rucksack, I found four coins in my pocket, and pressed them on the chauffeur with mumbled thanks. He was a white-haired, friendly and cheerful old man, a former coachman, I think. He had been telling me, over his shoulder on the way, how he too had loved wandering about as a young man. He looked surprised and distressed at this sudden unwanted largesse – he didn't in the least expect me to try to keep up with the Liechtensteins – and he said, with real feeling, '*O nein, junger Herr!*' and almost made as though to give the wretched coins back. Leaving him with his coronetted cap in his hand, scratching his head with a puzzled and unhappy look, I dashed in confusion into the station for cover and oblivion and watched him get slowly back in the car and drive off. The station master, who had exchanged friendly greetings too, headed for the office to sell me a ticket. Instead, I gave him an ambiguous wave, slunk out again and strode fast along the Vienna road. Looking back in a minute or two, I saw him standing on the platform, staring bemusedly at my dwindling figure. I wished I were dead.

From *A Time of Gifts* by Patrick Leigh-Fermor

A

General understanding

Reading a passage of this kind, extracted from the context of a book, is a little like solving a mystery in a detective story, but there should be sufficient clues for you to understand the writer's circumstances. Find evidence in the passage to answer the following questions before proceeding to the exercises below. The relevant lines in the text are given to help you discover the answers.

1 In which country was the writer (lines 12, 20, 29, 37)?
2 Which family was he staying with (line 28) and what evidence is there that they were very rich (lines 3–4, 10–11, 22, 28)?
3 How was he travelling around Europe (lines 14, 25–26)?
4 What do you imagine that he had told the family (lines 2–3) and how do we know that it was not true (lines 6–8)?
5 When had he made the mistake of inventing this story (line 19) and why was it a mistake to offer money to the chauffeur?

B

Unfamiliar words

In this passage there are a number of words that may be unfamiliar to you, used with great precision in the context. Use the aid given below to decide on their meaning.

1 **entangled** (caught up in obstacles) (line 2): how had the writer entangled himself in the situation?
2 **snugly** (line 4): contrasts with the weather outside.
3 **phantom rendezvous** (line 7): why was the rendezvous (meeting) phantom?
4 **cocooned** (line 10): a cocoon is the protective covering made by a caterpillar. Why is it appropriately used here?
5 **swished** (line 11): usually a sound like that of a horse's tail, or a long dress moving. Why is it used here for a car?
6 **recrudescence of last night's folly** (line 19): what had the writer done the previous night, and what was he doing now?
7 **pressed them on** (line 22): what additional meaning is conveyed by this, instead of 'gave them to'?
8 **largesse** (line 27): a generous gift. Why is it ironic here?
9 **coronetted** (line 30): what do you think the cap looked like?
10 **slunk** (line 36): from 'slink' (to move in a guilty or ashamed manner). What was the writer ashamed of?
11 **bemusedly** (line 38): how was the station master likely to react to the writer's behaviour?
12 **dwindling** (line 38): growing smaller. Why, in this context?

Reading for gist

Answer the following multiple-choice questions, choosing the answer that expresses most accurately what is suggested by the passage.

1 The writer was unwilling to be taken to the station by car because
A his hosts were worried about him.
B he was afraid of missing his train.
C he preferred to walk in such good weather.
D he really had no intention of catching the train.

2 The chauffeur's behaviour when they arrived at the station worried the writer because
A he thought he had lost his rucksack and stick.
B the man obviously intended to wait until he left in the train.
C he thought he would have to borrow money for the ticket.
D it was just starting to snow.

3 He tipped the chauffeur because
A he knew the man would not go away otherwise.
B he was very grateful to him.
C he was very nervous, and thought the man would go away.
D it was an easy way of getting rid of some small change.

4 The chauffeur was surprised and distressed by the tip because
A he did not think it was enough.
B it interrupted his story.
C he knew the writer was not as rich as his employers.
D it was not the custom for chauffeurs to receive tips.

5 The station master was puzzled by the writer's behaviour because
A he did not come into the station.
B he told him that he did not want a ticket.
C he replied to him in an unfriendly manner.
D he set off on foot towards Vienna.

Interpretation of text

Answer the following questions.

1 Why do you think the man mentioned in line 4 was dressed in green?
2 Why is the train described as 'unwanted' (line 7)?
3 Why are the coins the writer gave to the chauffeur described as 'wretched' (line 30)?
4 Why did the writer run into the station?
5 Why was the wave the writer gave the station-master 'ambiguous'?
6 Why did the writer wish he were dead as he walked away?

Words often confused

1 advertise, advise, announce, notice, warn (verbs)
Use each of these verbs *at least once* in the correct form to complete the sentences below, and note the structures in which the verbs appear.

– I __________ in the paper today that XYZ Ltd are __________ for a new marketing manager. They must be __________ Harry Phillips's job. I feel very sorry, because I __________ him to take it last year, but it proved too much for him, and the doctor __________ (or __________) him that if he did not rest he would have a heart attack.
– What a pity! He must have worked hard, because XYZ __________ record profits last week.

2 advertisement, advice, announcement, notice, warning (nouns)
Use each of these words *at least once* to complete the sentences below. Remember that **advice** is an uncountable noun.

1 The announcer reading the weather forecast read out a gale __________ for ships in the North Sea.
2 I am replying to your __________ in yesterday's *Times* for the post of marketing manager.
3 I'll always remember the kindness of my first boss, who always gave me such good __________.
4 Teachers seeking private classes are asked to check with the secretary before putting up their names and telephone numbers on the __________ board.
5 Here is an __________. The talk on *Hamlet* has been postponed until next Wednesday at 7 p.m.
6 – Let me give you a piece of __________. Never believe what you read in an __________. After all, it's just a way of making people take __________ of the product.
– True, but smokers don't take any __________ of the __________ (or __________) which the Ministry of Health prints on cigarette packets.

Vocabulary expansion

In the text you have just read, the chauffeur **scratched** his head, and the writer **waved** to the station master. What did these two actions represent?
In what circumstances might you do the following?

1 pat a child on the head
2 prick your finger
3 nod your head
4 shake hands
5 shake your head
6 shrug your shoulders
7 bite your lip
8 grind your teeth

Holidays Abroad

Read the three passages that follow one after another before answering any questions. Decide what their purpose is and why they were written, and explain what features of style and content lead you to your conclusions. Then give each passage a heading.

A

Theo Inniger is dynamic, cosmopolitan, and manages one of Amsterdam's finest hotels. His passions include sailing, France, and fine art (there's a regular exhibition in the hotel).

'I have an American Express Card myself, and would advise any one coming to Amsterdam to have one. It's certainly more convenient than carrying lots of different currencies – and a lot safer. You know you're not going to run out of funds, either. And you're more than welcome to use it here at the Pulitzer!'

The Pulitzer, one of the Golden Tulip hotels, is on Prinsengracht 315–331, and is an imaginative conversion of 17th century merchants' houses. Guests enjoy modern comfort, thoughtfully combined with the charms of yesteryear – vast oak beams, trim Dutch brickwork, winding corridors, and elegant courtyards.

The Pulitzer hotel is just one enchanting example of the many fine hotels in Amsterdam and around the world, where you can settle your bill with a signature and the American Express Card.

Today, the American Express Card is warmly welcomed by over 800,000 hotels, restaurants, stores, airlines, car hire companies, and other fine establishments worldwide, and there are over 1000 Travel Service Offices of American Express Company, its subsidiaries and representatives ready to help Cardmembers with travel advice and arrangements.

If you're not yet enjoying international financial services like these, with all the freedom and security they bring, complete the application form today.

B

The normal package holiday doesn't have a great deal in the package. You usually find yourself digging deep in your pocket to keep up with the cost of the extras.

Not so at Holiday Club International. Instead of a grasping hand, you'll find a helping hand. Most of the extras don't cost any extra. Because we own and operate our own private resorts, we can offer free activities and entertainment for the entire family.

Most of the fun is free

What other holiday includes all these extras in the cost? Free wine with main meals. Nightly cabaret and disco. Windsurfing, Sailing and pedalloes. Deck chairs on the beach. An incredible variety of sports, such as tennis, table-tennis, volley-ball and keep-fit classes.

As you'd expect, there's a nominal charge for water-skiing and horse-riding. But we do all we can to stop you dipping your hand in your wallet. Even the kids are looked after free of charge. In all of our resorts there's a children's playground, and our staff are trained in organising competitions and games for children.

Whatever type of holiday you choose, you'll get more for less with Holiday Club International. Speak to your travel agent or ask anyone who's been. Better still, phone or write for our free brochure which describes all of 1985's best holidays.

C

When you go to Ireland, you'll find a place of mountains, lakes and rivers.

A quiet land, so beautiful you'll want to stay forever.

But, the other beauty of it is, there's so much to enjoy besides.

There's fishing in some of the finest waters to be found anywhere, golf on courses that are famous throughout the world, pony trekking, skin diving and a multitude of other fascinating pastimes.

Perhaps the most beautiful thing of all is the warmth and hospitality you will meet wherever you go in Ireland.

There is accommodation ranging from top hotels, farm houses, guest houses and town and country homes to caravans and castles; always somewhere to stay where you will always be welcome.

You could cruise on one of our many waterways or even take to the roads in a horse-drawn caravan.

If ever there was a place of contrast, Ireland is it, and there are so many simple ways of getting there.

If you would like to know more about Ireland and the many places you can visit, simply send us the coupon and we'll send you our free brochure.

Just ask anyone who's been there.

G

Comparison of texts

Answer the following questions.

1 Passage A is an advertisement for
A a credit card.
B a hotel.
C both of them.
D neither of them.

2 Passage A is primarily aimed at emphasising
A the convenience and safety of using the credit card.
B the distinction of the people that use it.
C the kindness of the company's employees.
D the unique attractions of Amsterdam.

3 Passage B places its main emphasis on
A economy.
B holidays for young people.
C sport.
D holidays for people who want to look after themselves.

4 Passage C was probably placed by
A a hotel.
B a travel agent.
C a car hire firm.
D the national tourist authority.

5 Passage C stresses above all
A the quietness of the countryside.
B the kindness of the people.
C the opportunities for sport.
D the variety of means of travel available.

H

Use of language

First, look through each passage at the adjectives used, to gain a general impression of the stylistic content. Now answer the following questions in your own words.

1 What contrast is made in Passage A between the manager of the Pulitzer hotel and the hotel itself?

2 Why would this be likely to appeal to users of credit cards?

3 The word 'yesteryear' (line 16) is old-fashioned and poetic. Why do you think the copywriter used it here?

4 Which adjective is most frequently used in Passage B and why is this so?

5 Find three phrases in the first four paragraphs of Passage B that suggest other companies are greedy in contrast to the advertisers.

6 In the third paragraph find an example of exaggeration, and in the fourth paragraph find one of understatement. What is the advertiser's intention in each case?
7 Which phrase in the last paragraph summarises the impression the advertisers are trying to create?
8 In what ways does Passage C attempt to appeal to all classes and ages of people?
9 Which of the advertisements would be most likely to interest you if you were each of the following, and why?
a) a young couple who want a quiet honeymoon together
b) a young couple who want to stay up late and enjoy themselves
c) two friends who want to go on a walking tour
d) an American tourist on a package tour of Europe
e) a working class family with three children

Around the World in 80 Clichés

Read the passage below to gain a general impression of its content before attempting to answer the questions below.

Ever since he left office, **Mr Heath** has subjected his public to a kind of relentless reminiscence about his pastimes. Bachelors are such single-minded hobbyists. After *Sailing* and *Music* we have *Travels*, and before long no doubt we will be privileged to witness Mr Heath **signing even more titles** about other chaste recreations.

He is strong on scrapbook memorabilia–this present book contains the newspaper articles he wrote decades ago for the *Advertiser & Echo* (Broadstairs), tourist brochures, holiday snaps ('The picnic we had on our way from Warsaw to Lodz'), a forty-year-old Spanish letter of Authorization, and ancient Press cutings. But he is weak on detail of other sorts. For a man whose second favourite word is 'particularly' he is highly unparticular. The word most favoured in this book is 'agreeable': Bamberg was 'an agreeable place', Nairobi was 'Pleasant and agreeable', and **The Forbidden City**? Mr Heath does not equivocate: 'agreeable'.

This is almost entirely a record of happy days abroad, for however exotic or distant the place, what Mr Heath requires is a good meal, a hot bath, a night's sleep, solid comfort – no crowds, no awkward temperatures (he always reports whether a place was hot or cold). His time in Venice is typical: he spends his time 'exploring different churches' – the churches are not named; he eats 'meals' – no dishes are listed; he stays a 'hotel' – he doesn't say which one. And, 'I was captivated by Venice.' I was not captivated by Mr Heath's Venice.

But travel writing is a funny thing. The worst trips, in retrospect, make the best reading, which is why Graham Greene's *The Lawless Roads* and Kinglade's *Eothen* are so superb; and the most comfortable travel ('There was invariably split-second timing and exact positioning as they drew up at the steps leading to **the red carpet** and the welcoming party') becomes in the telling little more than chatting or, in Mr Heath's *Travels*, smug boasting. 'I wonder how many people in Europe know about **the Caprivi Strip**,' Mr Heath inquires, and lest anyone mistake this for a Dutch **fandango**, he adds, 'and how many people have been there?' Apart from the fact that he is saying 'I have and you haven't he says practically nothing about the place itself. Like so many of his destinations – like Venice, for goodness' sake – it is merely a name.

Mr Heath has been promoted as a man with wide interests. You name it, and he has sung it, or sailed in it or been there. He is a statemanly combination of **Toscanini** and **Joshua Slocum**, and now he is an indefatigable traveller. He laments that as an official visitor he has been unable to see much of 'the day-to-day life of the people'. And yet here he is in Kenya at the time of the **Mau Mau** troubles. He praises the **chintzes** at Nairobi's Norfolk Hotel, the carved doorways in the old Arab Quarter in Mombasa ('The only attractive part of the town') and the coconut trees. In a twinkling he has had enough of the day-to-day life of the people and he is up the coast: 'I enjoyed excellent bathing.' In Miramer on the Mediterranean, 'I could swim and sunbathe all day,' and on the little island of Gan, Mr Heath spends 'a few hours bathing in the translucent light-green water'. I would be willing to wager anything that his next book is called *Swimming*.

From an article by Paul Theroux in *The Sunday Times*

The title of the review: a parody of *Around the World in 80 Days*, by Jules Verne
Mr Heath: Edward Heath, British Prime Minister 1970–4, was well-known during his period of office for his hobbies, since he sailed a yacht and sometimes conducted choirs in concerts
signing even more titles: Mr Heath was renowned for his willingness to sign copies of his books
The Forbidden City: Peking
the red carpet: traditionally laid down to welcome distinguished visitors
The Caprivi Strip: a strip of land in Namibia separating Botswana from Angola
fandango: a dance, not normally associated with the Netherlands!
Toscanini: famous Italian conductor
Joshua Slocum: famous American sailor
Mau Mau: the Kenyan organisation that led the resistance against British rule in the 1950s, prior to independence
chintz: material used for curtains, furniture coverings, etc

I

Unfamiliar words

Decide on the most probable meaning of the following words and phrases in the context, using the aid given.

1 **relentless** (line 2): without pausing, without showing any mercy, or both at the same time?
2 **scrapbook memorabilia** (line 8): see examples that follow in the text.
3 **equivocate** (line 20): a) deceive himself b) hesitate
4 **captivated** (line 31): a) captured b) charmed
5 **in retrospect** (line 35): looking in which direction?
6 **split-second timing** (line 38): timed in what way?
7 **smug** (line 43): a) hesitant b) self-satisfied
8 **lest** (line 45): a) because b) in case
9 **In a twinkling** (line 63) refers to time or place? How long or how far?
10 **wager** (line 70): a) bet b) pay

J

Reading for gist

Answer these questions in your own words before looking at the multiple-choice questions below, and then link the answers together to form a summary of the passage.

1 Why does the reviewer criticise *Travels* in the second paragraph?
2 Why does he suggest that it is a record of 'happy days abroad'?
3 Why does he suggest that it is difficult to write an interesting travel book in situations like Mr Heath's?
4 What is his opinion of Mr Heath's statement that he had little opportunity to see much of the 'day-to-day life of the people'?
5 Why is he prepared to bet that Mr Heath will call his next book *Swimming*?

Now answer the following questions, comparing your answers already given to the choices available here.

6 The reviewer criticises *Travels* in the second paragraph primarily because it is
A disagreeable.
B full of quotations.
C out of date.
D vague.

7 He suggests *Travels* is 'a record of happy days abroad' because Mr Heath
A almost invariably had good weather.
B enjoyed Venice so much.
C had such interesting experiences.
D was mainly interested in his own comfort.

8 He goes on to say that it is difficult to write an interesting travel book if the writer
A does not explain exactly where he has been.
B has no difficulties to overcome.
C is so obviously pleased with himself.
D mentions places no one else has visited.

9 He thinks Mr Heath saw so little of the 'day-to-day life of the people' in the countries he visited because he
A had so many interests that he could not devote much time to travel.
B was kept away from them by his position as an official visitor.
C was not sufficiently curious about them to find out.
D was too busy fulfilling his responsibilities to enjoy himself.

10 He is prepared to bet Mr Heath's next book will be called *Swimming* because
A he has often been to the Mediterranean.
B he is such a good swimmer.
C he spends so much of his time on his travels bathing.
D it has a single-word title.

Use of language

Answer the following questions on the writer's choice of words in the passage.

1 What difference is made by the reviewer's writing 'subjected his public to . . .' (line 1) instead of 'treated his public to . . .'?
2 Why is Mr Heath's choice of titles for his books apparently evidence of his being a 'single-minded hobbyist'?
3 The use of the word 'privileged' in line 6 is ironic. Why?
4 Mr Heath is a bachelor. Why does the reviewer refer to 'chaste recreations' in line 7?
5 Why is it ironic that Mr Heath's second favourite word is 'particularly', and why is his frequent use of 'agreeable' a fault in the book?

Words often confused

1 memoir, memorandum, memorial, memory, recollection, reminder, reminiscence
Use each of these words *at least once* in the sentences that follow, in the plural form if necessary.

1 There was a procession of ex-servicemen to the War __________ on November 11th. The __________ was originally erected in __________ of those who died in the First World War, and while few people in the town have any personal __________ of them, it stands as a __________ to us of their sacrifice and a warning for the future.

2 Your __________ of the 28th about the publication date of the ex-Prime Minister's __________ has been acted on. Personally, I think he should have called them __________, since he makes little reference to his political life.

2 hobby, pastime, recreation
The writer uses these words interchangeably in context, but there are some differences between them in emphasis. Which would best describe the following?

1 jogging
2 doing jigsaw puzzles
3 stamp collecting
4 going for long walks in the country
5 making model aeroplanes
6 playing dominoes

3 course, dish, menu, plate, recipe
Use each of these words *once only*, in the plural if necessary, to complete the following.
Let's have a look at the __________ and decide on the first __________. The chef here recommends a number of __________. The prawn cocktail is particularly good, made according to a __________ of his own, though I can't understand why they serve it on a __________ instead of in a glass or a bowl.

House and Home

Introductory exercise

1 **Rooms:** where would you expect to find the following rooms in a house and what would they normally be used for?
   a) cellar
   b) loft
   c) lounge
   d) scullery
   e) study

2 **Furniture:** what would you expect to find in the following?
   a) a chest of drawers
   b) a safe
   c) a sideboard
   d) a wardrobe
   e) a bureau

3 **Eating and drinking:** what would you expect to be served in each of the following?
   a) a tankard
   b) a cup
   c) a glass
   d) a mug
   What is the purpose of a saucer?

4 **Receptacles:** Link the receptacle on the left with its most probable contents from the list on the right.

1 bucket	a) corned beef
2 can	b) flowers
3 flask	c) marmalade
4 jar	d) milk
5 jug	e) petrol
6 tin	f) water
7 vase	g) whisky

The Kitchen Sink

Read the following passage carefully before answering the questions that follow.

The kitchen is the housewife's workshop, the place where she has most scope for imagination and economy, for science and art. This is the battlefield upon which she must triumph or admit defeat. Let us suppose that our visit coincides with her return, laden, from the supermarket. As soon as she enters by the back door one defect in the kitchen plan is instantly apparent. For a feature of our age is the super-abundance of its wrapping paper. In the name of hygiene and paper-manufacturing dividends everything from the bread (which is dietetically worthless) to the eggs (laid weeks ago by battery-fed prisoners) must be protected by cardboard or paper, by cellophane or graphite. The daily accumulation is almost frightening in its mere bulk. But no one seems to have any plan for its disposal. Stuffing the paper into a sack hung behind the door, putting her purchases in the refrigerator or cupboard the housewife turns to an object which is central in her life: the Sink.

Fifty years ago the sink was an oblong, shallow trough of yellowish earthenware, placed far enough under a tap to allow for a bucket being filled there. Its sides were grooved and it was fitted with a waste-pipe and plug. When the time came to wash the dishes the first move was to boil a kettle and the second move was to pour hot water, diluted with cold, into a chipped enamel basin which was placed in the sink. Since those early days the March of Progress has introduced a second tap, which actually runs hot, and has altered the appearance and shape of the sink itself. It first became whiter and deeper, then it turned into stainless steel, the grooved wooden draining boards being transformed into shining metal or gaily-coloured formica, the old wooden plate racks turning into fibreglass or plastic.

What is surprising, however, is that the old basin (now also made in plastic) should remain; a smaller basin within a larger trough. But why? Why should not the sink be of the right size to begin with? Perhaps a hundred years of mental effort have at last produced a double sink, each half small enough to fill directly as a first step towards washing the dishes. But houses with double sinks are still the exception and those with plastic basins are still the rule. Nor is even the double sink complete, for the housewife needs to add, as she has always done, a triangular perforated vessel into which her wet trash and tea-leaves can be emptied. Without this the waste-pipe is liable to be blocked, as the designer of the sink should have realised. But why was no effort made to produce a sink that was complete in itself, needing no plastic afterthought? Why was not the required mesh incorporated in the original design? It is true that the waste-disposal unit is now on the market, but how long it has taken to introduce!

Seldom, in the story of human domesticity, has so little thought been devoted to a piece of equipment used by so many for so much of their time.

From *Mrs Parkinson's Law* by C N Parkinson

The last sentence is a parody of Sir Winston Churchill's tribute to the Royal Air Force: 'Never in the field of human conflict have so many owed so much to so few.'

A

Unfamiliar words

Decide on the most probable meaning of the following words and phrases in the context, using the aid given.

1 **laden** (line 6)
2 **super-abundance** (line 9)
3 **dietetically** (line 12)
4 **grooved** (line 24) an advantage for a draining-board
5 **chipped** (line 28) not when new, but quite soon afterwards because enamel chips easily
6 **wet trash** (line 50)
7 **afterthought** (line 55)
8 **mesh** (line 55) prevents the sink being blocked

B

Reading for detail

Choose the answer that best expresses what is stated in the passage. Note carefully the wording of questions 2 and 3.

1 One of the main problems facing the housewife who has been shopping is that
A she must find a way of getting rid of a lot of wrapping paper.
B she must unwrap everything she has bought.
C the bread she has bought is not of very good quality.
D there is an excessive concern with hygiene nowadays.

2 Which of the following features of the average sink has *not* changed during the last 50 years?
A The depth.
B The draining board.
C The material it is made of.
D The number of compartments.

3 In most cases, only one of the following processes in washing up is no longer necessary. Which is it?
A Boiling a kettle.
B Diluting the hot water with cold.
C Turning on the tap.
D Using a basin.

4 The writer's main complaint against the modern sink is that
A it is not deep enough.
B it is still necessary to use a basin when washing up.
C the waste pipe is not big enough for tea leaves to pass through.
D too much use is made of plastic.

5 The invention of the double sink
A causes more frequent blockage of the waste pipe.
B has made washing up easier.
C has solved all the housewife's problems.
D is no improvement on the traditional method.

Interpretation of text

Answer the following questions on the passage.

1 The writer explains the 'super-abundance' of wrapping-paper nowadays by saying it is done for the sake of 'hygiene and paper-manufacturing dividends'. Which two groups of people therefore recommend it, and for what reasons?
2 What are the 'battery-fed prisoners' referred to in line 13, and what methods of rearing them are being criticised here? Why does the writer criticise their products?
3 Which three phrases in the first half of the second paragraph are sarcastic tributes to twentieth-century technology?

Words often confused

extent, margin, range, scope, sweep
These words are best learnt in the idiomatic phrases where they often occur. Use each word *at least once* to complete the phrases given below.

1 marketing a wide ______ of products
2 to a certain ______
3 leave a ______ for error
4 offering unprecendented ______ for development
5 a ______ of options open to the Government
6 covering a broad ______ of history
7 the ______ of the damage following the hurricane
8 making a clean ______ by winning all the prizes
9 losing by a narrow ______
10 an outstanding ______ of colours available

E

Vocabulary expansion

1 bag, box, packet, sack, wallet

1 What would you expect each of these to be made of?
2 Which of the above would you expect to contain the following?
a) cigarettes
b) a credit card
c) coal
d) flour
e) matches
f) a purse
g) sweets
h) bank notes

2 chipped, cracked, flawed, fractured, shattered
All these words indicate something that is partly or completely broken.

1 Which one is stronger in effect than 'broken'?
2 Which would you apply most appropriately to the following?
a) someone's leg
b) the rim of a cup
c) a glass that has 'exploded' in small pieces
d) a window where there is a line through the glass
e) glass that is not quite perfectly made

3 junk, litter, refuse, scrap, trash
All of these words indicate rubbish of some kind. Complete the sentences below, using each word *at least once*.

1 When the English want to sound dignified, they use words of Latin origin, so dustmen, who used to empty dustbins, are now supposed to be engaged in ______ disposal!
2 After the accident, the car was written off, so it was towed to a ______ yard to be sold as ______ metal.
3 Instead of dropping your empty cigarette packets in the street, you should use the ______ bins provided.
4 Housewives in the USA throw their household rubbish away into the ______ can.
5 Bad novels are commonly called ______, suggesting they are cheap and nasty, but old objects without any value are called ______.

Three Rooms

The rooms described below belong to: a publisher; a composer of popular music; a writer and lawyer. Before answering the questions on the three passages, decide from the context which room belongs to which person.

A

His 12-roomed house, 140 years old, is surrounded by fields with post-and-rail fencing and an outstandingly beautiful garden. His room started out as a barn, then became part of a flat and is now in its third manifestation next to a studio filled with an array of electronics that must gladden the heart of the Electricity Board.

He had different acoustic needs in mind when he designed the room. 'The far end has cork on the walls so that if I want to practise – say with acoustic guitars – the sound is warm and close. If I move into the tiled section, the sound becomes lighter and there is more echo.' The ceiling, embedded with spotlights, is 'stepped' and covered with small ceramic tiles, glowing like mother-of-pearl and edged with scarlet beading whose colour picks up the bright red of the floor tiles.

From an article by Ena Kendall in the *Observer Magazine*

B

When we met at his country home near Henley, he had been up since 5am, as usual, to cope with it all. He lives in what was originally his father's house. The house is spacious, well-used and quite unpretentious.

His study used to be the garage in which his father's Morris Oxford reposed. He says of his room, 'It is wonderful to have a place where you can leave everything.' He is particularly fond of it because it is the only room in the house that does not have a view of the lush garden. 'The fewer distractions the better.'

He did not seem to have tidied up specially, unlike most of our subjects for this series so far. But, although there were a lot of things around, the overall impression was orderly. Rows of files were neatly stacked on one shelf and all tapes of the same size kept together. He has quite a selection of video tapes. He keeps those of his own plays and likes to tape opera. But he cannot actually work the video. 'There was a time when I was mechanically deft,' he said, 'but legend has now taken over and I have become totally hopeless about anything mechanical.'

He listens to music all the time as he is reading up on a case, correcting what he has written or just reading, but never when he is actually writing. 'I find it interferes with my own rhythm,' he explained.

From an article by Angela Levin in the *Observer Magazine*

C

His parties are noted gatherings of the **glitterati** and the big reception room-cum-library where they are held is a suitably distinguished setting. The flat where he has lived for the past 10 years overlooks the Thames and the exterior of the building gives only a hint of the grandeur inside. You have to be up early in the morning to catch him and as Freddie, his Filipino cook-housekeeper (female despite the name), led the way into the room, Ignazio, his Italian butler-chauffeur, was brushing up crumbs from the previous night's party and tut-tutting gently at some drink-spills on the carpet.

The room, good for parties because it absorbs large numbers effortlessly, is high, with sunken lights in the ceiling and tall windows at either end. As the almost identical brick and stone fireplaces suggest, it used to be two until the central dividing wall was removed. The red walls, the Turkey rugs, the sober dark grey of the sofas give it a solid masculine flavour, softened by the flower arrangements – that day a set piece of yellow irises, white lilies and beech leaves worthy of a cathedral, matched by smaller arrangements on the tables, all the work of a professional florist for the previous night's party.

From an article by Ena Kendall in the *Observer Magazine*

glitterati: a word invented to combine glitter (shine) and literati (figures of the literary world), meaning 'well-known literary figures'.

F

Comparison of texts

Answer the following questions.

1 Which of the rooms, if any, fulfils its original purpose?
2 Why is each room suitable for the purpose it is now used for?
3 Which of the rooms is likely to be the largest, and why?
4 What is the advantage of the first room having no view of the garden?
5 Why is it appropriate that the second room, B, should be a 'reception room-cum-library'?
6 Why is the material used for the walls important in the third room, C?

G

Reading for detail

The passage below is a composite picture of the three rooms described above. Read each sentence in turn and, without referring back to the texts, decide which room is being described in each case. Then check your answer carefully against Room A, Room B, and finally against Room C.

The room is part of an old house, and has a view of a beautiful garden. It had been tidied up before the interviewer arrived. It has a number of lights in the ceiling, and there are shelves on the walls. There are a number of carpets on the floor; the floor itself is made of tiles. The room is essentially practical, designed for work rather than pleasure or entertaining people.

Words often confused

1 **fertile, lush, luxurious, overgrown, prolific**
Use each of the following *at least once* to complete the sentences below.

He is a __________ writer, having published several novels and plays, with a __________ imagination. Despite his success, however, his house is not __________, but it lies in a beautiful setting not far from the Thames, where the __________ green grass of his lawn stretches away to meet the __________ fields beyond. He claims that the garden distracted his attention at first, because when he bought the house it was __________ with weeds.

2 **absent-minded, careless, distracted, inattentive, indifferent, preoccupied**
A person who is **distracted** is mad, but if his attention is **distracted**, he simply cannot concentrate. Which of the other adjectives best describe the following people?

1 a child who doesn't listen to the teacher in class
2 a man who drops cigarette ash on the carpet
3 a person who is so worried about something that he cannot pay attention to a conversation
4 a man who consistently puts on odd socks or one black shoe and one brown one
5 a person who is not concerned by what happens to someone working with him

I

Vocabulary expansion

overact, overcome, overhaul, overlap, overpower, overrate, overrule, overrun, overtake, overthrow
Look at the verbs above, all of which begin with the prefix *over-*, and then complete the sentences below, using each *once only*.

1 As Chairman of the Committee, I have power to __________ objections, unless they are supported by the majority.
2 The country has been __________ by the invading army.
3 It is forbidden to __________ on the inside lane.
4 When he reached the age of 18, he __________ his uncle in a bloodless coup. The regent escaped but was caught by his soldiers and __________ after a brief struggle.
5 My electric lawnmower has not been working properly, so I'm taking it in to be __________.
6 Some people think a lot of his music, but in my opinion it's __________.
7 His responsibilities __________ with mine, but we have worked out a sensible system for sharing them.
8 If he can __________ his unfortunate tendency to __________, he may be good enough to play Hamlet one day.

Lexical Progress Test 3

You must choose the word or phrase which best completes each sentence. For each question, 1 to 25, indicate the correct answer, A, B, C or D. The time for the test is 20 minutes.

1 I ________ to say anything unless I am allowed to speak to my lawyer.
A deny B neglect C refuse D reject

2 You're old enough to ________ your own living.
A earn B gain C gather D win

3 The paintings are hung in heavy gold ________.
A easels B frames C fringes D rims

4 The noise from the traffic outside ________ me from my work.
A annoyed B distracted C prevented D upset

5 We have ________ the post in the press and are awaiting applications.
A advertised B distributed C notified D reported

6 The car that had been following us ________ us and disappeared from sight.
A advanced B approached C overcame D overtook

7 The scene ________ me of my childhood.
A commemorated B recalled C remembered D reminded

8 Would you like to ________ the costume to see if it fits you?
A experiment B prove C try on D try out

9 We've met before. As a ________ of fact, it was last Christmas.
A case B matter C question D subject

10 His hens ________ a record number of eggs last year.
A deposited B laid C lay D spilled

11 The monkey jumped on the table and ________ the cups in all directions.
A distributed B scattered C separated D spaced

12 He was so angry that he ________ to call the police.
A advised B menaced C threatened D warned

13 Please put your empty cigarette packets and paper bags in the ________ bins provided.
A junk B litter C scrap D deposit

14 The curtains are on fire! Get a ________ of water quickly.
A bucket B mug C sink D tank

15 He was ________ by a bee when he went too close to the hive.
A bitten B pricked C stuck D stung

16 The Government are unlikely to ________ their opponents in the election.
A beat B gain C vote D win

17 The ________ control of the company is in the hands of the Board.
A massive B overall C predominant D unlimited

18 The conspirators were planning the ________ of the Government.
A demolition B disaster C overthrow D withdrawal

19 I'm surprised they are no longer on speaking terms. It's not like either of them to bear a ________.
A curse B disgust C grudge D resentment

20 When the cat is angry, its ________ stands up on end.
A feather B fur C hide D skin

21 You won't have any difficulty with the examination. You'll take it in your ________.
A duty B pace C step D stride

22 The service was held to ________ the sacrifice of those who died in the war.
A commemorate B memorise C remember D remind

23 He was hit by a bullet but luckily he was only ________ wounded.
A barely B little C merely D slightly

24 His ________ of the basic structures is good but his vocabulary is limited.
A grasp B grip C hold D seizure

25 I ________ him that I would not put up with any more of his insolence.
A announced B predicted C said D warned

The Past

Introductory exercise

Test your knowledge of twentieth-century history by matching the correct date in the left-hand column to the appropriate event in the right-hand column.

1903	The assassination of President Kennedy
1911	The first flight of the Wright brothers
1917	The end of the Second World War
1929	Hitler takes power in Germany
1933	Mount Everest climbed for the first time
1945	Nixon resigns because of Watergate
1953	Roald Amundsen reaches the South Pole
1963	The first landing on the Moon
1969	The Russian Revolution
1974	The Wall Street Crash

The Generation Gap in the 1920s

Read the passage below to gain a general impression of its meaning.

The cardinal facts for the historian of the inter-war period are, firstly, that the Second World War, as Churchill and a few others have constantly insisted, could have been avoided, and avoided by British action alone; and, secondly, that the progress of **the past fifteen years**, the ironing out of the worst of economic inequalities and a measure of social security for all, could have been achieved at infinitely less cost twenty years earlier to justify the faith of so many who had believed that was what they were fighting for. Of the generation that grew up immediately after the war, many believed that they were going to achieve both these objectives. Contemptuous of the Victorian values which still dominated English public life, they did not even think it was going to be very difficult. Those who have survived must inevitably seek to account for their failure. It is probably too early still to give any final answer; and the allocation of blame and responsibility is, in any case, an unprofitable exercise. But it is becoming possible to disentangle the facts from the special pleading and to give some coherent account of how that failure came about; and it is undisputably true that the first steps towards the disaster of 1939 were being taken before the rejoicings over the **Armistice** of 1918 had died away.

For 1918 produced in Britain a great gulf between two kinds of thinking. There is, in trying to define it, a grave danger of over-simplification: to see the division between the advocates of socialism and of free enterprise, or the division between those who believed in all that the **League of Nations** stood for and those who were sceptical about it, or even quite simply the division between two social systems and outlooks as represented by the elderly and the young, as the important division. It was not any one of these, but all of them together which led in the end to the misunderstandings and failures of the thirties. For, though these divisions did not ever precisely overlap, they did so nearly enough to produce a deep cleavage of outlook which left the nation at the critical moment incapable of action. The young people who reached maturity in the twenties and thirties had little sympathy with the nation's leaders who were struggling in every sphere to recreate as nearly as might be what seemed in retrospect the golden age of before the war. It was from the critics and debunkers of the ***ancien regime*** that the young took their tone. They learnt from **Keynes** to be ashamed of the **Treaty of Versailles**, to mistrust all politicians, and to perceive more and more clearly the fallacies which underlay their financial policies. If they read Mr Churchill's great account of the World Crisis it was to underline the mistakes and muddles and wastage it revealed; and when they looked around they saw the army and the navy, and even the RAF, still commanded by living replicas of the men so austerely condemned by **Captain Liddell Hart** as being directly responsible for the useless slaughter of their fathers. They looked to **Geneva** and not to **Downing Street** for a solution of the world's problems without, it must be said, considering very closely what action might be involved in enforcing international justice in a highly nationalistic age.

From *Britain's Locust Years* by William McElwee

the past fifteen years: 1945–60
The Armistice: the peace settlement of 1918
The League of Nations: the forerunner of The United Nations between the two World Wars
ancien régime: here refers to the previous system of government (before 1914), but generally associated with the French Government before the French Revolution of 1789
Keynes: famous economist
Treaty of Versailles: treaty ending the First World War, which laid harsh conditions on Germany
Captain Liddell Hart: military historian
Geneva . . . Downing Street: in other words, to the League of Nations rather than to the British Government

Unfamiliar words

Decide on the most probable meaning of the following in the context, using the aid provided.

1 **cardinal** (line 1)
2 **ironing out** (line 6) – what is the effect of ironing?
3 **allocation** (line 18)
4 **special pleading** (line 21) when pleading means 'making out a case for'
5 **came about** (line 22)
6 **rejoicings** (line 24 – usually singular)
7 **stood for** (line 31)
8 **sceptical** (line 32) compare the opposite
9 **cleavage** (line 39)
10 **debunkers** (line 46) see 'critics'
11 **muddles** (line 53) see words alongside
12 **replicas** (line 56) of the previous leaders
13 **slaughter** (line 58)

Reading for gist

Answer the following questions in your own words before attempting the multiple-choice questions below.

1 In what ways were the policies of British leaders in the 1920s and 1930s inadequate?
2 How soon were the false steps taken that eventually made the Second World War inevitable?
3 What was principally responsible for the misunderstandings and failures of the thirties?
4 Why were the young people who grew up in the 1920s unsympathetic towards the nation's leaders?
5 Why were they not altogether realistic in seeking a solution to the world's problems in Geneva?

Now answer the following questions, taking into account the answers you have already given. Only one answer is correct.

6 The writer claims that
A Britain was largely responsible for the outbreak of the Second World War.
B British policy could have prevented the Second World War.
C the Second World War would not have taken place if conditions in British society had been fairer.
D young people in 1918 thought that a fair society could be achieved within 20 years.

7 Britain's failure to prevent the Second World War can, in the writer's opinion, be traced to
A actions taken immediately after the First World War.
B the ignorance of the younger generation.
C the Victorian values that dominated public life.
D pointless arguments about who was to blame for what was happening.

8 The misunderstandings of the 1930s grew out of
A political divisions on class lines.
B disagreement over whether national or

international approaches to political questions should take precedence.
C the generation gap.
D all the above.

9 The most consistent error of the politicians of the 1920s was in
A behaving as if the ideal was to return to the pre-war situation.
B signing the Treaty of Versailles.
C not sacking generals who had lost battles.
D making a series of financial miscalculations.

10 The writer considers that the young were wrong in
A criticising politicians who were doing their best under the circumstances.
B listening to the debunkers of Britain's past achievements.
C believing that the League of Nations had power to keep the peace in the world.
D trusting in an international organisation rather than in their own government.

Words often confused

1 inquire (about/into), look for, search (for), seek
Study the examples below before attempting the exercise. In the exercise use each of the verbs listed above *at least once* in the correct tense to complete the sentences.

Almost everyone is **seeking (searching for/ looking for)** an answer to the question: 'What is the meaning of life?'
His research **seeks to** prove that children learn languages best if they begin at an early age.
The police organised a search party to **look for (search for)** the missing child. They **searched** the woods and **inquired** if anyone had seen her.
I was **searched** when I went through the customs because they thought I might be carrying a weapon.
The Government has set up an inquiry to **inquire into** the reasons for the accident.

1 A Royal Commission has been set up to ________ into the effectiveness of local government. In particular, the Commission is expected to ________ evidence to demonstrate whether the changes made in local authorities in the 1970s have improved services to the public. When I ________ about the composition of the Commission, a spokesman told me: 'The Commission is not ________ to prove that the present arrangement is unsatisfactory. It is simply ________ (or ________) for objective evidence on which to base its recommendations.'

2 I am within my rights as a citizen to ________ whether you have a search warrant. If you have, you can ________ the house, and ________ me, too, I suppose, though it would help us both if you told me what you are ________ (or ________) for.

2 blame (n. & v.), **fail** (v.), **failure** (n.), **fault** (n.)
Choose the correct word, and put verbs in the correct tense where necessary, in order to complete the sentences below, using each word *at least once*.
At the inquest of Mr Harold Simpson, 63, who died when the brakes in his brother's car ________ and it crashed into a tree, the Judge told James Simpson, 58: 'According to the medical evidence, your brother's death was due to heart ________. Consequently, it was not your ________ and you should not ________ yourself for it. But you are to ________ for ________ to notify the police of the accident immediately.'
NOTE: Look carefully at the sentence below, which shows the only expression in which **fail** is used as a noun.

I expect you all to be here at 9.00 tomorrow, **without fail**.

3 compel, enforce, persuade, urge
Study the constructions used with these verbs in the examples below before attempting the exercise. Then use each of them in the correct tense *at least once* to complete it.

A judge has power to **enforce** the law.
A judge has power to **compel people to obey** the law.
I **urged him not to break** the law, but I was unable to **persuade him not to do so.**

My duty is to ________ the law, and if I cannot ________ you to respect it by reasonable arguments, I will have to ________ you to do so by the use of force. I ________ you to pay attention to what I say and go home quietly. I am sure you will be ________ that what I am saying is common sense.

Vocabulary expansion

1 outbreak, outburst, outcome, outcry, outfit, outing, outlaw, outlay, outlet, outline, outlook, outpost, output, outrage, outset, outskirts

Outlook (lines 34 and 40) is used in the passage to mean a way of looking at things, an attitude. Look at the nouns, all of which begin with the prefix *out-*, and then complete the sentences below, using each *once only*.

1 At the __________ of the Second World War, few people realised that the seeds of disaster had been sown at the Treaty of Versailles.
2 From the __________, it was clear that the negotiations were doomed to failure, and there was little hope of a successful __________.
3 The company's __________ has risen sharply this year, and we are at last beginning to justify the initial __________ on modern plant and equipment, thanks to finding a new __________ for our products abroad.
4 She has bought a completely new __________ for the firm's annual __________ to Brighton.
5 There was a tremendous __________ in the popular press about *Hamlet* being performed at Stratford in modern dress, and many readers wrote to say that they had read of the experiment with a sense of __________, but an __________ of cheering from the audience greeted the first performance.
6 I can only give you a rough __________ of what the book will be like, because I have only written one chapter.
7 Robin Hood, who robbed the rich to feed the poor, is the most famous __________ in English folk tales.
8 He lives on the __________ of London, but when you hear him describe his train journey to his office every morning you would imagine he had to travel from some remote __________ in the Sahara Desert.

2 underestimate, undergo, undermine, understand, undertake

Underlie (line 51) meaning 'lie beneath' and **underline** (line 53) meaning 'emphasise' are both used in this passage. Look at the verbs above, all of which begin with the prefix *under-*, and then complete the sentences below, using each *once only*.

1 You shouldn't talk about him failing the examination. You'll __________ his confidence.
2 There is no point in __________ an opponent. I've never __________ why you always tell the press you are going to win before an important match.
3 It does not seem a very difficult job to do, so I am willing to __________ it.
4 The soldiers __________ a heavy bombardment as soon as they went into action.

Growing Up in a Small Town

Read the passage carefully before answering the questions that follow.

If I had known it, the whole future must have lain all the time along those **Berkhamsted** streets. The High Street was as wide as many a market square, but its broad dignity was abused after the first great war by the New Cinema under a green Moorish dome, tiny enough but it seemed to us then the height of pretentious luxury and dubious taste. My father, who was by that time headmaster of Berkhamsted School, once allowed his senior boys to go there for a special performance of the first Tarzan movie, under the false impression that it was an educational film of anthropological interest, and ever after he regarded the cinema with a sense of disillusion and suspicion. The High Street contained at 'our end' a half-timbered Tudor photographer's shop (from the windows the faces of the locals looked out in wedded groups, **bouqueted** and bemused like prize oxen) and the great flinty Norman church where the helmet of some old Duke of Cornwall hung unremarked on a pillar like a bowler hat in a hall. Below lay the Grand Junction canal with slow-moving painted barges and remote gypsy children, the watercress beds, the hillocks of the old castle surrounded by a dry moat full of cow-parsley (it had been built, so they said, by **Chaucer**, and in the reign of **King Henry III** it was besieged successfully by the French). The faint agreeable smell of coal dust blew up from the railway, and everywhere were those curious individual Berkhamsted faces which I feel I could recognize now anywhere in the world: pointed faces like the knaves on playing cards, with a slyness about the eyes, an unsuccessful cunning.

At the far end of the long High Street was the village of Northchurch and an old inn, the Crooked Billet. The name, perhaps because of some event which had happened there and had left an ambiguous impression in my mind from veiled adult conversation, always had for me a sinister ring (in the inn I was sure travellers had been done to death), and this gave the whole Northchurch village an atmosphere of standing **outside the pale**: a region of danger where nightmare might easily become reality. We were never taken there for walks, though this could well have had a natural explanation, for why should any nurse endure the two-mile trudge along the High Street, past the town hall, past the new King's Road, up and down which the commuters streamed twice a day to the station with their little attaché cases, past Mrs Figg's toy-shop where the children would certainly want to linger, past the sinister stained glass windows of the dentist, along the market gardens, with everywhere that odd gritty smell blowing up from the coal yards and the coal barges?

From *A Sort of Life* by Graham Greene

Berkhamsted: small town in Hertfordshire
bouqueted: an invented word, meaning 'carrying bouquets of flowers'
Chaucer: Geoffrey Chaucer (1340–1400), the most famous English mediaeval poet
Henry III: King of England from 1216 to 1272
outside (or **beyond**) **the pale:** outside the bounds of civilisation and therefore socially unacceptable

E

Unfamiliar words

Decide on the most probable meaning of the following in the context, using the aid provided.

1 **pretentious** (line 6) what sort of luxury would you expect to be afforded by this sort of cinema?
2 **half-timbered** (line 12) timber is wood prepared for building
3 **flinty** (line 15) flint is a sharp, hard form of stone
4 **helmet** (line 16)
5 **barges** (line 18)
6 **watercress** (line 19) what sort of bed?
7 **hillocks** (line 19)
8 **knave** (line 26) also called 'jack' and most English packs of cards carry a 'J' in the corner of this one
9 **trudge** (line 37) 'walk', but how?
10 **gritty** (line 43)

F

Reading for detail

Compare each of the statements made below in the multiple-choice questions, testing them for *true* or *false*, and decide which of the answers is correct. *Only one answer* is correct in each case.

1 For the writer, the dignity of Berkhamsted High Street depended on
A its acting as a market for the surrounding countryside.
B its width and architecture.
C the fact that it had such an effect on his future.
D the tasteful importation of a foreign architectural style.

2 The writer's father
  A believed that the cinema was a valuable aid to education.
  B had apparently not read any books about Tarzan.
  C permitted the older boys of the school to go to the cinema whenever they liked.
  D was suspicious of the cinema from the outset.

3 The local photographer's shop window was full of pictures of
  A people from the town on family occasions.
  B important figures in the history of the town.
  C animals displayed at cattle shows.
  D pictures of marriage ceremonies in the church.

4 The writer believes that the faces of Berkhamsted people
  A indicated that at heart they were gamblers.
  B showed their cleverness.
  C were different from those of people elsewhere.
  D were disagreeable, because of the humble jobs they worked in.

5 The writer distrusted Northchurch because
  A adults in his family talked about the village in a confusing way.
  B he had been told that travellers had been murdered in the inn.
  C his imagination led him to believe it was a place where terrible things happened.
  D the name suggested it was a dangerous place.

6 The main reason why children in the writer's family were never taken to Northchurch for walks was probably that
  A it would have been necessary to go past the Town Hall.
  B their nurse thought the walk would be long and irritating.
  C their nurse was superstitious.
  D their parents had warned the nurse about it.

7 An additional reason for not going to Northchurch for walks, from the nurse's point of view, was
  A the problem of having to watch the children looking at toys.
  B the risk of running into commuters.
  C the sinister atmosphere surrounding the dentist's.
  D the walk through the coal yards.

8 Berkhamsted Station, from the writer's description, was situated
  A at the end of the High Street.
  B beside the canal.
  C in the High Street.
  D up a road leading into the High Street.

G

Words often confused

1 fallacious, fallible, false, faulty

False can mean 'erroneous', where no deception is intended, or 'untrue', where it usually is intended. It occurs in a number of idiomatic phrases. The first letter of the associated noun is given in the sentences below. Complete the sentences.

1 The writer's father gained a false i__________ of the object of Tarzan films.
2 When I heard the bell ringing, I thought the hotel was on fire, but it turned out to be a false a__________.
3 When he was arrested, he gave the police a false n__________, but they subsequently established his identity.
4 'I am unworthy of this honour,' he said, on receiving the prize, but the broad grin on his face showed this was false m__________.

Now complete each of the sentences below, using the words listed above *at least once*.

5 The crash was due to the __________ brakes on the car.
6 Everyone can make a mistake. We are all __________.
7 He was convicted of perjury, which means giving __________ evidence at a trial.
8 Although it may seem logical to assume that the Earth is flat, you only need to study the sunset to realise that the argument is __________.
9 If you take a __________ step, I will kill you.

2 bear, endure, persevere (in/with), put up with, undergo

Endure can mean 'suffer without complaining' or 'last, in spite of difficulties'.

He **endured** the pain without crying out.
His work will **endure** for ever.

Use each of the other words listed above *at least once* in the correct form to complete the sentences below.

1 I'm tired of your complaints, and I'm not going to __________ your insults any longer.
2 He can't __________ the sight of blood.
3 She __________ an operation on her heart yesterday.
4 You must __________ what you are doing, and not give up at the first sign of failure.
5 Everyone has his cross to __________ in life and the boss is mine!

Vocabulary expansion

ditch, gutter, moat, trench, trough

Use each of the words listed *once only* to complete the sentences below, employing the plural form where necessary.

1 When the steering failed, I lost control of the car, and the next thing I knew was that I was lying in a ______ by the side of the country road.
2 In mediaeval times, castles were surrounded by ______ filled with water as a means of defence.
3 In the first World War, soldiers dug ______ as a means of protection.
4 The rain ran off the pavement into the ______.
5 The old horse ______ is still there, in the centre of the town, though now there are no longer any horses to drink from it.

Growing Up in a Village

Read the following passage to gain a general impression of its content.

The last days of my childhood were also the last days of the village. I belonged to that generation which saw, by chance, the end of a thousand years' life. The change came late to our **Cotswold** valley, didn't really show itself till the late 1920s; I was twelve by then, but during that handful of years I witnessed the whole thing happen.

Myself, my family, my generation, were born in a world of silence; a world of hard work and necessary patience, of backs bent to the ground, hands massaging the crops, of waiting on weather and growth; of villages like ships in the empty landscapes and the long walking distances between them; of white narrow roads, rutted by hooves and cartwheels, innocent of oil or petrol, down which people passed rarely, and almost never for pleasure, and the horse was the fastest thing moving. Man and horse were all the power we had – abetted by levers and pulleys. But the horse was king, and almost everything grew around him; fodder, smithies, stables, paddocks, distances, and the rhythm of our days. His eight miles an hour was the limit of our movements, as it had been since the days of the Romans. That eight miles an hour was life and death, the size of our world, our prison.

This was what we were born to, and all we knew at first. Then, to the scream of the horse, the change began. The brass-lamped motor car came coughing up the road, followed by the clamorous **charabanc**; the **solid-tyred** bus climbed the dusty hills and more people came and went. Chickens and dogs were the early sacrifices, falling demented beneath the wheels. The old folk, too, had strokes and seizures, faced by speeds beyond comprehension. Then scarlet motor-bikes, the size of **five-barred gates**, began to appear in the village, on which our youths roared like rockets up the two-minute hills, then spent weeks making repairs and adjustments.

These appearances did not immediately alter our lives; the cars were freaks and rarely seen, the motor-bikes mostly in pieces, we used the charabancs only once a year, and our buses at first were experiments. Meanwhile Lew Ayres, wearing a bowler-hat, ran his wagonette to Stroud twice a week. The carriage held six, and the fare was twopence, but most people preferred to walk. Mr West, from Sheepscombe, ran a cart every day, and would carry your parcels for a penny. But most of us still did the journey on foot, heads down to the wet Welsh winds, ignoring the carters – whom we thought extortionate – and spending a long hard day at our shopping.

From *Cider with Rosie* by Laurie Lee.

Cotswold: the writer was brought up in a village in the Cotswold Hills in Gloucestershire.
charabanc: motor coach
solid-tyred: this was before the days of pneumatic tyres
five-barred gates: large gates normally erected at the entrance to farmers' fields

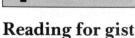

I

Reading for gist

Answer the following questions on the passage. *Only one answer* is correct.

1 What is astonishing about the writer's opening statements is that
 A he was 12 years old before he realised what was happening.
 B his childhood coincided with the last days of the village.
 C the changes he refers to came so late to the valley.
 D the traditional life of the village disappeared in so short a time.
2 The world the writer was born into was silent because
 A everyone had so much work to do in order to survive.
 B people seldom visited one another.
 C the villages were deserted and far apart.
 D there were no motor vehicles.
3 The effect of motor vehicles on the old people in the village was that they
 A screamed in panic, like horses.
 B were frequently knocked down or caught by the wheels.
 C were pleased to be able to travel about more.
 D were so astonished that they had heart attacks.
4 The buses in the village were an experiment at first, mainly because
 A of the competition from Mr Ayres.
 B of the competition from Mr West.
 C people regarded them as freaks.
 D people were so used to walking.
5 Most people went to the shops on foot because they
 A did not mind the rain.
 B did not trust the carters with their shopping.
 C had not far to go.
 D thought the carters charged too much.

Use of language

Answer the following questions on the writer's choice of words in the passage.

1 The writer speaks of people 'massaging the crops' (line 9). Why do you think he uses this metaphor to describe their care of them?
2 What impression of subsequent developments is given by the phrase 'innocent of oil or petrol' (line 12)?
3 Why does the writer refer to the world of his childhood as 'our prison' (line 21)?
4 Why did the first motor cars come 'coughing up' the road (line 24)?
5 In what sense can the hills around the village be called 'two-minute hills' (line 31)?
6 Why were the motor-bikes 'mostly in pieces' (line 34)?

Unfamiliar words

Decide on the most probable meaning of the following in the context, using the aid given below.

1 **rutted** (line 12) by cartwheels
2 **abetted** (line 15) levers and pulleys are simple means of raising and transporting heavy weights
3 **fodder, smithies** and **paddocks** (line 17) all have to do with horses
4 **clamorous** (line 25)
5 **demented** (line 27)
6 **seizures** (line 28)

Words often confused

adjustment, amendment, check-up, repairs, revision
Use each of these words *at least once* to complete the sentences below, in the plural where necessary.

1 There is nothing seriously wrong with him, but he thought it would be wise to go to the doctor for a __________.
2 The American constitution has never undergone a major __________, but there have been a number of __________ made to it from time to time.
3 The cost of the __________ to the house may be rather more than you expected, but I am willing to make a small __________ in your favour because of the time I have taken.
4 Although it is advertised as a new book, it is in fact a __________, with a few minor __________ on a number of pages.

M

Vocabulary expansion

Look at this sentence, taken from the text.

Then, to the **scream** of the horse, the change began (line 23).

Horses normally **neigh**, or **whinny** with pleasure, but on this occasion the writer wished to emphasise the animal's terror. Relate the verbs in the left-hand column to the sound made by the person or animal on the right.

1 groan	a) a wolf
2 howl	b) someone in pain
3 squeak	c) a child or dog wanting attention
4 squawk	d) someone mourning a person who is dead
5 roar	e) someone crying bitterly
6 sob	f) a mouse
7 wail	g) an angry bird
8 whine	h) a lion, or a car, with a powerful engine

The **fare** is what you pay when you go on a journey. When or for what purpose would you pay or receive the following?

a) alimony
b) an allowance
c) as annuity
d) a bill
e) a bonus
f) duty
g) a fee
h) a grant
i) interest
j) a legacy
k) maintenance
l) a pension
m) the rates
n) rent
o) royalties

Computers

Introductory exercise

Have you a computer at home? Do you learn from it, or do you use it mainly for entertainment? Do you find you spend hours with it? Do you play games like Space Invaders? How often? Do you find that you improve with practice?
Do you think that in future it will be possible to learn entirely from computers? Would you think this was preferable to going to school? Can you see any risks involved in the process?

The Case for Home Computers

Read this extract from an advertisement for a computer to gain a general impression of its content.

If you're already a computer expert, may we refer you to the box of technical specifications displayed opposite.

If you're not, may we refer you to the new Dragon 32 Family Computer. A computer so easy to understand, you won't understand why all the others seem so difficult.

USER-FRIENDLY?

You may have heard of the term 'user-friendly'. Reverting to plain English once more, this means simply that the computer will go out of its way to understand you, rather than vice-versa.

The Dragon 32 is so user-friendly, it practically licks your hand.

You tap (literally) its vast resources through a beautifully-designed keyboard that's as easy to use as a typewriter. On this keyboard, you type in a language which is surprisingly close to the English you talk every day. The Dragon 32 will receive your order. Understand it. Send it to the appropriate section of its massive brain. And then display the appropriate information on your screen. All before you can say **'gobbledy-gook'**.

FIRE YOUR IMAGINATION

Learning how to use the Dragon 32 won't cause you to experience any problems. Learning what you can use it for will cause you to experience something entirely different.

Delight. Surprise. Fascination. And challenge.

The Dragon offers a range of some of the most popular computer games in the world. From those celebrated space battles to mind-boggling adventures in seemingly unfathomable dungeons and caves.

As if by magic, a simple typed message will command the Dragon to create your own drawings. Then it will colour and paint them in 9 colours. And it's clever enough to create virtually any image you want – circles and arcs as well as straight lines.

The Dragon will also play and compose music with you, with a range of 5 octaves. And it works with any UHF TV or PAL monitor.

LEARNING THROUGH PLAYING

All of this makes the Dragon the ideal machine to build your children's interest in the world of computers as they become increasingly more vital. Schoolchildren already enjoy using computers.

The Dragon is the first computer specifically for the family – so by enjoying yourselves at home, you and your children can soon become expert enough to create your own programs.

From an advertisement for Dragon Computers (abridged)

gobbledy-gook: meaningless technical jargon

Reading for gist

In answering the questions, bear in mind the advertiser's intention, as well as the words that are used. Choose the answer that best reflects the aims of the advertisement. *Only one answer* is correct.

1 Readers who know nothing about computers are advised to
A ask the company for an instruction manual.
B consult an expert.
C refer to the technical specifications listed.
D study the computer itself.

2 The purpose of emphasising the term 'user-friendly' is to
A blind the reader with science.

B explain the range of the computer's resources.
C reassure readers that they will be able to operate the computer.
D suggest that the computer will respond to them like a dog.

3 The main intention of the paragraph headed 'Fire Your Imagination' is to convince readers that they will
A be able to create things for themselves.
B be able to play games like Space Invaders.
C have wonderful fairy-tale adventures.
D not have to solve problems.

4 The educational principle behind such computers is that children
A are much better at using them than adults.
B can learn best through playing games.
C prefer them to doing real work.
D will all become computer experts.

5 The specific advantage of the Dragon, according to the advertisement, is that it
A allows parents and children to learn together.
B can be programmed without previous practice.
C is specially designed for young children.
D is the easiest machine on the market to program.

Use of language

Answer the following questions in your own words.

1 Why is 'user-friendly' not 'plain English', but why is it not 'gobbledy-gook' in the context, either?
2 What image is created by the phrase 'practically licks your hand', and why is it used here?
3 In what sense is it 'literally' true that the user can 'tap the resources' of the computer?
4 What is the advantage of the language used in this machine being 'surprisingly close to the English you talk every day'?
5 Why is it important that although the adventures in dungeons and caves are 'mind-boggling', they are only 'seemingly unfathomable'?

Words often confused

1 experience (n. uncountable and countable), **experiment** (n.), **experience** (v.), **experiment** (with) (v.)
Use the words above in the correct form *at least once* in the sentences.

– For this job we need someone with a lot of __________ in dealing with unusual situations and people. What interested us in you was your journey across Mongolia and the book you wrote about your __________ there. Why did you go there?
– Partly as an __________, to see whether I could survive in such conditions, but also for the __________. I think it helped me to grow up. In a sense I was __________ a great feeling of satisfaction, to think that I could do what I had planned to do.

2 alive, living, requisite, viable, vital
Vital usually means 'indispensable, absolutely necessary', but it can also mean 'full of life,' (note the noun, **vitality**). Use each of the words above *at least once* to complete the sentences below.

1 It's of __________ importance that I should contact him immediately. It's a matter of life and death.
2 If you want a new passport, you must complete the __________ forms.
3 It is surely an exaggeration to say it is __________ for everyone to be able to handle computers. In any case, what matters most is to decide whether the educational systems based on them will be __________ in schools and the difficulties involved can be overcome.
4 He's the __________ image of his father. He looks just like him. He has the same __________ energy. I wish his father were still __________. He would be so proud of him!

Vocabulary expansion

a connoisseur, a consultant, a specialist, a veteran
An **expert** is someone who knows a great deal about a subject. Each of the words listed above is used to describe a particular kind of expert.
Which would you use to describe the following people?

1 Harold Anstey is a famous doctor. He is a heart __________, and __________ to several London hospitals.
2 Jimmy Budd has played football 84 times for England.
3 Rachel Connolly has the finest collection of porcelain in the country, and dealers ask her advice.
4 Brian Dalton is an economist. He is an expert on business management, and is employed as a __________ by many companies.
5 General Sir Alan Everett spent 42 years in the army, and fought in both world wars.

The Invasion of the Space Invaders

Read the passage below carefully, both for the general impression and for points of detail, before attempting the exercises.

It was in Japan, naturally, that the plans for the Invasion were first formed. High up in the spectral tower block of Taito Inc., teams of computer experts and game psychologists doodled and mused until, in 1978, they unveiled the legendary screen; a squad of fat silver insects, chugging its way down towards a lone tank, which fires and then dodges back between the four green shields. Within months of the Space Invaders' landing, no one in Japan could use a public telephone or buy a **subway** ticket: all the coins were nestling in the bellies of the video games. Obviously the idea was a natural for Japan – where (due to the sardine-can overcrowding) everyone is always invading everyone else's space. The big question was whether the appeal of the game was exportable. It was, and the rest is history.

Nowadays, in Silicon Valley, California, and its equivalents across the globe, morale is high, even idealistic. The **hip** young heroes of Atari, for instance, are convinced that they stand on the very brink of evolutionary breakthrough. The development of the video games is seen as roughly equivalent to mankind's slow crawl from the primal broth of creation. 'The computer,' says Atari's Steve Jobs, 'is one of the pinnacles of Western rational thought. Computers bring together physics, electronics, chemistry and mathematics; they bring logic, and philosophy, information theory, all that. And the people working on these computers possess a passion about the discovery and creation of something. It's a passion that I have only seen matched in people pursuing what they consider to be the truth of their existence. It's the same purity of spirit I have experienced in monks.'

Jobs speaks wise words – in theory, anyway. Take the notion of teaching special relativity with video games. It is possible to programme any set of physical laws into the 'microworld' of the **customised** TV screen. As was the case with the educational science-fiction stories of the mid-century, it is instructive to alter the ratios so that the laws are more noticeable than in everyday life. 'So on the screen,' says a physicist, 'you make the speed of light be 10 miles an hour, put in some gravity, make it a game, and kids will start learning special relativity, the same way they learn to calculate parabolas without knowing what a parabola is, or what calculating is, in order to catch a baseball.' The game already exists, at the Massachusetts Institute of Technology, and has been used with encouraging results.

Consider the following, a game of the future. I quote from an instructive article by Paul Trachman in the *Smithsonian*: You have a 10-year reign as a king and you have so much grain, so many people and so much land. You can buy or sell land for grain, but you can't plant more acres than you have people to work at farming them. If you don't feed your people enough, they start to die. If they die, you can't plant as much grain anymore, and you may get into a downward spiral. But if you plant too much and store it, rats eat some of it . . .

And so on. If such a game were mass-produced and unleashed on the arcades, what would it be called? **Malthus?** ***The Social Contract*?** No, it would be called Ratter; it would have **loony-tune** rodents that winked at you between bites; it would have a farmer with a **funfair** hammer and a farmer's wife who jumped on a stool every time a rat squeaked; it would have a big grinning cat which scored a lump of cheese every time you . . .

The predictions of the video egg-heads are grand and stirring; at the time of writing, though, all the trends in the industry stubbornly point the other way.

From *Invasion of the Space Invaders* by Martin Amis

subway: (USA): underground (UK)
hip (USA): up to date and self confident
customised(USA): adapted for the purpose of the computer

Malthus: British economist who predicted the population explosion in the world in the early 19th century
***The Social Contract*:** book by Jean-Jacques Rousseau, the French-Swiss philosopher of the 18th century
loony-tune: accompanied by snatches of music, as in a cartoon
funfair: fairground, or amusement park

E

Unfamiliar words

Decide on the most probable meaning of the following in the context, using the aid provided.

1 **spectral** (line 4) a spectre is a ghost
2 **doodled** and **mused** (lines 6–7)
3 **chugging** (line 10) noise and movement
4 **dodges** (line 12)
5 **nestling** (line 18)
6 **bellies** (line 18) really stomachs, but here. . . ?
7 **brink** (line 34)
8 **broth** (line 39) really soup, but here. . . ?
9 **pinnacles** (line 41) what sort of point?
10 **unleashed** (line 105) what animal is often held on a leash?
11 **stirring** (line 120) moving, but in what way?

F

General understanding

Answer these questions, taking into account the writer's view in general terms, but also checking the statements made carefully against the text to see whether they are *true* or *false*. *Only one answer* is correct.

1 The success of Space Invaders in Japan was predictable because
A the game was made there.
B the Japanese are aggressive by nature.
C people could imagine in fantasy that they had more space.
D people are so overcrowded that they need to get out of the house to the amusement arcades.

2 Those who devise video games in places like Silicon Valley
A are only interested in profit.
B are primarily concerned with the export market.
C believe they are capable of revolutionising man's abilities to learn.
D pretend they are helping to educate people.

3 Jobs compares those working on video games to monks because
A they are so creative.
B they are so dedicated.
C they are so passionate.
D they live alone in cells.

4 It is necessary to change the ratios of physical laws in video games
A to make the games enjoyable.
B to make it easier to recognise the concepts.
C to separate them from everyday experience.
D because they must be visible on TV screens.

5 The writer's criticism of companies using video games like the one referred to in the *Smithsonian* is that the games
A are not designed to teach anything.
B are old-fashioned in concept.
C are not satisfactorily programmed.
D are vulgarised, and lose their value.

G

Words often confused

1 moral, morale, morality
Complete the sentences below, using each word *at least once*, in plural form where necessary.

1 The __________ of the troops was high before the battle, because they were confident of winning.
2 The __________ of the story is that it doesn't take two to make a quarrel, as the proverb says, but only one.
3 If there is one thing that irritates me it is to hear people preaching to me about the __________ of my actions, when their own __________ leave a good deal to be desired.

2 assure, convert, convince, persuade
Complete the sentences below, using each verb *once only* in the correct tense. Note the construction used in each case.

1 I __________ you that what I am saying is true.
2 He spent a long time __________ them to change their minds, and eventually __________ them that they should give up the strike, because it was not in their own interests.
3 At one time he was a bitter opponent of our ideas, but now he has been __________ to our point of view.

Vocabulary expansion

The computer experts in Japan **unveiled** the new video game. In other words, they disclosed the secret of it and presented it to the public. What sort of thing would you expect to **unwrap**, or to **unpack**, and what sort of person could be **unmasked**?

Mary Poppins in the Chip

Read the following passage, comparing its attitude towards computers with the previous two and concentrating on the way in which it is written.

Usually **at this time of year** I write about toys, games and **things that go bump down the chimney**. I don't particularly want to, being by nature something of a kill-joy when it comes to party games, but it's a question of expediency. Already my desk is awash with a load of fascinating new games which, say the accompanying blurbs, will delight all ages from eight to eighty-eight.

For instance, there's Quadwrangle, an absorbingly wit-picking board game which lasts just as long as you can keep track of the five dice and eight plastic counters essential for effective play. Unfortunately this constituted roughly 20 minutes in my case, since the Arnold ménage, as well as accommodating an eight and an 88-year-old, also shelters a delinquent three-year-old whose chief preoccupation is flushing small objects like cash, car-keys, contact lenses and Quadwrangle counters down the lavatory.

The last box I almost discarded without even bothering to open, since its name alone was a turn-off. It was called the Talking Computer System. Regular readers of this column will know my feelings about computers and my altogether inept attempts to come to grips with the New Technology. So I was just about to ditch the Talking Computer System when a breezy lady telephoned and said had I got her computer for three-year-olds and did I need any help in operating it? A computer for *three-year-olds*. Ye gods, where will it end? I asked numbly if there was any chance of its being flushed down the lavatory and set out for the breezy lady's office behind Fleet Street.

For a full hour and a half I sat crosslegged in front of a small plastic box about the size of a telephone and learnt to do what a three-year-old will apparently pick up in five minutes. It's like the old lady in the flat next door who has to ask the neighbourhood kids to open her child-proof medicine bottles and give them a shilling for their pains. To be fair, it wasn't *that* difficult once Mr Pullman, 'who markets the toy' had shown me exactly where to put my finger when the talking computer said 'Find the flower.' The reason I sat there so long was that there are 21 different programmes. The voice, female, takes a little getting used to but no matter how many times you punch five when she asks 'What is two times two?' she never raises her voice. Mr Pullman said the chip inside the computer was so complex it took seven-man-years to perfect, and the only reason it retails at £50 instead of £150 is that it is made in Hong Kong where they don't worry about **PAYE**, **National Insurance** and junk like that.

I went home. I hauled the delinquent out of the lavatory along with a set of antique coffee spoons and sat him in front of the Talking Computer System. He didn't jam the keys on the calculator, he didn't wrench the hands off the clock. 'Find the cat,' said **Mary-Poppins-in-the-chip** – and good grief, he found the blessed flower. If I start saving now he could have one next Christmas. Mr Pullman says he'll have a whole lot of new programmes for it by then.

From an article by Sue Arnold in the *Observer Magazine*

at this time of year: not long before Christmas
things that go bump down the chimney: Father Christmas is supposed to drop Christmas presents down the chimney
PAYE: Pay As You Earn, the British income tax system
National Insurance: compulsory contributions by workers and employers towards state aid in the event of sickness, unemployment, etc.
Mary-Poppins-in-the-chip: the voice of the computer sounds like the kindly, authoritative child's nurse, Mary Poppins, in the film which starred Julie Andrews. 'The chip' means the microchip in the computer

Unfamiliar words

Decide on the most probable meaning of the following in the context, using the aid provided.

1 **kill-joy** (line 6)
2 **awash** (line 9) normally used of ships when waves sweep over them, but here?
3 **blurbs** (line 12) give information, but of what kind?
4 **wit-picking** (line 15) it tests one's wits
5 **keep track of** (line 17)
6 **ménage** (line 23) or in plain English?
7 **turn-off** (line 35)
8 **ditch** (line 42)
9 **breezy** (line 44) a breeze is a refreshing wind, but here ?
10 **numbly** (line 50) numb means without feeling, because of cold, for example, but here?
11 **jam** (line 94)
12 **wrench** (line 96) what would you expect a destructive three-year-old to do with typewriter keys and the hands of a clock?

Interpretation of text

Answer the following questions about the passage in your own words.

1 Why is it a 'question of expediency' for a practising journalist to write about new games just before Christmas?
2 Why did the experiment of playing Quadwrangle only last 20 minutes in the Arnold household?
3 What is the point behind the selection of objects that the three-year-old flushes down the lavatory?
4 Why did the writer almost discard the Talking Computer System without opening it, and what prevented her?
5 Why is 'three-year-olds' (line 48) printed in italics, and what is 'it' in the phrase 'where will it end'?
6 What was the point of the question the writer asked before setting out for the office in Fleet Street?
7 In what way is the example of the old lady next door relevant to the writer's experience with the Talking Computer?
8 What is the joke behind the suggestion that the voice of the computer sounds like Mary Poppins?
9 How long are 'seven man-years' (line 82)?
10 Why is the Talking Computer so cheap?
11 What do you imagine the writer's three-year-old son was about to do with the coffee spoons, and why is the fact that they were 'antique' important?
12 What reactions do the expressions 'good grief' and 'the blessed flower' (lines 98–100) indicate in the mother's mind?

Words often confused

discard, discharge (from), dispense with, lay off, reject, replace, substitute (for), write off

Use each of these verbs *at least once* in the correct form in the sentences below, and pay attention to the constructions in which they are found.

1 When he was completely cured, he was __________ hospital.
2 We are reluctant to __________ his services, because he has worked for us for so long, but like so many people nowadays, he is being __________ by more efficient machines.
3 The fall in production over the past year has caused 200 workers to be made redundant, and a further 500 have been __________ temporarily, pending an improvement in world conditions.
4 He was __________ for military service because he had flat feet.
5 The manager has been forced to __________ Jones from the team against France next Wednesday because he is unfit. He will be __________ in the eleven by Matthews. Cannon is standing by, and may be __________ for another forward during the game.
6 After the crash, the car was __________ by the insurance company.
7 He was __________ the army because of ill health.
8 After careful consideration, she __________ her original plan to trump the king of diamonds and __________ a heart instead.

Education

Introductory exercise

What special facilities are available in your country for people who want to become actors, dancers, musicians, painters, etc? What subjects do they study and how soon do they give up normal academic subjects?

Is it possible to study a variety of subjects at university that are not available at school? What sort of subjects are studied? Are they all aimed at professional qualifications, such as law and medicine, or are there degree courses in subjects like drama?

The Royal College of Music

Read the following passage, both to gain a general idea of its content, and also so that you will be prepared to answer questions on points of detail.

'For all you know, I might have a tremendous burning talent,' warns the heroine of ***Brief Encounter***, as the camera pans on to a serenading lady cellist in a teashop trio. 'Oh dear no,' comes the reply, 'you're too sane and uncomplicated.'

For a place where talent rarely falls below combustion point, the Royal College of Music is good at not encouraging the cinema stereotype of what it means to be an artist. In fact, the college is too close to the profession it serves to be anything but a breeding ground of serious hard work: there's not time, and very little room, for temperament. The proof of industry is quite audible on weekdays during term, when the whole building generates a comfortable din of unco-ordinated noise, as pervasive as the English academic smell of polish and cooked cabbage that haunts the corridors.

The overall impression is that the college has outgrown its premises as well as its soundproofing, even though the building in Prince Consort Road has been extended twice. A hundred years ago, when the Royal College came into official existence, it was on a much smaller scale and housed in what is now the Royal College of Organists – a florid piece of 19th-century fantasy beside the Albert Hall.

Most students come here straight from school, which is often at a younger age than the current director, Sir David Willcocks, would like: 'Singers in particular we encourage to come later, because the voice doesn't really develop until 20–23. But in practice we accept people before then, rather than see them go elsewhere. If you tell someone to come back in three years' time, and he goes off and gets a good job, why should he then risk giving it up to become a student?'

Willcocks likes to keep his students for as long as possible; and one of the major policy decisions taken since he came to the college in 1974 has been to increase the length of the basic performers' course by a fourth year. 'The only ones who could properly go into the profession after three years are wind players, because their standards are astonishingly high these days. Otherwise, my advice is usually to stay here for four years and then perhaps take a specialist course abroad.'

The most critical recommendation of all – for a student to abandon the idea of a professional performing career – is one that Willcocks rarely has to make. It's in the nature of a conservatoire that progress, or lack of it, is public knowledge; and, given some sensitivity to the competition, most students find their own level without having to be told, 'You know when you've done well,' said one battle-scarred soprano, 'because nobody speaks to you.'

In fact the great majority do carry on with music after they leave the college, but not necessarily in the form they had expected. Conductors may end up ***répétiteurs*** in provincial opera houses; solo singers may be swept into the chorus; some are absorbed by arts administration or the BBC, and many become teachers. In all cases, even those who give up music altogether, Willcocks is insistent that they haven't failed: 'Music is a discipline in itself, a training of the mind.'

From an article by M J White in the *Observer Magazine*

Brief Encounter: film made by David Lean and starring Trevor Howard and Celia Johnson, later remade with Richard Burton and Sophia Loren

répétiteurs: pianists who play for the rehearsals of operatic or choral productions

A

Unfamiliar words

Decide on the most probable meaning of the following words and phrases in the context, using the aid given.

1 **pans** (line 4)
2 **serenading** (line 5)
3 **teashop trio** (line 6)
4 **din** (line 23)
5 **pervasive** (line 24)
6 **sound-proofing** (line 30) for what purpose?
7 **florid** (line 39) a building that is a fantasy
8 **wind players** (line 66) what sort of instruments?
9 **conservatoire** (line 78)
10 **battle-scarred** (line 85) usually from wounds received in battle, but here?

B

Reading for gist

Answer the following questions in your own words before referring to the multiple-choice questions which follow. Then link your answers together to provide a summary of the passage.

1 What is the popular idea of the artist, as expressed in films?
2 What impression is given by the Royal College of Music on a normal working day?
3 What is the attitude of the director towards students who come straight from school?
4 Why is it seldom necessary for him to recommend that students should give up music?
5 What sort of careers do students eventually follow?

Now answer the following questions. *Only one answer* is correct.

6 The speaker in *Brief Encounter* did not believe the heroine could be an artist because she was not
A professionally trained.
B sensitive enough.
C talented.
D temperamental.

7 The main complaint keen students might make about conditions at the Royal College of Music is that
A the building smells terrible.
B the course is unco-ordinated.
C the course is too long.
D there is not enough room to practise.

8 Sir David Willcocks's policy in accepting students is to
A discourage singers.
B give students time to develop their ability.
C make the course last as long as possible.
D refuse those who come straight from school.

9 He rarely needs to recommend that students should give up music because
A he knows they would not listen.
B he believes that music is valuable training for everyone.
C other students stop talking to them if they have no talent.
D they realise themselves what their real standard is.

10 Most students at the College
A achieve their original ambitions.
B adapt their ambitions to circumstances.
C become music teachers.
D eventually give up music.

Words often confused

1 fit, healthy, sane, sound

Use each of these words *at least once* to complete the sentences below, without repeating the same word in a sentence.

1 – You are still fairly __________ for your age, but you don't take much exercise, and so you're not as __________ as you should be. I realise you have too much work, but the only __________ attitude to adopt is to recognise that you need relaxation, too.
– Thank you. That seems to me to be very __________ advice.

2 While I would hesitate to suggest that he was insane when he killed himself, the verdict must be that he was mentally disturbed, and therefore not of __________ mind at that moment.

3 I doubt if I will be __________ enough to play tomorrow.

2 humour, mood, temper, temperament, tendency

Use each of these words *at least once* in the sentences below, employing the plural form where necessary.

1 When I made those criticisms, I expected him to lose his __________, but he accepted them with good __________ and even made a joke about them.

2 I'm not in the __________ to put up with any of your displays of artistic __________ today.

3 He has a __________ to take offence at the smallest thing. In fact, he is in one of his __________ now, sitting in the corner there, sulking. His brother, on the other hand, has a good sense of __________, though he, too, has a terrible __________ when roused.

D

Vocabulary expansion

1 outclass, outgrow, outlive, outnumber, outweigh

The verb **outgrow** can have two meanings.

a) 'grow too large for'. In the context of the passage, the college had **outgrown** its building.

b) 'to leave behind as one grows older'. Children **outgrow** their childish habits as they reach maturity.

Complete the sentences below, using each of the above words *once only*, in the correct form.

1 The College has long __________ the building in which it was originally established. At first it was intended only for boys, but girls are now admitted and in fact they __________ the boys, because we receive far more applications from them.

2 He did his best, but his opponent was so much better than he was that he was soon __________.

3 I have a few complaints to make about the job, but on the whole the advantages __________ the disadvantages.

4 Krushchev was popularly reported to have said that the Soviet system would 'bury' ours, whereas he actually said it would __________ ours, which is not quite the same thing!

2 abdicate, desert, forsake, give up, part with, renounce, secede, vacate, withdraw

The verb **abandon** means to 'leave definitively'. The words listed above are all similar in meaning to 'abandon'. Look at the sentences below and choose the most suitable verb(s) to complete each one. Use each verb, *at least once*, in the correct form.

1 The King was obliged to __________, and to __________ his throne in favour of his younger brother.

2 During the American Civil War, the Southern States __________ from the Union.

3 You must not __________ hope. I will never __________ (or __________) you, whatever happens.

4 He was court-martialled for having __________ from the army.

5 It was my mother's ring, and I would be unwilling to __________ it, so I must decline your offer.

6 In the face of such a determined attack, he ordered his men to __________ to more strongly defended positions on the hill.

7 Guests are required to __________ their rooms in the hotel by 12.00.

8 Unless there is some sign of a positive desire to reach agreement, my delegation will __________ from the conference.

Footsteps to Fame

Read the following passage, noting details but concentrating primarily on the way in which it is written.

'I hope you won't mind my asking you a tiny favour,' said my week-end-in-the-country hostess. 'Victoria is taking part in a dancing display at the village **hall** this morning and I promised we'd go and watch.'

'How lovely,' I lied. 'I can't think of a nicer way to spend a Saturday morning in Sussex. What sort of dancing is it? **Square?**' Victoria is 10 and like a milk churn in build.

'I believe it's called *soubrette*,' replied my **hostess.** 'They've all learnt a dance at ballet classes. Victoria's is called Catching Butterflies.'

As if on cue there came a heavy footfall on the stairs and the little lepidopterist herself appeared in **lace-trimmed** smock and lace-trimmed bonnet wielding a lace-trimmed butterfly net with the innate grace of a miner heaving his **pick**. She appeared to have difficulty walking beneath the weight of all those frills, like a giant human **doily**, but maybe butterflies go for it. Anyway we piled into the Volvo with the **Labradors** and headed for the village.

I heard a brief item on the radio the other day that following the huge success of that TV series 'Fame', about the New York High School for the Performing Arts, stage schools in this country have been inundated with stage-struck kids wanting to be **Shirley Temple**.

I speak from bitter experience because half a century ago I did exactly the same. I clamoured to be a ballet dancer and was sent off to a special boarding school where we danced every day. At the end of every term there was a show and my mother used to say she couldn't bear to watch 10-year-olds simpering and strutting on stage as we were taught to do: it was shameless.

In the village hall, behind a desk stacked with certificates headed Bronze, Silver and Gold Medal Awards, sat the adjudicator, ex-Royal Ballet dancer Mr Robin Paige-Palmer. The curtains opened and Mrs Frimmond, the ballet teacher, appeared. The first item, she announced, was in the bronze medal section with Charlotte Gilroy 'Going Fishing'. The lady at the piano tore into a merry polka and Miss Gilroy entered left, skipping, and for three minutes attempted to land a fish the size (to judge by the strain on her face) of **Moby Dick**.

She was followed by a positive fleet of small, aspiring bronze medallists. After the fish came the butterfly-catchers, 16 in all, followed by 10 haymakers, 8 strawberry-sellers, 5 flower-pickers and 1 Fairy Who Painted The Apples Red.

'Why is Camilla Fenn the only Fairy Who Painted The Apples Red?' I asked my neighbour, as Mrs Frimmond staggered across the stage with a fully grown tree hung with **Golden Delicious.**

'Because her mother used to be a professional dancer and choreographed the number herself.' she replied, 'Camilla is going to a stage school next term.'

Camilla tripped on, **all tinsel and tiara**, tapping the apples with a silver wand, and I was suddenly transported to my own dancing schooldays. The same coyness, the same arch smile, the same exaggerated facial expressions. It was, as my mother had said, shameless, but the audience loved it. You could feel respect rising from them, respect for a true professional. Afterwards all the bronze medallists lined up on stage and Mr Paige-Palmer commented on their work at some length.

Then Mr Paige-Palmer turned to Camilla Fenn, the Fairy Who Painted The Apples Red. Here, said Mr Paige-Palmer, was a true artist. Her technique was exceptional, her presence magnetic and her feeling for the role so poignant that he doubted there was one of us who had not been moved by the performance. A Congratulatory Honours for Camilla then and, no doubt, a one-way ticket to Broadway.

From an article by Sue Arnold in the *Observer Magazine*

Square: square dances are normally danced in the USA to the accompaniment of country and western music
lace-trimmed: lace is a material commonly used to decorate the borders of clothes
pick: a miner's tool used for digging out coal
doily: a small, round piece of linen, lace or paper, usually with frills
Labradors: presumably the family took these large dogs with them
Shirley Temple: archetypal child star of the 1930s
Moby Dick: the white whale in Herman Melville's novel of the same name
Golden Delicious: a type of apple, golden in colour
all tinsel and tiara: wearing shining imitation finery and a horseshoe-shaped headdress of imitation jewels

E

Unfamiliar words

Decide on the most probable meaning of the following words and phrases in the context, using the aid given.

1 **lepidopterist** (line 13) the technical term for the role the little girl was playing
2 **smock and bonnet** (line 14) imagine the dress and hat she was wearing
3 **frills** (line 18) what sort of decoration?
4 **go for it** (line 19)
5 **stage-struck** (line 25)
6 **skipping** (line 43) what sort of movement?
7 **land** (line 44) here, the object of fishing
8 **choreographed** (line 56)
9 **wand** (line 60) carried by a fairy
10 **coyness** (line 62)
11 **arch** (line 62) the smile that goes with coyness
12 **lined up** (line 67)
13 **presence** (line 72) used technically here, for what sort of artistic effect?
14 **poignant** (line 73)

F

Interpretation of text

Answer the following questions in your own words.

1 How do we know the writer was being sarcastic in expressing her enthusiasm about going to the village hall?
2 Why did she suggest that Victoria might be suited for square dancing?
3 Why was it appropriate that Victoria arrived as if 'on cue'?
4 How does the use of 'heavy footfall' emphasise what the writer has previously said about Victoria and make the idea of her dancing sound grotesque?
5 What is ironic about the use of the words 'innate grace'?
6 Why did Victoria look like 'a giant human doily'?
7 Why did the writer's mother object to the performances at the end of every term at her school?
8 What gave the writer the impression that the first contestant was trying to catch a whale?
9 Why should she have been followed by 'a fleet' of other aspirants?
10 Why did Mrs Frimmond 'stagger' across the stage?
11 What struck the writer as 'shameless' about Camilla's performance, why did it attract the audience and what criticism of child stars is suggested by the use of the word?
12 Why may Camilla one day obtain 'a one-way ticket' to Broadway?

Use of language

Much of the humour of this passage depends on the substitution of one word for another. Find the words used instead of the following and say what difference the word chosen makes. The paragraph in which the word appears is given in brackets.

1 said (2)
2 carrying (4)
3 got into (4)
4 begged (6)
5 smiling (6)
6 walking (6)
7 started playing (7) (two words)

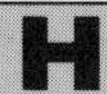

Vocabulary expansion

An **adjudicator** judges performances in dancing. In what circumstances would you rely on the judgement of the following?

1 a juror
2 a referee
3 a reviewer
4 a surveyor
5 an umpire

Lexical Progress Test 4

You must choose the word or phrase which best completes the sentence.
For each question, 1 to 25, indicate the correct answer, A, B, C or D.
The time for the test is 20 minutes.

1 I've had enough of your insults. I won't __________ your behaviour any longer.
A hold up B persevere C put up with D support

2 The negotiations are going well and we are confident of a successful __________.
A outburst B outcome C output D overflow

3 I'm in no __________ to listen to your complaints this morning.
A attitude B feeling C mood D opinion

4 He used to live in the centre of the city but now he has moved to the __________.
A brink B district C frontier D outskirts

5 We need someone __________ in all branches of the business.
A accustomed B experienced C experimented D used

6 We __________ the whole area for hours but could not find them.
A chased B enquired C searched D sought

7 We cannot grant you a licence until you have filled in the __________ forms.
A authoritative B fit C requisite D viable

8 The taste __________ in my mouth for a long time afterwards.
A insisted B lingered C loitered D prolonged

9 He is so __________ in his work that it would be a pity to disturb him.
A absorbed B attentive C consumed D intent

10 The plan presents some difficulties, but they are __________ by the advantages.
A overbalanced B overlooked C outweighed D prevailed

11 I want you here tomorrow morning at 9 o'clock, without __________.
A fail B failure C fault D miss

12 I __________ him to reconsider his decision before it was too late.
A enforced B indicated C said D urged

13 Before the bill was passed in Parliament, a number of __________ proposed by the opposition were debated.
A adjustments B amendments C removals D reviews

14 Despite the advances made in recent years, women are still __________ in most professions by about three to one.
A outclassed B outnumbered C overcome D superseded

15 Many lawyers are able to command large __________ for their services.
A bills B grants C fees D rates

16 The __________ of the soldiers was high before the battle, because they were confident of victory.
A mood B moral C morale D temper

17 He __________ from the Committee because he disapproved of the way in which it was being run.
A renounced B replaced C retracted D withdrew

18 The new car was __________ to the public for the first time yesterday.
A opened B unpacked C unveiled D unwrapped

19 He was __________ for military service because he had flat feet.
A discarded B dispensed C discharged D rejected

20 I expected him to lose his __________ when I made those remarks, but he accepted them with a good grace.
A disposition B humour C mood D temper

21 The King was obliged to __________, and a republic was proclaimed.
A abdicate B forsake C renounce D vacate

22 Despite his unimportant post in the Government, he __________ great power.
A draws B manages C sways D wields

23 I __________ with him to abandon the ship before it was too late.
A appealed B begged C claimed D pleaded

24 His father paid him __________ while he was at university.
A alimony B an allowance C a pension D the rates

25 The children from the ballet school performed a __________ dance.
A graceful B gracious C precise D smart

Advertising

Introductory exercise

The fifteen advertising slogans printed here are meant to advertise cars, home computers and insurance policies.

1 Divide them into three groups, five slogans for each topic.
2 Decide which human emotions, e.g. aggression, fear, greed, they appeal to in each case, or what sort of feeling, e.g. comfort, convenience, freedom from worry etc., they are trying to instil.
3 Decide whether any pattern emerges for each group.

1 After a lifetime's slog one's entitled to relax and play a little golf.
2 Ask any child at school why it's worth £199.
3 Before we made it clever we made it simple.
4 Change pies in the sky into things you can buy.
5 Do you get a feeling of power when you leave the office?
6 Even more icing on the cake for our policyholders this year.
7 Have you got what it takes to be a pensioner?
8 Is your child's future clear?
9 It's tough on the streets.
10 Luxury need not stop where adventure begins.
11 Interest this high is a rare sight. Don't let it get away.
12 Quick to reach 60, slow to grow old.
13 Soon English won't be the only common language of British schoolchildren.
14 Takes your family, your luggage, and your breath away.
15 The first thing we had to figure out was how soon it was going to pay for itself.

Changes in the Art of Persuasion

Read the passage below to gain a general impression of its content before answering the questions below.

Stephen Leacock described advertising as the science of arresting the human intelligence long enough to get money from it. But the sellers don't have it all their own way; over the last twenty years or so, those who attempt to influence what we buy have had to change their tactics. They used to persuade us to buy only a particular brand or product, but the great mushrooming of products which has accompanied growing economic prosperity has forced them to adopt more subtle approaches. Brand loyalty had been exposed as a marketing myth – it is now acknowledged that even where we have a strong preference for a particular brand, we still like to flirt with rival products, especially when they are new. This aspect of purchasing behaviour is extremely robust, and may answer a basic need for variety. However, in the economic recession of the 1970s there were signs of a revival of campaigns designed to establish brand loyalty: only Persil mums are caring mums, and we can all spot the chap who drinks Guinness – he's the calm, relaxed one in the corner, content to wait for the head on his beer to subside. The techniques have become more sophisticated, but the aim of these campaigns is very long-standing.

The other major change in the tone of advertising campaigns in recent years has less flattering implications for us as buyers. In the 1950s and 1960s, advertisements were packed with information about the product, on the assumption that we decided what to buy on rational grounds; 'unique selling propositions' were brought to our attention, and our TV screens were filled with actors who exuded integrity as they made us offers no sensible person could possibly refuse. But surveys of people's voting habits carried out by sociologists have been seized on by admen as evidence that rational persuasion is wasted on us. The pollsters' pursuit of the floating voter has turned out to be something of a wild-goose chase. It now appears that most of us vote according to long-standing emotional loyalties, and only rarely change our minds in response to events. So advertisers, assuming that we buy as we vote, have tended to abandon campaigns which appeal to reason and calculation in favour of advertisements designed to play on our unconscious motivations and associations. It is difficult to evaluate the effectiveness of advertising (we don't know how well the product would have sold without advertisements) but the standard of qualitative market research – the investigation of our underlying motivation – is so poor, from a scientific point of view, that it is hard to believe in the picture sometimes conjured up of the consumer as a marionette who simply makes purchases according to the wishes of the omnipotent advertising and marketing men who pull the strings.

From *Habits* by John Nicholson

A

Unfamiliar words

Decide on the most probable meaning of the following in the context, using the aid given below.

1 **mushrooming** (line 8)
2 **a marketing myth** (line 11)
3 **flirt with** (line 13) usually used for relations between the sexes, but here?
4 **robust** (line 16)
5 **caring mums** (line 20) who care about what?
6 **exuded** (line 32)
7 **pollsters** (line 37)
8 **the floating voter** (line 37) floating between what?
9 **a wild-goose chase** (line 38)
10 **conjured up** (line 52) what is a conjuror?

B

Reading for gist

Answer the following questions on the passage in your own words before attempting the multiple-choice questions which follow.

1 What was the basic aim of advertising in the past, and what circumstances caused advertisers to change their approach?
2 When advertisements stressing brand loyalty reappeared in the 1970s, were they still of the same kind as before?
3 What kind of image did advertisers attempt to project in TV commercials in the 1950s and 1960s, and on what assumption was it based?
4 How did research into people's voting habits cause advertisers to modify their approach?
5 What effect has the new approach to advertising had on the public, and what does it consist of?

Link your answers together to produce a brief summary of the passage, and then use this information to answer the multiple-choice questions.

Now answer the following questions. *Only one answer* is correct.

6 Traditional advertisements
 A assumed people would never change their minds.
 B deliberately created a marketing myth.
 C relied on people's ignorance.
 D underestimated the appeal of novelty.

7 When brand loyalty was emphasised again in the 1970s
 A it proved that the advertisers' original assumptions had been correct.
 B it was because the recession had reduced the choice available.
 C advertisers concentrated on psychological approaches.
 D it was used to sell more sophisticated products.

8 The approach of advertisers on TV in the 1950s and 1960s depended primarily on
 A flattering the customer.
 B good-looking actors.
 C indicating the advantages of using the product.
 D people's voting habits.

9 The study of people's voting habits persuaded advertisers that
 A people are seldom influenced by reasonable arguments.
 B people do not really know why they buy things.
 C people's preferences for products are determined by the way they vote.
 D polls are an unreliable guide to public opinion.

10 The writer thinks that the new trend in advertising
A has justified the advertisers' confidence in it by proving so effective.
B has probably not affected sales as much as people believe.
C has successfully demonstrated that we are ruled by our emotions.
D has transformed consumers into robots.

C

Words often confused

1 adopt, designate, decide, elect
Use each of these verbs *at least once* in the correct form to complete the sentences below, paying attention to the structures used.

1 In view of the results of public opinion polls, advertisers __________ a new strategy.
2 As they could not have children of their own, they __________ two orphans.
3 Once the President had __________ to retire, he attempted to __________ Vice-President Ramos as his successor, but the Senate were not prepared to accept this, insisting that the new President should be __________ by popular vote.
4 Although he had been __________ President, Ramos __________ to stand for election.

2 detect, exhibit, expose, reveal
Use each of these verbs *once only* to complete the sentences below.

1 His paintings have been __________ at the Royal Academy.
2 The press campaign __________ the President's dishonesty, __________ that he had taken bribes.
3 He had also tapped ministers' telephones in order to __________ any signs of disloyalty.

3 detection, disclosure, exhibition, exposure, revelation
Use each of the above *once only* to complete the sentences below, in the plural form where necessary.

1 They are sensitive instruments designed for the __________ of minerals under the ground.
2 The photograph would have been better if you had given it a longer __________.
3 The __________ of modern art will be held at the National Gallery.
4 Questions have been asked in the House of Commons, seeking to discover whether the sensational __________ in the popular press referring to the Minister's conduct constitute a __________ of classified information.

4 compose (oneself), relax, resign (oneself to), rest, stay
Use each of these verbs *at least once* in the correct form to complete the sentences below.

1 After a full and active life, I must now __________ myself to gardening and reading books.
2 At least you'll be able to __________ (or __________) and take things easy. The trouble with you has always been that you've never been prepared to __________ still. You've been so busy that you've never let things __________.
3 He was overcome by emotion but had time to __________ himself before the award was made to him.
4 He is buried in Westminster Abbey, where his body __________ in a marble tomb.
5 When I was a child, we always used to __________ at a hotel by the seaside, when my father took a few days off to __________, playing golf and enjoying himself while my mother and I __________ ourselves to following him round the course.

5 chronic, deep-seated, durable, immemorial, inveterate, long-standing
These adjectives occur most frequently in certain idiomatic phrases. Use each of the words above *once only*, to complete the phrases below.

1 a __________ arrangement
2 an __________ enemy
3 __________ resentment
4 __________ and hard-wearing
5 a __________ illness
6 from time __________

D

Vocabulary expansion

ebb, evaporate, set, shrink, slump, wane
These verbs are all associated with the idea of growing smaller, or disappearing. Which would you apply in the following cases?

1 clothes washed in the wrong way
2 moisture rising in the heat
3 the moon growing smaller
4 the stock market, or business, collapsing
5 the sun disappearing over the horizon
6 the tide going out

Television Advertising

Read the following passage carefully before answering the questions that follow.

When the 1954 Television Act made it mandatory for the different television companies to see that any advertising they carried conformed to the ITA's Principles of Television advertising, Parliament in effect was creating two quite separate standards of advertising. This double standard has continued ever since.

On the one hand is television advertising, every piece of which is scrutinized beforehand by a central committee and compelled to comply with an increasingly demanding set of rules, the infringement of which could lead to direct action by the Government. And on the other hand is the rest of advertising with no overall scrutiny of individual advertisements, an undemanding code and responsibility to an authority whose expenses the industry pays and whose members it appoints.

It should be emphasized that this double standard is not merely theoretical. In practice it appears even more clearly in the contrast between the leisurely operation of 'self-discipline' in advertising as a whole and the precise and often very tough way the programme companies' censoring committee deals with the commercials which are submitted to it. At first sight this censoring committee looks like yet another of those *ad hoc* creations which British media owners have been in the habit of setting up to enforce their own views of the standards of the advertising they accept. In itself it has no legal obligation to censor anything. (Under the Television Act it is the Independent Television Authority which is ultimately responsible for seeing that the legal minimum for commercials is actually imposed, just as each of the eleven independent television contracting companies in the country has no obligation to see that any commercials it broadcasts conform to it.)

But in practice it was found that the only way of making sure that they did conform was for the separate companies to join forces to vet all television commercials centrally and to impose a single standard of interpretation for the whole country. The copy committee of the Independent Television Companies Association was the organization set up to do it and at present deals with just over seven thousand separate television commercials a year.

The Independent Television Authority has the last word over any disputed or particularly difficult decisions, and also sees all projected commercials before they are finally accepted. This participation of the Authority in the work of scrutinizing commercials has recently been stepped up after criticisms that the programme companies were being left too much freedom in the work of censorship. But in fact the day-to-day work of scrutinizing commercials continues to be done by the ITCA, and however anomalous the idea may seem of having the bulk of the censoring done by the same people who are trying to sell television time to the advertisers, it is hard to fault the efficiency with which they have done their work.

From *The Persuasion Industry* by John Pearson and Graham Turner

E

Unfamiliar words

Decide on the most probable meaning of the following in the context.

1 **mandatory** (line 1)
2 **leisurely** (line 16)
3 **vet** (line 30)

4 **projected** (line 37)
5 **stepped up** (line 40)
6 **anomalous** (line 43)

F

Reading for detail

Compare each of the statements made below with the passage and decide which of the answers is correct. *Only one answer* is correct in each case.

1 The 1954 Television Act laid down that
  A all television advertisements must observe certain standards.
  B all television advertisements should be scrutinized beforehand by a central committee.
  C Parliament should approve all television advertisements.
  D There should be separate standards of advertising on television and elsewhere.
2 Advertisements outside television
  A are censored as strictly as TV advertisements.
  B are scrutinized at the industry's own expense.
  C are submitted for scrutiny to employers of the advertising industry.
  D must conform to a fairly easy-going code of practice.
3 The censorship of television commercials is legally the responsibility of
  A an ad hoc committee set up by British media owners.
  B the advertising industry.
  C the Independent Television Authority.
  D the programme companies' censoring committee.
4 Before the copy committee of the Independent Television Companies Association was set up, advertisements were scrutinized
  A by each company individually.
  B only by the ITA.
  C to see if they satisfied advertisers.
  D to see if they satisfied media owners.
5 The copy committee of the Independent Television Companies Association was set up
  A to ensure that the same standards were applied on all independent television channels.
  B to make sure that the companies scrutinized advertisements on their programmes.
  C to protect advertisers from prosecution.
  D to see that the independent television companies conformed to the ITA's standards.

G

Words often confused

1 explore, inspect, investigate, keep under observation, observe, scan, scrutinise, take stock of

Use each of these verbs in the correct form *at least once* to complete the sentences below, paying particular attention to the contexts in which they are commonly found.

1 The official asked to _____ our tickets, and _____ my travel warrant with minute attention before agreeing that it was valid for the journey.
2 The doctor is not sure what is wrong with her, so he has suggested that she should go into hospital and be _____ for a few days.
3 We are prepared to _____ every avenue in order to reach agreement.
4 They have installed electronic equipment at the airport to _____ people's luggage. Since then we have _____ that passengers have been more careful about packing objects subject to customs duty in their cases.
5 Having _____ the whole of the area around the source of the river, they decided to pitch camp to _____ the situation before deciding whether to turn back.
6 We are _____ a number of complaints from our customers about goods not being properly _____ before leaving the factory.

2 authoritative, compulsory, demanding, inquisitive, requisite

Use each of these words *at least once* to complete the sentences below, paying attention to the context in which they are found.

1 It is _____ to wear a seat belt in many countries nowadays when driving a car.
2 'What's it got to do with you where I was and who I was with? Don't be so _____!'
3 He spoke in such an _____ manner that he was clearly master of his subject.
4 You cannot obtain a licence until you have filled in the _____ forms.
5 I doubt if you will find the examination very _____. You should be able to take it in

your stride. The first three questions, remember, are ________, but after that it's a matter of completing the ________ number from a choice of ten.

3 **appeal (to/for), apply (to/for), resign (oneself to), submit (to), surrender (to)**
Submit has two meanings.
a) to present (a case, an application, etc.) for consideration
b) to give way to stronger power or authority
Use each of the verbs listed above *at least once*, in the correct form, to complete the sentences below, paying close attention to the structure and context in which the verbs are used.

1 When he ________ for the job, he was requested to ________ three copies of his application form.
2 He ________ his post, rather than ________ to an inspection of his management of the company's affairs.
3 The colonel ________ for help, but when it became clear that this would not be forthcoming, he ________ himself to the inevitable and ________, with all his men.

Advertising Standards

Read the following passage, comparing it to 'Television Advertising' (page 100). Be prepared to answer some detailed questions on it.

DO ADVERTISEMENTS SOM

The short answer is yes, some do.

Every week hundreds of thousands of advertisements appear for the very first time.

Nearly all of them play fair with the people they are addressed to.

A handful do not. They misrepresent the products they are advertising.

As the Advertising Standards Authority it is our job to make sure these ads are identified, and stopped.

WHAT MAKES AN ADVERTISEMENT MISLEADING?

If a training course had turned a **7 stone** weakling into **Mr Universe** the fact could be advertised because it can be proved.

But a promise to build 'you' into a 15 stone he-man would have us flexing our muscles because the promise could not always be kept.

'Makes you look younger' might be a reasonable claim for a cosmetic.

But pledging to 'take years off your life' would be an overclaim akin to a promise of eternal youth.

A garden centre's claim that its seedlings would produce 'a riot of colour in just a few days' might be quite contrary to the reality.

Such flowery prose would deserve to be pulled out by the roots.

If a brochure advertises a hotel as being '5 minutes' walk to the beach', it must not require an Olympic athlete to do it in the time.

As for estate agents, if the phrase 'overlooking the river' actually means 'backing onto a ditch', there would be nothing for it but to show their ad the door.

HOW DO WE JUDGE THE ADS WE LOOK INTO?

Our yardstick is The British Code of Advertising Practice.

Its 500 rules give advertisers precise guidance on what they can and cannot say. The rules are also a gauge for media owners to assess the acceptability of any advertising they are asked to publish.

The Code covers magazines, newspapers, cinema commercials, brochures, leaflets, posters, circulars posted to you, and now commercials on video tapes.

The ASA is not responsible for TV and radio advertising. Though the rules are very similar they are administered by the Independent Broadcasting Authority.

WHY IT'S A TWO-WAY PROCESS

Unfortunately some advertisers are unaware of the Code, and breach the rules unwittingly. Others

4 There is no reason why you should __________ to such treatment. You can demand a retrial, __________ to the court for legal aid, and even if the trial goes against you, __________ to the House of Lords, if necessary.

4 the bulk (of), the majority (of), the whole (of)

The bulk of (uncountable) } mean 'the greater
The majority of (countable) } part of'.

The whole of is also uncountable.

Complete the sentences below, using one of these three phrases.

1 The __________ of the consignment will not reach us before the end of the month, but the __________ of it has already been delivered.

2 The __________ of students attending the school go on to university, though of course not all of them achieve the standard required.

3 At the moment, the __________ force of our endeavour is directed towards the prevention of smuggling. In the __________ of cases, we are concerned with drugs and the __________ of what is found consists of consignments sent by sea.

7 stone: about 45 kg
Mr Universe: the world champion in body building
15 stone: about 95 kg

From an advertisement by The Advertising Standards Authority

IMES DISTORT THE TRUTH?

forget, bend or deliberately ignore the rules.

That is why we keep a continuous check on advertising. But because of the sheer volume, we cannot monitor every advertiser all the time.

So we encourage the public to help by telling us about advertisements they think ought not to have appeared. Last year 7,500 people wrote to us.

WHAT DO WE DO TO ADVERTISERS WHO DECEIVE THE PUBLIC?

Our first step is to ask advertisers who we or the public challenge to back up their claims with solid evidence.

If they cannot, or refuse to, we ask them either to amend the ads or withdraw them completely.

Nearly all agree without any further argument.

In any case we inform the publishers, who will not knowingly accept any ad which we have decided contravenes the Code.

If the advertiser refuses to withdraw the advertisement he will find it hard, if not impossible, to have it published.

WHOSE INTERESTS DO WE REALLY REFLECT?

The Advertising Standards Authority was not created by law and has no legal powers.

Not unnaturally some people are sceptical about its effectiveness.

In fact the Advertising Standards Authority was set up by the advertising business to make sure the system of self-control worked in the public interest.

For this to be credible, the ASA has to be totally independent of the business.

Neither the chairman nor the majority of ASA council members is allowed to have an involvement in advertising.

Though administrative costs are met by a levy on the business, no advertiser has any influence over ASA decisions.

Advertisers are aware that it is as much in their own interests as it is in the public's that honesty should be seen to prevail.

If you would like to know more about the ASA and the rules it seeks to enforce you can write to us at the address below for an abridged copy of the Code.

The Advertising Standards Authority

If an advertisement is wrong, we're here to put it right.

ASA Ltd, Dept. T, Brook House, Torrington Place, London WC1E 7HN

Unfamiliar words

Decide on the most probable meaning of the following in the context.

1 **pledging** (line 34)
2 **akin** (line 36)
3 **yardstick** (line 59)
4 **gauge** (line 66)
5 **unwittingly** (line 90)
6 **monitor** (line 97)
7 **back up** (line 110)
8 **contravenes** (line 123)
9 **levy** (line 155)
10 **abridged** (line 169)

I

Reading for gist

Answer the following questions. *Only one answer* is correct.

1 The main responsibility of the Advertising Standards Authority is
  A to appeal to the public for help in maintaining standards.
  B to censor all new advertisements.
  C to do their best to ensure that misleading advertisements are withdrawn.
  D to draw advertisers' attention to the content of their advertisements.

2 An advertisement is judged to be misleading if it
  A claims to have turned a weakling into a he-man.
  B employs flowery language.
  C exaggerates the possible benefits of a product.
  D makes claims that can be proved false.

3 The Authority appeals to the public for help because
  A it is unable to maintain a continuous check on advertisements.
  B many advertisers are unaware of its Code of Practice.
  C many advertisers deliberately break the rules.
  D there are so many advertisements that it is impossible to keep a check on all of them.

4 The power the Authority has over advertisers who break the rules is that it can
  A force them to withdraw the advertisement.
  B provide evidence to show that it breaks the Code.
  C remind publishers of the Code of Practice.
  D virtually ensure that publishers will not accept the advertisement.

5 The Authority claims to be effective because it
  A devised the Code of Advertising Practice.
  B has legal jurisdiction over advertisers.
  C is mainly composed of impartial people.
  D is paid for by the advertising business.

J

Use of language

Answer the following questions in your own words.

1 Why is it appropriate for the Authority to talk about 'flexing our muscles' in line 27, and what does the phrase mean here?
2 What is suggested by 'a riot of colour' (line 40) and why is it unlikely that the claim would be valid?
3 What do you understand by 'flowery prose' (line 43), and why would it deserve to be 'pulled out by the roots'?
4 In what circumstances do you normally 'show someone the door', and why would this be appropriate for the estate agent's advertisement described in line 56?
5 In what sense is dealing with misleading advertisements 'a two-way process' (line 85)?
6 What is the difference between 'breaching' the rules and 'bending' them (lines 89–92)?
7 Why do you think the writer used the phrase 'Not unnaturally' instead of 'Naturally' in line 135?
8 Is the sentence beginning 'Neither the chairman. . .' (line 149) grammatically correct?
If so, why?

Words often confused

allege, attribute, certify, claim, entitle, reclaim, stipulate, testify

Use each of these verbs *at least once* in the correct form to complete the sentences below, paying attention both to the structures used and the contexts in which they are commonly found.

1 The defendant is __________ to have expressed his intention to rob the house, and we have a number of witnesses prepared to __________ to that effect.
2 We are obliged to confiscate your camera unless you can provide evidence that it was not bought abroad. If you can produce a document from the shop, __________ that it was bought here, of course you will be __________ to __________ it. You __________ (or __________, which would suggest it was a lie) that you bought it here, but I have to follow the rules, as __________ in my instructions.
3 I would now like to play a composition __________ 'The Rustle of Spring'.
4 The painting was at one time __________ to Leonardo da Vinci, but it has now been proved to

have been painted by a pupil of his.

5 My client __________ that he is __________ to the property, since his uncle's will __________ that it should only pass to the other members of the family if he was unable to maintain it in its present condition.

Vocabulary expansion

batch, bouquet, bunch, clump, flock, gang, herd, quorum, quota, shoal, squad

The text on page 102 (line 10) refers to **a handful** of advertisers who break the Code of Advertising Practice. **A handful** means 'a small number'. All the words listed above are group words, like 'handful'. Use each word *once only* to complete the following sentences.

1 a __________ of articles (part of the complete delivery)
2 a __________ of cows
3 a __________ of fish
4 a __________ of flowers (or a __________) Is there any difference between the two words?
5 a __________, meaning a quantity limited by law, rationing, etc.
6 a __________, meaning a sufficient number present for the vote to be valid.
7 a __________ of sheep
8 a __________ of soldiers, policemen, etc.
9 a __________ of thieves
10 a __________ of trees

Adventure Then and Now

Introductory exercise

Look at the list of events on the right. You will see events in the left-hand column and dates in the right. Can you put the correct date alongside the event? Do you know who was the first person to perform the feat? The first person or people to reach:

the North Pole	1858
the South Pole	1909
the source of the Nile	1911
the top of Mount Everest	1969
the Moon	1953

Sturt's Exploration in Central Australia (1845)

Read the following passage carefully, paying attention to detail and noting down any words you do not understand.

Sturt in his dealings with the **blacks** is something of a rarity among Australian explorers. He did not despise them or reject them. He treated them with kindness and tried to understand them, and in return he found them to be a gentle, friendly people – embarrassingly friendly, in fact, since they invited the explorers to sleep with their grubby wives. They were, he said, an under-nourished but merry people who sat up laughing and talking all night long. Being naked they suffered very much from the cold at night, and at this point he split his blanket so that he could give half to a shivering old man. He notes that they were adept at foretelling the weather from the position of the moon, and that in sight and smell they were keener than a dog.

The tribes they had first encountered on their way up from **Menindie** were rather a **scrawny** lot, and very primitive; on seeing a horseman for the first time they had thought that man and beast were one creature like the mythical **Centaur**, and they had run off in astonishment when the man had dismounted. But here, on this green watercourse, they were a much more vigorous breed, the men **six feet tall**, and although by tribal law their front teeth had been knocked out, many of them were handsome. They netted fish and dived for mussels in the waterholes, they brought down birds with their spears, and from the seed of a plant they called nardoo they made a rough kind of flour that was baked into cakes.

Sturt questioned the tribesmen whenever he could, and now, by signs and by moving their arms in the manner of paddling a canoe, they indicated that there were indeed great stretches of water further to the east. With renewed hope the party went on and found that the watercourse continued to divide itself into many different channels and waterholes. With its grass and heavy timber the country was much more promising than anything they had previously seen. On November 1 they arrived at a lake with seagulls flying above it, and still further east they came on other great pools indigo blue in colour and very salty. Here in the wilderness they interrupted a strange scene: a group of seven men crying bitterly. Nothing could make them explain the occasion of their grief, they cried and cried and would not stop, and in the end Sturt was obliged to go on his way, having left them a present of his greatcoat.

A few days later, when they were 120 miles upstream from their original starting-point, they came on a crowd of some 400 blacks, more than they had ever seen before. The men were very fine, no tribal scars on their bodies, no bulging stomachs among them, and no missing teeth. They were very friendly once they got over their fear of the horses. They came forward with gifts of ducks and flourcakes, and held up troughs of water for the horses to drink. But they also blasted Sturt's hopes for the last time: from this point on they said the stream diminished, and nothing lay further to the east but the desert. Riding out in that direction Sturt came on a swamp, and beyond this he was confronted by an endless plain.

From *Cooper's Creek* by Alan Moorehead

Sturt: Charles Sturt (1795–1869), the first explorer to reach Central Australia during his journey from Adelaide to the Simpson Desert (1844–6) – see map above

blacks: usually called aborigines in Australia

Menindie: see map above

scrawny: an uncommon word, meaning thin and bony

Centaur: in Greek mythology, a horse with a human body, arms and head in place of its neck and head

six feet tall: about 1.85m

Unfamiliar words

Decide on the most probable meaning of the following in the context.

1 **grubby** (line 5)
2 **merry** (line 6)
3 **adept** (line 9)
4 **mussels** (line 18)
5 **spears** (line 18)
6 **seagulls** (line 27)
7 **bulging** (line 36)
8 **troughs** (line 38)
9 **blasted** (line 39)
10 **swamp** (line 41)

Reading for detail

Answer the following questions, comparing each of the statements made below with the text. *Only one answer* is correct in each case.

1 The first tribes the explorers met ran away because they
A thought they had seen a Centaur.
B were afraid of horses.
C were savage.
D were surprised to see the man and the horse separated.

2 The tribesmen Sturt met near the watercourse
A fished in boats.
B grew plants in order to make cakes.
C had had all their teeth knocked out.
D were much better-looking than those he had seen earlier.

3 Sturt's party were much more hopeful as they proceeded because
A the tribes were more communicative.
B there were signs of water further ahead.
C they had canoes.
D they saw lakes further to the east.

4 The group of 400 blacks Sturt met next were different from the others because they were
A friendly.
B good-looking.
C healthier.
D not frightened.

5 Their effect on Sturt was
A depressing.
B encouraging.
C exciting.
D negligible.

C

Interpretation of text

Answer the following questions in your own words.

1 Why were Sturt and his companions 'embarrassed' by the friendliness of the aborigines (line 4)?
2 If Sturt had taken aborigines with him as guides, what do you think would have been their most useful characteristics for him?
3 What were the seven men Sturt met crying for, and why do you suppose he gave them his greatcoat?
4 Why would the fact that the last tribe Sturt met did not have 'bulging stomachs' have been a sign that they were healthier (line 36)?
5 What do you suppose Sturt reported back when he returned to Adelaide about the prospects for colonists in central Australia?

Words often confused

1 exception, foreigner, freak, rarity, scarcity, stranger

All of these words except **scarcity** could apply to a person, and **foreigner** and **stranger** (as a noun) can *only* be used for people. In the text, **rarity** and **exception** are the same. Complete the sentences below, using each word *at least once*, in the plural where necessary.

1 __________ are normally expected to go through a different door at the Passport Office here.
2 Occasional __________ of nature, such as calves with two heads, may occur, even when breeding has been thoroughly supervised.
3 The __________ of strawberries on the market was caused by the late frost.
4 I liked all his films, with the __________ of the last one.
5 This village is so far away from the main road that a __________ is considered rather a __________. The first time I walked into a pub here, they spoke to me very slowly, as if I were a __________ and might not understand. That's nothing. The way they looked at me you would have imagined I was a __________, with green ears or something like that. But there was no point in taking __________ to them staring at me. There's such a __________ of places to eat around here that I put up with it and ordered some lunch.

2 **exceptional, foreign, rare, scarce, strange**
Now use the adjectives above *once only* to complete the sentences below. Note the construction used with **scarce**.

1 He has a wonderful collection of __________ coins from all parts of the world, and the collection is valuable, because some of them are very __________.
2 Although people found his manner __________ when they first met him, it was obvious that he had __________ ability.
3 Melons are __________ at this time of year.

3 **arrive (at/in), contact, encounter, find, meet, reach**
Use each of these verbs *at least once* in the correct form to complete the sentences below.

1 I'm afraid your message didn't __________ (or __________ me) before I left the house; otherwise I would have gone to the airport to __________ you.
2 – Can you put me through to Mr Murphy, please? I've been trying to __________ (or __________) him all morning.
– I'm sure he's in the building somewhere. I'll see if I can __________ him.
3 During his travels, Sturt __________ a number of tribes wandering about the desert. He always showed his good intentions by going forward alone and unarmed to __________ them, and __________ that they always responded in a friendly manner.

4 **chance, circumstance, event, occasion, opportunity, reason**
In the context, **occasion of** means 'cause of' or 'reason for' (line 30). Note the other examples given of its use, and then complete the sentences below, using each of the words listed *at least once* in the plural where necessary.

I have met him on several **occasions**.
This is not a suitable **occasion** for proposing such a thing.
I've had no **occasion** (or **reason**) to complain about the service.
He was not used to speaking in public, but when he found that he could not avoid it, he **rose to the occasion** and spoke very well.

1 I had no __________ of warning him beforehand about the fact that no microphone was available; under the __________ he did very well, because everyone heard his speech quite clearly.
2 The only __________ why he entered was to get some practice; he has no __________ of winning on this __________.
3 In normal __________ I would be free to meet you, but in the __________ of your plane being late, or if by __________ I can't find anyone to take my place, please contact me as soon as you arrive.
4 If I had the __________ (or __________) to go to Japan for a holiday, I would take it. I have only had __________ to visit the country once before, on business, and on that __________ I was so busy that in the __________, I couldn't see much of the country. That's the main __________ for my wanting to go back there.

E

Vocabulary expansion

1 **breed, caste, clan, sect, tribe**
Which of these words would you apply to the following?

1 a type of dog
2 a Scottish family group or closely-knit group of friends
3 people having a special form of religious belief or form of worship
4 a group of natives living together in the jungle
5 a social group, particularly with religious reasons for the social division, as in India.

2 **carve, chop, crack, divide, split**
Split implies 'divide by breaking or tearing' (e.g. Sturt's blanket, line 8). Which verb would you consider most appropriate for breaking or cutting in the following circumstances?

1 cutting down a tree
2 breaking the resulting logs in two
3 cutting the meat at table for everyone
4 breaking nuts
5 separating the atom in nuclear physics
6 allotting money among one's relations in one's will
7 using a whip
8 in mathematics

A Modern Crossing of Australia

Read the following passage carefully, paying attention to detail, and comparing it with the one on page 106.

Out back of Bourke there is still next to nothing. You can draw any number of lines from that New South Wales farming community in a generally northerly to westerly direction along which your **kookaburra** could fly 2000 miles without seeing so much as a house. That is how big and how empty **the outback** is.

It has also always seemed to me a pretty compelling reason for going there. And so, at 6.30 a.m. on a grey winter's dawning in a **downtown** Sydney bus station I find myself checking in for a coach camping tour of Australia.

About the camping there had never been much doubt. It saves money and besides, by definition, is the only way to see the empty places. The big dilemma had been whether to sign on for a slick high-mileage bus tour such as this, or to fly out to the centre of Australia and there to join a smaller group for a more leisurely and intimate 'safari' in a four-wheel-drive vehicle, usually a converted lorry, much of it off the roads altogether. But cost, a desire to see as much of Australia as possible, and, let's be honest, doubts about my ruggedness, had all argued in favour of the bus.

The driver concludes his welcome with the words 'this is an experience, not a holiday'.

Too right. And for the first few days I am not at all sure that it is one which is going to be enjoyable even in retrospect. We rush from campsite to campsite from dawn to dusk, living mostly on tinned food. And it is cold at night.

Still, the evenings are spent pacing echoing provincial towns; and Australia must be the most hospitable country on earth. Local clubs have permanent 'welcome' signs up for passing strangers. At Coober Pedy, an **opal** mining town, where they live underground to escape the summer heat, I find myself in a café full of Greek miners trying to teach our Australian Greek cook her own **grandmaternal** tongue. I catch the whiff of hilarious improbability which often marks great adventures. That night we sleep underground; but for warmth, in the entrance to an abandoned mine.

Things are definitely looking up by the time tradition, apparently, requires that we get out and push the coach over the state line into Northern Territory. We are on dirt roads much of the time now: John, our impeccable coach captain, **guns** us down them at a steady 60 mph.

Goodies come thick and fast now: Ayer's Rock, the world's largest monolith and beyond any doubt the star of the outback. It is no longer as remote and silent as it was. When I climb it at 4 p.m. there are already 263 signatures in the book at the top for that day, two quite separate entries from persons each claiming to be first up with a skateboard. Yet it still inspires an almost religious awe in all who experience it. Waiting for dawn or sunset feels like a scene from ***Close Encounters***. I had expected to report that the rock felt alive. In fact it felt wise.

The stations (ranches) in these parts are the size of a British county: 2500 square miles is nothing special. It must be 100 miles to the nearest house. The world could end, but here you would never know.

A modern-day expedition on Ayer's Rock

From an article by Mark Ottaway in *The Sunday Times Magazine*

Out back of: beyond (UK)
kookaburra: an Australian bird, also called the laughing jackass
the outback: the interior of Australia
downtown: central (UK)
Too right: quite right (UK)
opal: a precious stone
grandmaternal: presumably the cook's grandmother was Greek
guns: (slang) drives aggressively
Goodies: (slang) highspots of the trip
Close Encounters of the Third Kind: Film made by Stephen Spielberg

F

Unfamiliar words

Decide on the most probable meaning of the following in the context.

1 **dilemma** (line 21)
2 **leisurely** (line 26)
3 **ruggedness** (line 32)
4 **dusk** (line 41)
5 **whiff** (line 56)
6 **hilarious** (line 56)
7 **thick and fast** (line 69)
8 **monolith** (line 71)
9 **awe** (line 79)
10 **ranches** (line 85)

G

Reading for detail

Answer the following questions, comparing each of the statements made below with the text. *Only one answer* is correct.

1 The phrase 'by definition' (line 19) implies that
A camping is cheaper.
B camping is essential because of the distances covered.
C the writer had never had any doubts about camping.
D there are no houses in the outback.

2 If the writer had chosen the alternative trip to the coach tour, he would
A have been more comfortable.
B have had a longer holiday.
C have seen more of Australia.
D not have had to pay so much.

3 In the provincial towns the writer visited, people
A are pleased to see new faces.
B do not usually speak English.
C have no places of amusement.
D sleep underground.

4 The travellers were obliged to get out on the border of Northern Territory because
A the coach became overheated.
B the coach had broken down.
C the coach captain had taken the wrong road.
D it was the custom.

5 In comparison with Sturt's journey over a hundred years before the main difference appears to have been the absence of
A people.
B aborigines.
C birds.
D water.

An Early Balloon Voyage

Read the following passage carefully, paying attention to detail and noting down any words you do not understand.

Nottingham Journal 2ND SEPTEMBER 1786

Leeds, August 29

On Wednesday, at forty minutes after one o'clock, the gallant **Lunardi** fulfilled his engagement to the public by ascending with his Royal Balloon from Kettlewell's Orchard, behind the Minster, York, amid the acclamations of several thousand spectators. **The ascension** was truly sublime, the balloon rose to a prodigious height, so as to be distinctly seen in every part of the town and took a N.E. direction. A very dark cloud for some minutes obscured the intrepid **Aeronaut** from the gazing multitude, who had, however, soon the pleasure of again observing his progress at a great distance, through the trackless atmosphere. Mr Lunardi's dexterity in filling his balloon, which was done in little more than eighteen minutes, and every part of his conduct throughout the business, merited great praise and afforded the highest satisfaction to every beholder. Mr. Lunardi descended an hour after his ascent in a corn field, and observing the people flocking from every quarter towards him, by which he was apprehensive that the corn would be **injured**, he thereupon rose again; and went out of sight.

At three o'clock he finally descended between two hills at a place called Grenock in the parish of Bishop Wilton, about 18 miles from York. A few shepherds came to his assistance after he was perfectly anchored and the number of his rustic visitors increasing, he discharged the inflammable air from the balloon, and with their assistance packed it up. Robert Denison, Esq., who had **rode** after him from his home at Kilnwick Percy, arrived in time to give proper directions for conveying the balloon safe to that place, and having accommodated Mr. Lunardi with his horse, took him home to dinner and afterwards most politely brought him in his own chaise and four to that city. Though it was night when they entered the town, the anxiety of the people for Mr. Lunardi's safety had been so great and the joy they felt on his appearance such that they took the horses from the carriage and drew him through the streets to his lodgings in triumph. Soon after Mr. Lunardi dressed, and paid his respects to the ladies and gentlemen in the Assembly Rooms, where he was received with the warmest expressions of welcome and applause. Mr. Lunardi when at a great elevation from the earth, experienced very inclement weather, had rain, hail and snow, and was also in the midst of electrical clouds.

From *News from the English Countryside* 1750–1850 by Clifford Morsley

Lunardi: Vincent Lunardi, an attaché from the Neapolitan embassy, had made the first balloon ascent in England two years earlier
ascension: (modern English) ascent
aeronaut: (modern English) balloonist
rode: (modern English) ridden
injured: we would now say 'damaged', using injured only with regard to people in such a context

Unfamiliar words

This passage, written two hundred years ago, uses a number of words and expressions that a modern journalist would write differently. Turn the following into acceptable modern English.

1 **forty minutes after one o'clock** (line 2)
2 **amid** (line 5)
3 **the acclamations** (line 5)
4 **multitude** (line 9)
5 **atmosphere** (line 11)
6 **merited** (line 14)
7 **highest** (line 15)
8 **beholder** (line 15)
9 **thereupon** (line 18)
10 **drew** (line 34)
11 **elevation** (line 38)
12 **inclement** (line 39)

Reading for detail

Answer the following questions, comparing each of the statements with the text. *Only one answer* is correct.

1 During Lunardi's first ascent, the balloon
A could be seen everywhere in the town.
B disappeared from sight, and was not seen again in York.
C was always visible from the town.
D was in the air for 18 minutes.

2 Lunardi took off again because he
A had landed in a corn field.
B was concerned for the farmer.
C was afraid his balloon would be damaged.
D wanted to afford the crowd another view of an ascent.

3 His second landing was apparently made
A in another corn field.
B in a field used by sheep.
C in the middle of a village.
D next to a big house.

4 The balloon was temporarily housed at
A Grenock.
B Bishop Wilton.
C Kilnwick Percy.
D York.

5 When Lunardi arrived in York, the crowd
A followed his carriage through the streets.
B carried him in triumph on their shoulders.
C pulled the carriage through the streets themselves.
D welcomed him in a formal ceremony.

Words often confused

1 carry out, discharge, fulfil, perform
The meanings of these verbs overlap within the general context of 'doing an action', **fulfil** always suggesting successful completion. Nevertheless, one or other is usually preferred in combination with certain nouns. Complete the sentences below, using each verb *at least once* in the correct form, and paying attention to the related nouns in the phrases.

1 Although the cast __________ the play quite well, the overall effect on stage did not __________ our expectations.
2 He __________ his promise by __________ his debt to us.
3 He defended his action in shooting the man who was found in the camp by saying he was only __________ orders.
4 In accordance with our benefactor's will, we have __________ our obligation to him by __________ research into the causes of cancer.
5 The successful candidate said that his party had been elected to __________ the task of reconstructing the country and would __________ its responsibilites to the people, __________ the undertaking to do so made in its programme.
6 He threatened to sue us for the libel but fortunately he did not __________ his threat.

2 arise, rise, arouse, raise
The last two verbs always have a direct object, while the first two never do. **Arise** means 'present itself' or 'result (from)'; **arouse** means 'wake up' or 'provoke into activity'. Complete the sentences below, using each verb *at least once* in the correct form, and bearing this information in mind.

1 He __________ to address the meeting and what he said __________ such strong emotions in the audience that he was forced to __________ his hand to call for silence.
2 A number of problems have __________ in the factory, largely because the firm has refused to __________ the workers' wages, which has naturally __________ their resentment.

3 The Government __________ the hopes of the electorate before the election by saying that prices would not __________.

4 If we feel compelled to __________ objections to the Government's procedure, it is because they have deceived the voters. If they had told the truth, these problems would not have __________.

3 assemble, congregate, crowd, flock, gather

Congregate and **flock** are not found with a direct object. The meanings frequently overlap, as in the examples given, but in the sentences that follow there is a distinction in normal usage. Look at the examples and then complete the sentences, using a different verb in each case, in the correct form.

A large number of people **assembled/congregated/gathered** outside the Town Hall.

As the speaker left the hall, people **congregated/crowded/gathered** round him.

1 The hall was __________ with people.

2 When Lunardi landed, people __________ towards his balloon.

3 His campaign __________ support throughout the country the longer it went on.

4 These instructions will tell you how to __________ the machine.

4 assembly, congregation, crowd, flock, gathering

Which of these nouns would be the appropriate one to use in the following contexts?

1 a football __________

2 a __________ of sheep

3 an informal __________ of experts

4 a __________ in church

5 the legislative __________ of a country

Ballooning for Fun

Read the passage below to gain a general impression of its content, and in particular as a contrast to 'An Early Balloon Voyage' (page 112).

'Report to Ashton Court, Bristol at 06.00 hours,' said Tessa Tennant of the Hot Air Balloon Company.

'But that's dawn,' I protested.

'All the best balloon flights are made at dawn,' she explained. 'There is less wind then and you can't fly in wind.' My own view was that none of the best anything could possibly happen at dawn, but anyway I rolled up at the appointed time, still rubbing the sleep from my eyes, on a big field near Bristol.

I found the Hot Air Balloon Co's Range Rover and my pilot, the incredibly handsome Robin Batchelor. 'I'm a 20th-century **buccaneer**!' he told me. Gosh. Meanwhile I had to help hold the balloon open while he inflated it with the fan. Our balloon proved to be blue and grey and called Alka Seltzer, though I felt secretly rather envious of Coppertone nearby, which was all gold and tan, and the Mr Gas balloon shaped like a gas flame.

When our Alka Seltzer was fully inflated, Robin told me to hop into the basket. It was really just a laundry basket with room for two people to stand, and space in the corners for the propane gas cylinders. These fuel the burner which heats the air in the balloon to make it rise. Our take-off, when it came, was so gentle I hardly noticed it: one moment we were on the ground, and the next we were looking down on trees.

Most of the other balloons had gone off east into the sunrise, but I remarked to Robin that I thought it would be rather nice to go west, and land on my parents' lawn near Salisbury. He looked at me as if I were crazed and started talk—ing very slow—ly and carefully like someone on ***Playschool***. 'You can't actually *steer* a balloon, you know. It *blows*. With the *wind*.' Ah. Somehow, although I had theoretically known that, I had not entirely grasped the implications.

'You mean we can't control where we go – eek!'

Robin explained kindly that we could control it to the extent of going up or down, thus avoiding **power lines** for instance (eek eek!). Or if we needed to come down very quickly, for instance if we were drifting into **controlled air space** (eek eek eek!), he could pull the ripcord to open the top of the balloon. But going west when the wind was blowing east – no.

D'Arlandes, the first man ever to go up in a balloon, reported afterwards, 'The silence surrounding us surprised me,' but I was more surprised by the noise. First there was the hiss of the burner, and the occasional woosh when Robin turned the flame up, and then there was Robin's radio which was meant to keep us in touch with our **retrieve crew** on the ground. Robin identified himself as 'Birdman' and our retriever (his girlfriend in the Range Rover) as 'Turkey', but although we talked to what seemed like the entire car-owning population of Bristol, we never got through to Turkey.

From an article by Lynn Barber in the *Sunday Express Magazine*

buccaneer: (in this context) adventurer
Playschool: a TV programme for small children
power lines: electricity cables
controlled air space: air space reserved for the flight paths of military or civil aeroplanes
retrieve crew: those who drive to collect the balloon where it lands

Interpretation of text

This passage, written by a woman journalist, is part of an article explaining the attraction of ballooning as a weekend sport. The writer pretends to be a helpless female. Before answering the questions below, find four ways in which she does this. Then answer the questions.

1 What were the writer's first reactions to the balloon flight, and why did she feel like that?
2 Why do you think she was 'secretly envious' of other balloons (line 23) and how does this confirm the impression she is trying to create in general terms?
3 Why are the words 'talking' and 'slowly' printed with spaces in lines 46 and 47 and how does this relate to the writer's wish to visit her parents?
4 What three possible disasters was the writer envisaging by making use of the word 'eek' to express fright?
5 Why did Robin talk to 'what seemed like the entire car-owning population of Bristol' (lines 81–2)?
6 What is it necessary to do before one can take off in a balloon, and how is it done? How is it possible for the balloon to take off? How much control has the balloonist got over the direction in which he is flying and the height at which he flies? Why was Robin's balloon noisy compared to the original balloons?
7 In comparison with Lunardi's flight (page 112), in what ways have the risks increased and in what ways have they decreased? How far is Robin justified in calling himself 'a 20th -century buccaneer'?
8 How far are the reactions of people nowadays to balloonists the same as they were 200 years ago, and how far and why are they different?

L

Words often confused

contradict, object (to), obstruct, oppose, protest against/to, refuse, resist
Use each of these verbs *at least once* in the correct form to complete the sentences below.

1 Don't __________ me! I know what I'm talking about, and you don't!
2 He was arrested for __________ the police in the course of their duty.
3 He __________ his innocence, but the judge __________ to accept his explanation.
4 I couldn't __________ the urge to __________ him when he made such a ridiculous statement. I __________ to people saying things without checking their facts and __________ to listen to reason.
5 We __________ the use of force to further our cause, but we feel justified in __________ against force being used to remove peaceful demonstrators whose only crime has been to __________ the road to the base by lying down in the middle of it.
6 He has always been __________ to the marriage, so it was not surprising that he __________ his consent.
7 I __________ to the management because my view of the stage was __________ by a pillar.
8 When they realised that the force __________ them outnumbered them by three to one, they were on the point of losing heart but the captain encouraged them to __________ until help arrived.

Language

Introductory exercise

Study the sentence below, which is an example of official language and compare it with the 'translation' into straightforward English below it. Then attempt to 'translate' the other official sentences given.

Enquiries concerning the condition of patients may be effected by personal application to the hospital or by telephone.
You can find out how a patient is either by calling at the hospital or by ringing up.

1 The course should be well within the competence of students who have been pursuing the preliminary course of English studies, which is of two years' duration.
2 It is not the normal practice of this bank to offer customers extended credit without adequate financial safeguards.
3 I am not permanently employed at the present moment because I have been unable to encounter a post commensurate with my ability and interests.
4 The local authority is fully cognizant of the need to make adequate provision for senior citizens in laying the foundations of its prospective housing programme.
5 While proceeding on my customary beat along Charing Cross Road, I apprehended an individual in suspicious circumstances, and was obliged to take him into custody when he was unwilling to give a satisfactory account of his presence outside the bank.
6 Our failure to obtain a renewed vote of confidence from the electorate on this occasion is indicative not of disenchantment with our policies but of the worsening world situation.
7 The refusal of management to contemplate a readjustment of annual increments for teachers will oblige many of them to take private classes in order to augment their income.
8 I am not altogether unaware of the fact that my disinclination to discuss the reasons for my resignation may give rise to conjecture.

Decline of the English Language

Read the following passage to gain a general impression of its content, and then study the way in which the argument is organised before answering the questions which follow.

Most people who bother with the matter at all would admit that the English language is in a bad way, but it is generally assumed that we cannot by conscious action do anything about it. Our civilization is decadent and our language – so the argument runs – must inevitably share in the general collapse. It follows that any struggle against the abuse of language is a sentimental archaism, like preferring candles to electric light or **hansom cabs** to aeroplanes. Underneath this lies the half-conscious belief that language is a natural growth and not an instrument which we shape for our own purposes.

Now, it is clear that the decline of a language must ultimately have political and economic causes: it is not due simply to the bad influence of this or that individual writer. But an effect can become a cause, reinforcing the original cause and producing the same effect in an intensified form, and so on indefinitely. A man may take to drink because he feels himself to be a failure, and then fail all the more completely because he drinks. It is rather the same thing that is happening to the English language. It becomes ugly and inaccurate because our thoughts are foolish, but the slovenliness of our language makes it easier for us to have foolish thoughts. The point is that the process is reversible. Modern English, especially written English, is full of bad habits which spread by imitation and which can be avoided if one is willing to take the necessary trouble. If one gets rid of these habits one can think more clearly, and to think clearly is a necessary first step towards political regeneration; so that the fight against bad English is not frivolous and is not the exclusive concern of professional writers.

Modern writing at its worst does not consist in picking out words for the sake of their meaning and inventing images in order to make the meaning clearer. It consists in gumming together long strips of words which have already been set in order by someone else, and making the results presentable by sheer **humbug**. The attraction of this way of writing is that it is easy. It is easier – even quicker, once you have the habit – to say *In my opinion, it is not an unjustifiable assumption that* than to say *I think*. If you use ready-made phrases, you not only don't have to hunt about for words; you also don't have to bother with the rhythms of your sentences, since these phrases are generally so arranged as to be more or less euphonious. When you are composing in a hurry it is natural to fall into a pretentious, latinised style. Tags like *a consideration which we should do well to bear in mind* or *a conclusion to which all of us would readily assent* will save many a sentence from coming down with a bump. By using stale metaphors, similes and idioms, you save much mental effort, at the cost of leaving your meaning vague, not only for your reader but for yourself.

From *Politics and the English Language* by George Orwell

hansom cabs: horse-drawn cabs for two passengers commonly used in the 19th century

humbug: dishonest language, meant to deceive

Unfamiliar words

Decide on the most probable meaning of the following in the context, using the aid given.

1. **abuse** (line 5)
2. **archaism** (line 5)
3. **indefinitely** (line 13) – what is not definite about it?
4. **take to drink** (line 13)
5. **slovenliness** (line 16)
6. **reversible** (line 17)
7. **frivolous** (line 22)
8. **gumming** (line 26) – what is gum used for?
9. **euphonious** (line 33)
10. **pretentious** (line 34) – what does it pretend to do?

Reading for gist

Answer the following questions on the passage.

1. What arguments are advanced by those who think the English language cannot be prevented from declining?
2. In what way, according to the writer, does the relationship between language and thought operate?
3. What can be done to reverse the process, and who should be responsible for doing it?
4. What benefits would result from this?
5. Why do so many writers use long, empty phrases instead of short, clear ones?

Link your answers together to provide a summary of the passage, and use the information to answer the multiple-choice questions that follow, finding answers that mean more or less the same as what you have written.

6 It is commonly believed that nothing can be done to halt the decline of the English language because
A language cannot be altered by conscious effort.
B people are too lazy to do anything about it.
C it is old-fashioned.
D there are so many bad writers.

7 According to the writer, the abuse of language
A is the cause of foolish thoughts.
B is the result of foolish thoughts.
C both of these.
D neither of these.

8 The solution would be for
A people to think clearly.
B people to take more interest in politics.
C everyone to become more conscious of what is good and bad English.
D good writers to set a better example.

9 As a result of that,
A people would appreciate literature more.
B people would be better equipped to judge political issues.
C the language would become more beautiful.
D the language would no longer be the concern of professional writers alone.

10 The increasing use of ready-made phrases
A is a conscious effort to deceive the public.
B is a sign of laziness.
C is due to their being more effective.
D indicates that the level of education in Britain has fallen.

Words often confused

abolish, annul, cancel, demolish, disallow, dispose of, do away with, execute, exterminate, get rid of
Use each of the above *at least once* in the appropriate form to complete the sentences below, noting the contexts in which they appear.

1 The Pope __________ the marriage because the king and queen had had no children.
2 He was offside when he scored, so the referee __________ the goal.
3 Unfortunately, his company has __________ the order for books.
4 The police have ordered people to keep clear of the area while the tower is being __________.
5 A new poison has been developed to __________ (or __________) (or __________) the rats in the area.
6 I never expected to be able to __________ the pictures for such a good price.
7 Police leave has been __________ this weekend because of the risk of violent demonstrations in the city.
8 The Government has decided to __________ (or __________) the tax on playing cards.
9 The leader of the rebels was __________ in front of a large crowd and afterwards his followers were systematically __________.
10 The poor dog was so old and blind that it seemed kinder to __________ it than allow it to live in misery.

D

Vocabulary expansion

contaminated, flat, mouldy, old-fashioned, polluted, rotten, rusty, stale
Orwell refers to 'stale metaphors' (line 36), meaning expressions which have to some extent lost their original impact. Look at the adjectives above, all of which are used to describe something which is past its best, and use each word *once only* to complete the sentences below.

1 Beer goes __________ if you don't put the top back on the bottle.
2 The water supply can be __________ by effluent from factories by the river.
3 A bicycle left in the rain goes __________.
4 Customs no longer in vogue are __________.
5 Food not properly packed can be __________.
6 Cheese left in the air for a long time goes __________ while bread becomes hard and __________.
7 Fruit not picked in time becomes overripe and eventually __________.

The Effect of Language on Juries

Read the following passage carefully, and study the chart in order to answer detailed questions on its content.

Experimental psychologists have put forward two very different accounts of the process of remembering. According to the first, memory consists of a series of snapshots which we view whenever we wish to recall some past experience or item of information. If you ask how memories get **laid down**, exponents of this theory would say that we behave like the character in Christopher Isherwood's play who said: 'I am a camera with a shutter open, quite passive'. In essence, the theory describes both the laying-down and the recall of memories as passive and objective processes, and it is the view of memory presumably held by the people responsible for deciding what is admissible as evidence in a court of law, where great importance is attached to the recollection of eye-witnesses at the scene of a crime or an accident.

Unfortunately, it is now clear that this is not how memory works at all; moreover, it seems certain that the acceptance of what is known to be an erroneous view of the memory process is frequently responsible for miscarriages of justice. Consider the following experiment carried out by psychologists at the University of Washington, in Seattle.

People were shown films of traffic accidents, and then asked to estimate the speed at which the vehicles involved had been travelling. The experimenters posed this question in one of five slightly different ways: some subjects were asked 'About how fast were the cars going when they hit each other?', while, in the other four phrasings, the word 'hit' was replaced by 'contacted', 'bumped into', 'collided with', or 'smashed into'. The graph opposite leaves little doubt that the alteration of a single word in the question had a significant effect on the average speed estimated. The average estimated speed produced by observers who were asked how fast the cars were travelling when they made contact with each other was less than 32 mph; those who had heard the evocative phrase 'smashed into' suggested an average speed of more than 40 mph. Nor is this all. A different group of subjects subsequently watched a film of a traffic accident, and were then asked either, 'About how fast were the cars going when they smashed into each other?' or, 'About how fast were the cars going when they hit each other?'; alternatively, some subjects were asked nothing at all about the speed of the cars. A week later, the observers were summoned back, and a further series of questions posed, including, 'Did you see any broken glass?' Twelve per cent of those who had been asked nothing about the speed of the cars the previous week, and 14 per cent of those who had answered the milder form of the question, said that they had seen broken glass, whereas 32 per cent of those who had been exposed to the question involving the words 'smashed into' said that they had noticed it. In actual fact, no broken glass had been shown in the film, so these results seem to provide overwhelming evidence against the view that our perception of events in any way resembles the action of a camera. They also make it clear that when we are remembering an event, we actively reconstruct it rather than passively watch a 'film' made at the time of its occurrence.

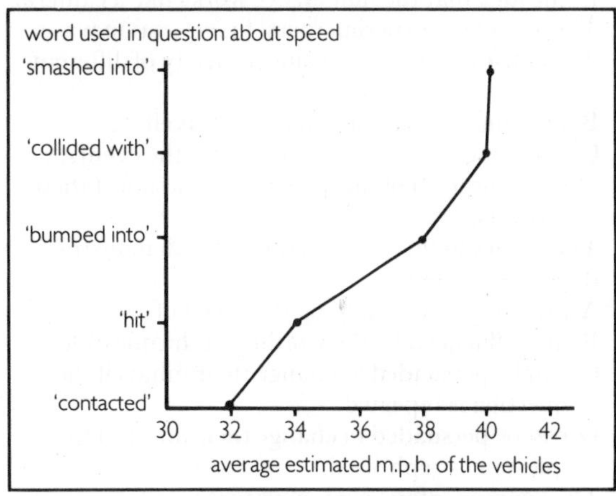

From *Habits* by John Nicholson

laid down: here, established

The speeds mentioned in the text and shown in the graph range from 48 kilometres per hour (30 m.p.h.) to 67 kilometres per hour (42 m.p.h.)

E

Unfamiliar words

Decide on the most probable meaning of the following in the context, using the aid given.

1 **snapshots** (line 4)
2 **exponents** (line 7)
3 **erroneous** (line 21)
4 **miscarriages** (line 22)
5 **posed** (line 28)
6 **evocative** (line 40) what sort of feeling did it call forth?
7 **summoned** (line 49)
8 **milder** (line 54)

F

Reading for detail

Answer the following questions, comparing each of the statements made below with the text. *Only one answer* is correct.

1 The use of eyewitnesses' accounts as evidence in trials is based on
A the fact that most people have reliable memories.
B the fact that they are passive observers.
C the assumption that we can remember what we have seen as a series of pictures.
D the idea that the human eye works like a camera.

2 The aim of the experimenters' first question was to
A confuse observers by using a variety of different terms.
B find out how fast the cars were travelling.
C encourage observers to dramatise the events.
D see if the form of the question would affect their answers.

3 The replies to this series of questions demonstrate that most witnesses
A are incapable of judging the speed of cars.
B are influenced by the wording of the question.
C can be persuaded to change their minds if the question is repeated.
D can be persuaded to change their minds if the question is rephrased.

4 The experimenters' next move was to
A ask the same observers the questions again, using different words.
B ask a different group the same questions.
C ask a different group a different range of questions.
D ask a different group, using only the two most extreme forms of the question.

5 The replies to the second series of questions demonstrate that witnesses' memories are unlikely to be wholly reliable because
A language can influence imperfect recollection to produce an inaccurate picture in their minds.
B they invent a dramatised version of the events as they watch them, and this is what they remember afterwards.
C they can easily be persuaded to change their minds by the form of the question.
D they rely on their ears rather than their eyes in making judgements of this kind.

G

Words often confused

characterise, impersonate, personify, resemble (verbs), **characteristic, impersonation, personification, resemblance** (nouns)
Use each of the above *at least once* in the correct form to complete the sentences below, the nouns in plural where necessary.

1 In many ways, he takes after his father. Although he does not __________ him physically, he has inherited many of his __________, such as his habit of gazing into space when he is thinking.

2 The comedian did a wonderful __________ of the President. Every gesture was so typical of him that you would have thought there was a physical __________ between them.

3 It is not so much his ability to __________ great historical figures of the past, like Mark Antony, that __________ his acting, as his skill in conveying abstract qualities. As Horace in Corneille, he was the __________ of heroism.

4 The ancient gods and goddesses all had different __________, but many of them __________ others from different mythologies. Diana and Artemis, for example, both __________ chastity, and this __________ is extended through their association with hunting.

Language and Censorship

Read the following passage, primarily as a comparison with the two previous ones in this unit, to see what parallels can be established between them, and note in particular the use of words to produce an effect.

Those who think of librarians as quiet, gentle people will be surprised to learn that for some time now the correspondence columns of that indispensable journal, the *Assistant Librarian*, have contained appeals to librarians to censor the material on their shelves and to exercise a similar censorship in their selection of new books.

Nor is that all. In the *Assistant Librarian* for March 1978, there is an article which not only comprehensively expresses the views to which I have been drawing attention, but is such a magnificent compendium of mental sludge that it sums up to perfection the kind of notion that is running through our society today like a science-fiction bacillus for which there is no known cure. It is in fact by a senior librarian; his name is Keith Harrison, and his article appears under the innocuous title 'Community Stock'.

Mr Harrison begins by declaring that 'it's books that I'm into' and goes on to make clear that he is interested in what his local community 'is all about and where it's at' – a statement of faith which hardly leads to the belief that it is literacy that Mr Harrison is into or that the English language is where he's at. Nor is this a trivial point: I have rarely read anything that made as clear as Mr Harrison's article does the connection between the corruption of language and the corruption of thought.

'Public librarians,' he tells us, 'have a long and rather depressing history of impartiality' – a history of which he can certainly claim not to be part. 'Impartiality is OK,' he goes on, 'if you don't believe any one thing very strongly.' I always thought it was OK if you did believe things very strongly, provided one of those things was that views opposed to your own should also be heard. But Mr Harrison seems alternately amused and outraged at such an attitude. The 'quality of life' which he seeks to improve, after all, 'is about open-ended enlightenment rather than restrictive formal education', so that he advocates 'deliberate entertainment rather than gently philanthropic culturizing'.

And having heard the word culture, he reaches for his gun. 'How easy is it in your local library,' he asks indignantly, 'to find quickly a colourful and fun paperback of jokes, cartoons, puzzles or quizzes?' Not easy enough, it seems for Mr Harrison; but stocking the shelves with comics is only a start; we must also remove literature (he calls it 'literature', the quotation marks being there to make clear that it is something to be despised) and replace it with material, which, as well as being politically acceptable, will *not* be of 'lasting literary merit', since 'Novels of lasting literary merit can be scant in pleasure-potential'. For, after all, 'spreading worthwhile human values is surely more important than promulgating tedious literary worth.' By now we have an alarmingly clear picture of Mr Harrison's mind. Political judgements should dictate which non-fiction books are stocked; one of the worst dangers in a library is a balanced range of opinions; impartiality is only suitable for those with no opinions of their own; those equipped with strong views have the right and indeed the duty to suppress views they do not themselves hold; literary worth is tedious; and 'as socially committed community workers, we are surely responsible for the human values and attitudes reflected in the novels we buy.'

The truth is that the expressed contempt for knowledge displayed by Mr Harrison is exactly equal to his unconscious contempt for the people, who cannot be trusted, and therefore cannot be allowed, to read books he disapproves of, so that these must be removed from the shelves before the people are allowed in. And his contempt for knowledge extends to those who possess it: 'librarians . . . may indeed know a great deal about books, but is this really the right basis for deciding what to buy and what to tear up?' Well, I would have thought it was a good start.

From *Taking Sides* by Bernard Levin

Synonyms

Find words in the context that have approximately the same meaning as the following.

1 idea
2 harmless
3 unimportant
4 proposes
5 get rid of
6 boring
7 frighteningly
8 decide

Use of language

The writer correctly points out Mr Harrison's use of jargon and deliberately slang usage in English. Translate the following phrases into the kind of English that would be acceptable to the writer (and to George Orwell – see page 116).

1 It's books that I'm into. . .
2 . . .what his local community is all about and where it's at
3 open-ended enlightenment
4 gently philanthropic culturizing
5 scant in pleasure-potential

Note that the sentence beginning 'How easy is it. . .' (line 64) is appallingly written and not to be imitated, any more than any of Mr Harrison's other sentences. By 'a colourful and fun paperback of jokes,' he means 'a colourful, entertaining paperback full of jokes', etc.

Interpretation of text

Answer the following questions.

1 Find three adjectives in the first two paragraphs that are used to mean the opposite of what the writer really believes, and say how the context indicates that they are not meant to be taken at their face value.
2 What is the writer's intention in repeating Mr Harrison's form of words in the clause beginning 'a statement of faith. . .' (line 32)?
3 Why does the writer, referring to Mr Harrison, say, 'a history of which he can certainly claim not to be part' (line 44)?
4 Why does Mr Harrison write the word 'literature' in inverted commas (line 73)?
5 What sort of political opinions does Mr Harrison consider 'politically acceptable' (line 77)? Acceptable to whom?
6 Which sentence in the passage suggests the same conclusions about good writing as those expressed in the passage by George Orwell (page 116)?
7 How is the writer's definition of impartiality different from Mr Harrison's and why is his opinion about believing things strongly also completely different?
8 What sort of idea does Mr Harrison appear to have of the reasons why creative writers produce 'novels of lasting literary merit'?
   a) To spread worthwhile human values.
   b) To entertain the public.
   c) To put forward their political ideas.
   d) To show off their literary technique.
9 In what way does Mr Harrison's contempt for knowledge indicate a contempt for the public?
10 In what way does it indicate a contempt for librarians?

Words often confused

1 **advice (against/of), ban, disagree (with), disapprove (of), react (against), remonstrate (with)**
Use each of the above *at least once*, in the correct form, to complete the paragraph below, paying particular attention to the preposition used.

1 Although we __________ of political demonstrations in principle because we believe they lead to violence in many cases, we have no power to __________ them unless we have evidence that violence will take place. On this occasion, we __________ the organisers of the risks and __________ with them when they insisted on going ahead with it. Of course it is unfortunate that those who strongly __________ with the attitudes of the demonstrators feel that the march itself is a kind of provocation and __________ against it with violence. It is easy enough for liberals to quote Voltaire's noble words: 'I __________ with everything you say, but I will defend to the death your right to say it'. Unfortunately, we live in a world where a

number of political activists believe that anything they ________ of should be ________.

2 **cure** (v. and n.), **make amends (to/for), prescribe** (v.), **prescription** (n.), **redress** (v. and n.)
These words are best learnt in a series of idiomatic phrases in the contexts where they most commonly occur. Complete the sentences below, using each *once only* (those which are both nouns and verbs twice) in the correct form.

1 The doctor ________ this remedy not as a ________ for my cold, but in the hope that it would alleviate the irritation, so now I am taking the ________ to the chemist's.
2 He instituted a legal action against the landlord, seeking ________ for the abuses he had been the victim of.
3 I realise I was unfair to you, and would like to ________ to you for it. I know that a few words of apology may not be enough to ________ your resentment against me, but at least they may do something to ________ the balance.

Lexical Progress Test 5

You must choose the word or phrase which best completes each sentence, For each question, 1 to 25, indicate the correct answer, A, B, C or D. The time for the test is 20 minutes.

1 These pictures are being framed for the art __________ next week.
A exhibition B exposition C exposure D portrayal

2 The Board __________ advertisements very carefully before allowing them to be shown on television.
A estimates B explores C scrutinises D visualises

3 If you find it difficult to make both ends meet, you can __________ to the University for an additional grant.
A apply B ask C propose D submit

4 The shopkeeper replaced the defective components, although it was not __________ for him to do so.
A authoritative B demanding C obligatory D requisiite

5 The __________ of strawberries on the market has been caused by the late frost.
A drought B exception C rarity D scarcity

6 I don't __________ to know everything, but I'm not a fool.
A claim B classify C confess D permit

7 Following the elections, a completely new situation is likely to __________.
A arise B arouse C raise D rise

8 He was arrested for __________ the police in the course of their duty.
A contradicting B objecting C obstructing D protesting

9 He was not used to speaking in public, but when the opportunity presented itself, he rose to the __________.
A chance B circumstance C event D occasion

10 When the fire alarm went, everyone was told to __________ outside in the courtyard.
A assemble B crowd C mobilise D unite

11 The referee __________ the goal because of a previous infringement.
A annulled B demolished C disallowed D disqualified

12 The Government __________ the demonstration because it was likely to lead to violence.
A banned B disagreed C disapproved D disqualified

13 I was about to say something, but __________ the temptation.
A challenged B obstructed C resisted D struggled

14 The new machines will enable us to __________ production by 20 per cent.
A grow up B raise C rise D run up

15 We will accept your cheque, although it is not our normal __________.
A intention B occasion C practice D state

16 His phone must be out of order. We've been unable to __________ him.
A arrive at B contact C meet D transmit

17 The salary is £10,000 a year, with annual __________ of £500 for ten years.
A annexes B bonuses C increments D prizes

18 The football __________ burst over the barriers and attacked the players.
A congregation B crowd C flock D gathering

19 He is looking for a job __________ with his abilities.
A applicable B appropriate C commensurate D suitable

20 His sentence was reduced on the __________ of failing health.
A bases B causes C grounds D reasons

21 Your appointment will take __________ from 1st October.
A action B date C effect D fact

22 The Government have failed to make __________ for old people in their budget.
A admittance B assistance C conditions D provision

23 Her parents __________ of her action.
A approved B conformed C consented D endorsed

24 This encouraging news enabled us to go on with __________ hope.
A novel B recurrent C renewed D renovated

25 This fabric is likely to __________ if washed with normal detergents.
A grumble B shrink C squeeze D wither

Finance

Introductory exercise

Test your knowledge of financial terms by completing each of the paragraphs below, using each word given above the paragraph *once only*.

1 Banks

account, balance, black, charges, cheques, commission, credit, current, demand, deposit, interest, loans, rates, red, statement

The main business of banks is to borrow money from customers and lend it to others at advantageous interest [1]__________. If you have a [2]__________ account, they will not pay you [3]__________ and in some cases you will have to pay bank [4]__________; on the other hand, you can draw out the cash on [5]__________. After all, it's your money! If you have a [6]__________ account, you receive interest on condition that you leave the money in the bank for an agreed period of time. You must notify the bank in advance to withdraw money, though in practice this is not usually difficult. The bank charges interest on [7]__________ of money and [8]__________ on services, such as providing travellers' [9]__________. You can ask the bank at any time, to tell you what the [10]__________ is in your account. At frequent intervals, the bank sends you a [11]__________ of your [12]__________. If it is in [13]__________ (in the [14]__________), the statement arrives on an agreed date; if it goes into the [15]__________ and you owe the bank money, they normally advise you sooner!

2 The Stock Exchange

bid, bonds, capital, currency, dividend, expenditure, investment, investors, price, profitable, profits, rate, shares, speculative, stockbrokers, trusts

The Stock Exchange is a place where dealers buy and sell [1]__________ in companies on behalf of customers. They also deal in other forms of [2]__________, such as __________, which are loans raised to finance countries' or companies' future [4]__________, and usually pay a fixed [5]__________ of interest, though the value of the bonds themselves may rise or fall according to the value of the [6]__________ in which they are held. Most small [7]__________ rely on [8]__________ to advise them on which companies are likely to make big [9]__________ in the coming year. What are called [10]__________ investments are those in which investors hope to make a big profit in a short time, and then sell the shares. This often happens if a company has made a take-over [11]__________, offering a high [12]__________ for shares, in order to gain control of another. Because it is easy to lose money on the Stock Exchange as well as gain it, and gains are penalised by [13]__________ Gains Tax, many people prefer to invest for longer periods in safe companies that pay them a [14]__________ once or twice a year. This is a percentage of the firm's profit. Others attempt to spread the risks by investing in Unit [15]__________, which are operated by experts who invest in a number of different companies, the value of the units rising if the overall investment has proved [16]__________.

Prospects for a National Economy

Read the following passage to gain a general impression of its content before studying the vocabulary in more detail.

Prospects for a National economy

THE NORWEGIAN economy is enjoying a moderate, export-led recovery, having apparently passed the low point in the cyclical trough last summer. Prospects for growth this year are being revised upwards – Gross Domestic Product (**GDP**) could rise by 2–3 per cent in 1984 according to the latest forecasts – and last year's overall performance also proved to be far stronger than earlier thought.

Between 1971 and 1981 the growth GDP averaged 4.3 per cent a year – buoyed in the latter part of the period by steeply rising production of oil and gas – and the country achieved a growth rate substantially higher than the **OECD** average of 3.1 per cent or the 2.6 per cent of the European OECD states. Again last year Norway outperformed the OECD average with a growth in GDP of 3.3 per cent following the virtual stagnation of the two previous years.

The picture is distorted, however, by the strong surge in oil and gas production last year to 55m tonnes, an increase of 15 per cent thanks to the faster than expected rise in output from the giant Statfjord Field. Oil activities have assumed an overwhelming importance in the Norwegian economy – their share in GDP rose to 18.5 per cent last year from 17 per cent in 1982 – and the oil sector now outshines the contribution of manufacturing industry, which accounts for only 13.7 per cent.

In terms of employment the oil sector still plays a subordinate role, however, and to secure jobs it is vital that Norway manages to solve some of the more **intractable** problems facing its mainland industry.

Last year the fall in the GDP of industries producing for the domestic market was even greater than in the two previous years, the result mainly of a decline of more than 15 per cent in shipbuilding output. Overall manufacturing production fell by 1 per cent. It was in decline from the spring of 1981 and only began to show signs of picking up again last summer.

By the last quarter of 1983 manufacturing production was showing a rise of 2 per cent over the corresponding period of 1982 but the overall figures conceal big differences in the performance of various sectors of industry. Production in the export industries rose far more strongly than output in the sheltered sectors or those competing with imports.

From an article in the *Financial Times* by Kevin Done

GDP: The amount of money generated by production and sales within the national economy

OECD: Organisation for Economic Co-operation and Development

intractable: difficult to resolve

A

Unfamiliar words

A number of words in this passage are no doubt familiar to you in other contexts but are used here with a specific meaning within the field of economics. Decide on their precise meaning here, using the aid given.

1 **recovery** (line 2) from what?
2 **trough** (line 4) clearly nothing to do with horses drinking, but think of the shape of it and relate it to a graph.
3 **revised upwards** (line 6) why should forecasts be more favourable?
4 **performance** (line 10) in what sense could an economy perform well or badly?
5 **growth** (line 14) of what, in economic terms?
6 **buoyed** (line 15) a buoy floats on the surface of the water as an indication to shipping; how can rising production buoy an economy?
7 **stagnation** (line 25) suggests still water in a pond, but what is suggested here?
8 **surge** (line 28) a rise, but of what kind?
9 **outshines** (line 38) compare the statistics
10 **picking up** (line 57)

B

Reading for gist

Answer the following questions in your own words before attempting the multiple-choice questions below.

1 What is the general impression experts have now of the Norwegian economy?
2 How has the Norwegian economy performed over the past 10–15 years in comparison with that of other OECD states?
3 What is the factor that 'distorts' the picture of the Norwegian economy (line 27)?
4 Why is it so necessary for Norway to solve 'some of the more intractable problems facing its mainland industry' (line 46)?
5 Which sectors of Norwegian industry have most reason to be confident about the future, and which have the least?

Now answer the following questions, basing your choices on the answers you have already given.

6 According to the experts, the present state of the Norwegian economy indicates that
A the economic crisis is now a thing of the past.
B record growth levels can be expected in 1984.
C their previous forecasts were too pessimistic.
D the country is at last exporting more than it imports.

7 In comparison with other OECD states, the best performance of the Norwegian economy
A was in the 1970s.
B was in 1982.
C was in 1983.
D is expected in 1984.

8 The main problem remaining for economists, however, is that
A manufacturing production is falling.
B output of oil and gas has risen faster than expected.
C the economy is heavily dependent on oil.
D the price of oil has fallen.

9 From a political point of view, the main danger is that
A fewer people are now working in export industries.
B overall manufacturing production is still falling.
C there is unemployment in the oil industry.
D the oil industry does not employ large numbers of people.

10 The future looks bright for those employed in
A all branches of manufacturing industry.
B firms concentrating on exports.
C firms producing mainly for the home market.
D shipbuilding.

C

Words often confused

1 achieve, bring about, carry out, perform, succeed (in)

Use each of the above *at least once* in the correct form to complete the following sentences.

1 He said he would sue us if we printed the story in the newspaper but I don't believe he will __________ his threat.
2 He has always wanted to be recognised as a great actor, and he has finally __________ his ambition by being chosen to play the part of Hamlet. The play will be __________ in London next month.
3 He has been __________ research for many years on the causes of the disease and has finally __________ in isolating the virus. Apparently, this virus __________ a change in the nervous system. He is now trying to develop an antidote. Let us hope that he __________.
4 I asked you to __________ (or __________) a perfectly simple task and all you have __________ (or __________ in doing) is to make a complete mess of things.

2 account for, assign (to), attribute (to), derive (from), explain (to)

Use each of the above *at least once* in the correct form to complete the following sentences.

1 He said that he found it difficult to __________ (or __________) his success, but he __________ it to the encouragement he had received from his friends.
2 His interest in Chinese art __________ from his stay in Peking when he was __________ to the embassy there many years ago.
3 The play, which is __________ from Boccaccio, was first __________ to Shakespeare in the eighteenth century, but the critic concerned could not __________ why no one had previously referred to it as his.
4 We __________ the best room in the hotel to him and when he complained about the noise, __________ to him that all the rooms facing the street have the same problem, but he preferred to move to a little room at the back. There's no __________ tastes.

Local Authority Bonds

Read the passage below carefully in order to answer detailed questions on its content.

Local authorities don't always manage to lay their hands on enough **ratepayers'** cash and Government grants to cover their spending. To bridge this embarrassing gap, they issue what have come to be called over-the-counter local authority bonds.

These bonds have three notable virtues: the rate of interest is fixed (and so won't change, whatever **interest rates** do after you've made your purchase), there are no buying or selling charges or hidden extras, and your capital is returned when a bond's life ends. In other words, you know before you invest what your reward will be.

Some bonds allow you to invest as little as £100, others require £10,000-plus. The most popular are the £500 and £1,000 varieties. Because there's no restriction on the total sum you can invest, you can buy any number of the really big bonds, or a combination of big and small. Note, though, that the interest rate varies with the size of the bond and with the length of its life. As a rule, the biggest bonds with the longest life are the best payers. Interest rates have recently been ranging from 8 per cent gross on bonds with lives of less than one year to 11 per cent on bonds lasting five years and upwards.

Interest is paid gross only on bonds with lives of less than one year. For the remainder, it is paid after basic rate tax of 30 per cent has been deducted, although people not liable to tax can obtain a refund from the Inland Revenue. Most bonds pay interest at six-monthly intervals, but a few pay it in a lump sum at the end of a bond's life. Some bonds with lives of less than one year even offer monthly payments.

At any given time, between 150 and 250 local authorities are vying for investors' attention. To find out which bonds best meet your needs, ring the Loans Bureau, CIPFA Services, on 01–828 7855 between 3.30 and 5 p.m. Mondays to Fridays. The bureau also publishes a weekly list of all the bonds on the market, and you can get this by sending £2.50 and a large stamped, addressed envelope to the Loans Bureau, CIPFA Services, 232 Vauxhall Bridge Road, London SW1V 1AU. You can expect the list to vary every week because the rates of interest paid are constantly changing.

When you have chosen the bond most suited to your pocket, telephone the relevant local authority, check that the bond or bonds which interest you are still available, and, if so, say you wish to invest. They will be only too happy to answer any further questions and help you complete the transaction.

VERDICT

An ideal investment for non-taxpayers and for anyone wanting a guaranteed interest rate some way ahead. Your money is tied up, though, during a bond's life. Rates of interest now being paid are very competitive with other risk-free investments, so this is a good time to buy.

From an article by John Davis in the *Observer Magazine*

ratepayers: those who pay taxes (rates) to the local authority. Rates are paid by householders and businesses in the area

interest rates: the level of percentage interest required by a bank on money borrowed

Unfamiliar words

Decide on the most probable meaning of the following in the context.

1 **gross** (line 37)
2 **deducted** (line 41)
3 **vying** (line 51)
4 **transaction** (line 76)
5 **tied up** (line 81)

F

Reading for detail

Answer the questions, comparing each of the statements made below with the text. *Only one answer* is correct.

1 If you invested £1000 in local authority bonds at 8% for six months, when the bond expired, you would have earned
  A 4% of your capital.
  B 4% of your capital, less sales charges.
  C the standard rate of interest on your capital at the time of the sale.
  D the standard rate of interest on your capital at the time of the sale, less sales charges.

2 Assuming that you had over £10,000 to invest for a long period, your best plan would normally be to buy
  A the 500 and 1000 varieties of bond.
  B a combination of big and small bonds.
  C a large bond.
  D short-life bonds, and then reinvest.

3 As an average taxpayer, if you had invested in a bond for six months, you would
  A have to pay 30% tax on what you had earned.
  B receive the full rate of interest.
  C have to reclaim tax already deducted to receive it.
  D usually be paid interest once a month.

4 The first step for anyone deciding to invest in local authority bonds should be to
  A ask the local authority for advice.
  B ask the local authority if they have suitable bonds available.
  C ask the Loans Bureau for advice.
  D send a stamped, addressed envelope to the Loans Bureau.

5 The writer recommends local authority bonds because
  A the money will be safe for a long time.
  B they pay the highest rates of interest.
  C they are free from risk.
  D they combine good interest rates with security.

Use of language

Answer the following questions.

1 Does 'to lay their hands on' (line 2) mean to borrow, to obtain, or to take?

2 What is the 'gap' referred to in line 6, and why is it 'embarrassing' to local authorities?

3 Why do you imagine the local authority bonds referred to are called 'over-the-counter' bonds (line 7)?

4 What does 'and upwards' mean in line 35?

5 What is a 'lump sum' (line 46) and how does this method of payment differ from the normal method?

Words often confused

1 bill, charge, cost, debt, price

Use each of the above *at least once* to complete the following sentences, in the plural form where necessary. Note in particular the idiomatic phrases in which they are used.

1 The __________ of living has risen so fast recently that many people have got into __________.

2 The Minister of Finance said that when he took __________ of the economy 18 months ago, the country was in __________, and he had realised that it was his responsibility to reduce this amount at all __________. Politically, his measures had been unpopular, and this was a high __________ to pay for national solvency; they had increased unemployment and the Unions had been quick to count the __________ in terms of jobs. But the country had to pay its __________, (or __________) like any individual. He had introduced __________ control to cushion the effect on ordinary people, and he now felt that the sacrifices were justified, since the economy was showing a clean __________ of health for the first time in many years. Asked if a relaxation in controls would mean that __________ would go up, he replied that he had no intention of allowing this to happen as long as he was in __________.

3 As I was a friend of the shopkeeper's, he let me have the radio at __________ __________.

2 bound to, liable (to), likely (to), probable, subject (to)

Liable is an adjective only used as a complement, not before the noun.
Bound to, meaning 'certain to', is a past participle used in the same way.
Subject to, in these examples is also used like this, but can be used adverbially, as in the sentence below.

The plans have been made, **subject to** your approval.

Complete the sentences below, using the most appropriate word, and using each *at least once*.

1 Profits made on investments on the stock exchange are __________ (or __________) to Capital Gains Tax.
2 It seems __________ (or __________) that the weather will improve over the weekend.
3 Because of the fog, trains are __________ to delay.
4 Because of the fog, trains are __________ (or __________) to be delayed.
5 Everyone said before the game that Liverpool were __________ to win and the other side had no chance, but now the __________ (or __________) result is a draw.
6 He is planning to take over the rival company, but his bid is not __________ to succeed.
7 His father's will was __________ to death duty being paid, and on top of that it appears his father was in debt and he will be __________ for the debts.
8 I realise you are __________ (or, __________) to colds, but you're not __________ to catch cold if you wrap up warmly.

3 deduct, diminish, reduce, subtract

Use each of the above *at least once* in the correct form to complete the following sentences.

1 It used to be possible for businessmen to __________ their expenses from the sum liable to taxation, but this is no longer true. Consequently, private individuals in business have tended to __________ their expenditure on meals, for example.
2 If you __________ 34 from 80, what is the result?
3 This diet helps people to __________ their weight.
4 The war has considerably __________ (or __________) the country's natural resources, and it will soon be __________ to importing food. The problem is that its currency has __________ in value, so it will be very expensive.

4 assure, confirm, ensure, guarantee, insure, reassure

Use each of the above *at least once* in the correct form to complete the following sentences, paying particular attention to the constructions used and the contexts in which they appear.

1 Of course there is no way in which we can __________ (or __________) that the plan will be successful, but I __________ you that we are making the maximum effort to achieve it.
2 I rang the bank to give them my instructions, and was asked to __________ them by letter.
3 Of course the watch is __________ for a year by the makers, but I have also __________ it, because it is very valuable.
4 Although the girl at the enquiries counter in the airport pointed out that the flight arrival times are not __________, I was not __________ until news arrived __________ an earlier report that the plane had been late taking off from Brazil.
5 I __________ to repay the debt in three months' time, and I __________ you that I will do so. I hope that you now feel __________.

Money Problems

Read the extracts from readers' letters below, studying them in detail for the vocabulary contained and comparing the problems raised.

MONEY HELP! EXTRA

1)

Q I rent my house and want to borrow some money from my bank in order to install central heating. Will I be able to get tax relief on the interest I pay on this money, or is this only given to those who borrow money to improve their homes?

A You should get tax relief. Under the legislation, it is available on loans taken out to finance home improvements if you own property rights, whether as an owner or a tenant. Don't pay your bills with an overdraft, though. Overdrafts (unless they count as business expenses) can't be 'qualifying' loans – this is, loans on which one can get tax relief on the interest. Credit card debts don't qualify, either.

Of course, for any loan to qualify the money borrowed must be used to genuinely improve your home. The installation of central heating or double glazing is OK, for example, but, if one is merely carrying out repairs or re-papering the walls, the loan interest incurred won't usually be eligible for tax relief.

2)

Q My father, who lives in Switzerland, has recently given up driving and has offered me his car as a free gift. I understand that cars brought into the country from the Continent are subject to import levies and 15 per cent VAT. Would I have to pay these on a second-hand (and free) car?

A Sadly, yes. You'll be liable for any Customs duties and VAT (based on the vehicle's second-hand value). You would escape the fiscal fury only if you yourself had owned and used the car abroad for at least 12 months. Even then, though, you'd have to keep the vehicle for two years after you had brought it into this country.

3)

Q You mentioned demonetised coins last month. I believe that some charities, such as Oxfam, are happy to accept these (and foreign coins of small value, too) because they are able to collect enough to make exchange worthwhile.

A Yes, Oxfam says it welcomes any type of foreign coin, demonetised coins and stamps. All is grist to its mill. The stamps (and some of the foreign coins) are made into packs and sold. The rest of the foreign coins are exchanged at banks and, in the case of the demonetised coins, sold back to the Royal Mint. You can either cart your goodies to an Oxfam shop, or send them to the Oxfam Stamp and Coin Unit, Murdock Road, Bicester, Oxford OX6 7RS.

4)

Q Where can I get a simple form of will document, so that everything can be left to my wife?

A At a stationer's shop. If you are drawing up your own will, though, do ensure that your testamentary intentions are unambiguous, and that the document is properly signed and witnessed. Rumour has it that lawyers make hay – and a great deal of money – from carelessly drawn home-made wills. The Consumers' Association's publication 'Wills and **Probate**' (£4.95 from bookshops) is worth getting to help you leap over the pitfalls which have trapped more than one unwary **DIY** will-maker.

5)

Q Is it true that old age pensioners don't have to pay capital gains tax? If it isn't, how does one tell the taxman that a capital gain has been made.

A I am afraid OAPs are liable to capital gains tax just like everyone else – much to the chagrin, no doubt, of some of our senior citizen captains of industry. There is a section on one's tax return relating to gains made during that tax year. Any **CGT** bill is usually due for payment on 1 December, following the tax year in which the gain has been made. Remember, though, that the first £5,300 of gains are free of tax in this tax year.

From Joanna Slaughter's 'Money' page in the *Observer Magazine*

VAT: Value Added Tax
CGT: Capital Gains Tax
Probate: the process of proving a will legal
DIY: Do it yourself

Unfamiliar words

Decide on the most probable meaning of the following in the context, using the aid given.

1 **overdraft** (line 16) a draft is what you draw from a bank
2 **levies** (line 40)
3 **fiscal** (line 47)
4 **demonetised** (line 54) when do coins cease to be money?
5 **grist to its mill** (line 64) what happens to everything Oxfam receives?
6 **cart your goodies** (line 69) you would in fact probably not use a cart, and 'goodies' here does not mean sweets, though it does mean presents
7 **make hay** (while the sun shines) (line 85) do you know what this proverb means?
8 **pitfalls** (line 91)
9 **unwary** (line 92)
10 **chagrin** (line 102) how do you imagine they feel?
11 **senior citizen** (line 103)
12 **captains of industry** (line 104)

Reading for gist

Read each letter again to decide what the problem is and then answer the questions below. Only one answer is correct in each case.

1 The first reader wants advice on
A borrowing some money from a bank.
B obtaining an overdraft.
C deducting the loan from taxable income.
D avoiding tax on the interest on the loan.

2 The second reader could only avoid tax on the car
A if it had been a free gift.
B if it had been second-hand.
C if he or she had been driving it abroad.
D if he or she had been the owner-driver for a year abroad.

3 Oxfam is willing to accept demonetised coins (third letter) because it can
A exchange them at a bank.
B sell them to a bank.
C sell them to the Government.
D sell them abroad.

4 If you want to make a will, it is essential to
A get an official form from a stationer's shop.
B consult a lawyer.
C have witnesses to your signature.
D obtain the publication 'Wills and Probate'.

5 Capital Gains Tax is payable
A at the end of the tax year.
B during the following tax year.
C except by retired people.
D on all gains made in the tax year.

Comparison of texts

Answer the following questions, in multiple-choice format, by comparing the letters referred to.

1 The only reader whose question is answered in a completely reassuring way is the one who wrote
A letter 1.
B letter 2.
C letter 3.
D letter 5.

2 The only reader who can derive no comfort at all from the reply is the one who wrote
A letter 1.
B letter 2.
C letter 3.
D letter 5.

3 How many of the correspondents are hoping to save money by asking for advice?
A All of them.
B Four of them.
C Three of them.
D Two of them.

4 In how many cases are the correspondents hoping to save money by avoiding taxation?
A All of them.
B Four of them.
C Three of them.
D Two of them.

5 If you had to guess the age of the correspondents (excluding the author of letter 3), judging entirely from the kind of problem they raise, which would be the most likely order, the oldest first?
A 1–5–2–4
B 2–1–4–5
C 4–2–5–1
D 5–4–1–2

Human Relationships

Introductory exercise

1 **Engagement:** What is the difference between a **boy-friend/girl-friend** and a **fiancé/fiancée**? What do you call the second pair, taken together? What outward signs normally show that they are engaged in your country?

2 **Marriage:** What do you call the two most important figures in a wedding, and what do you call the close friend who accompanies him and the friend or friends who accompany her? What do they become after the wedding?

3 **Friendship:** In what social or professional circumstances would you refer to someone as the following?

a) an acquaintance
b) a colleague
c) a comrade
d) a companion
e) a playmate
f) a work-mate
g) a team-mate
h) a partner
i) a collaborator
j) an accomplice

Making Friends

Read the following passage to gain a general impression of its content.

Social psychologists are used to hearing that their experiments are a waste of time because they just prove the obvious, and tell us what we always knew. But there is a very simple and effective riposte to this accusation. The trouble with folk-wisdom (what we always knew) is that it tends to come in pairs of statements, both of which are 'obviously' true, but which – unfortunately – are mutually exclusive. For example, we all know that too many cooks spoil the broth. But wait a minute: don't many hands make light work? Similarly with friendship: birds of a feather flock together, but what about the attraction of opposites? Experiments may not be as much fun as intuitions, but they sometimes tell us which proverbs are actually true, or (more often) in what circumstances which apply.

There is one other preconception to be removed before tackling the question of whom we like and love, whom we find attractive and make friends with. Why bother to study an area in which we are all expert practitioners? Surely we can all make friends and organise social relationships naturally, without any resistance from behavioural scientists? Well, if you believe that, have a word with a **marriage guidance counsellor**, a psychiatrist, or someone involved in industrial relations.

Research on friendship has established a number of facts, some interesting, some even useful. Did you know that the average student has 5–6 friends, or that a friend who was previously an enemy is liked more than one who has always been on the right side? Would you believe that physically attractive individuals are preferred as friends to those less comely, and is it fair that physically attractive defendants are less likely to be found guilty in court? Unfortunately, such titbits don't tell us much more than the nature or the purpose of friendship.

In fact, studies of friendship seem to implicate more complex factors. For example, one function friendship seems to fulfil is that it supports the image we have of ourselves, and confirms the value of the attitudes we hold. Certainly we appear to project ourselves onto our friends; several studies have shown that we judge them to be more like us than they (objectively) are. This suggests that we ought to choose friends who are similar to us ('birds of a feather') rather than those who would be complementary ('opposites attract'), a prediction which is supported by empirical evidence, at least so far as attitudes and beliefs are concerned. In one experiment, some developing friendships were monitored amongst first-year students living in the same hostel. It was found that similarity of attitudes (towards politics, religion, and ethics, pastimes and aesthetics) was a good predictor of what friendships would be established by the end of four months, though it had less to do with initial alliances – not surprisingly, since attitudes may not be obvious on first inspection.

The difficulty of linking friendship with similarity of personality probably reflects the complexity of our personalities: we have many facets and therefore require a disparate group of friends to support us. This of course can explain why we may have two close friends who have little in common, and indeed dislike each other. By and large, though, it looks as though we would do well to choose friends (and spouses) who resemble us. If this were not so, **computer dating agencies** would have gone out of business years ago.

From an article in *New Society* by John Nicholson

marriage guidance counsellor: someone employed to help married couples who have problems
computer dating agencies: agencies that help people to get in touch with people of the opposite sex on the basis of their personalities and interests being alike

Unfamiliar words

Decide on the most probable meaning of the following words in the context.

1 **riposte** (line 5)
2 **comely** (line 38)
3 **titbits** (line 40)
4 **disparate** (line 70)
5 **spouses** (line 76)

Reading for gist

Answer the following questions. *Only one answer* is correct in each case.

1 Experiments conducted by social psychologists are frequently criticised because
  A people believe they already know what the results will be.
  B the results often disprove popular beliefs.
  C they are not much fun.
  D they tend to produce contradictory results.

2 Research into the reasons for friendship is thought to be unnecessary because
  A it is only possible if a wide variety of experts are employed.
  B it is too complex a subject to be scientifically investigated.
  C no one has any difficulty in making friends.
  D we all believe we are capable of dealing with it ourselves.

3 Research on friendship has demonstrated that
  A every student has five or six friends.
  B judges are always influenced by a pretty face.
  C ugly people find it harder to make friends than beautiful people.
  D we tend to grow fond of people if we dislike them at first sight.

4 Studies of friendship have indicated that in seeking friends we
  A are looking for sympathy.
  B insist on them having similar attitudes to ourselves.
  C think they resemble us more than they really do.
  D want to be flattered.

5 The experiment conducted on students living in a hostel suggested that
  A in the long run, people get on better with those who are like them.
  B it was impossible to predict which friendships would develop.
  C students immediately recognised others with similar attitudes and interests.
  D students split up as soon as they discovered differences in attitudes.

Use of language

The passage mentions three well-known proverbs in the first paragraph. Find them and explain what they mean in simple language as general comments on life. Then explain the following in the same way.

1 The proof of the pudding is in the eating.
2 You shouldn't kill the goose that lays the golden eggs.
3 A bird in the hand is worth two in the bush.
4 Absence makes the heart grow fonder.
5 Marry in haste and repent at leisure.
6 Once bitten, twice shy.
7 Familiarity breeds contempt.
8 Don't put all your eggs in one basket.
9 More haste, less speed.
10 A friend in need is a friend indeed.

D

Words often confused

1 amusement, enjoyment, entertainment, fun, joke

Use each of the above *at least once* to complete the sentences below, employing the plural form where necessary.

1 It is wrong to make __________ of people who cannot defend themselves.
2 The unfortunate accident to one of the trapeze artists spoiled our __________ of the circus.
3 The children played a __________ on the French teacher by balancing a bucket of water on the door, and to their great __________, he was soaked to the skin. 'It's no __________!' he said angrily. 'This is my new suit.'
4 Cinemas used to be charged __________ tax on the price of the seats, but I don't think they are now.
5 He's said to have a dining room that holds 600 people, and an orchestra that plays for the __________ of his guests during dinner.
6 I went to one of his parties once but it wasn't much __________. He spent most of his time making __________ at other people's expense. Of course, if you listen to him without showing the least sign of __________, he doesn't like it. 'Why are you looking so upset?' he says. 'I didn't mean it. I only said it in __________.' He's just the sort of person who loves playing practical __________ on other people, but hates it if anybody plays one on him.

2 inaugural, initial, original, primary, principal

Use each of the above *at least once* to complete the sentences below, paying close attention to the contexts in which they are most commonly found.

1 The President's __________ address, when he took up office, was of __________ importance to the media because of what he might say about the world situation, but in fact contained no __________ ideas. The __________ item of interest was his __________ forecast of government spending during the first year after his election, but of course that may well be modified in the coming months.
2 This is a copy of El Greco's __________ painting, which is in the Prado, but it conveys his use of the __________ colours, red, blue and yellow, perfectly.
3 In the __________ stages of their occupation of the continent, the __________ inhabitants of Europe settled along the estuaries of the __________ rivers.

E

Vocabulary expansion

The passage describes students living in a **hostel**. What sort of people would you expect to find living in the following?

1 barracks
2 a hotel
3 a hovel
4 an inn
5 lodgings
6 a mansion
7 a tenement
8 a shanty
9 a tent
10 a wigwam

Matchmakers

Read the following passage carefully, paying attention to detail and noting down any words you do not understand.

I WAS born in a society – the Ireland of 40 years ago – in which marriages were still made by a matchmaker. It was characteristic of the country, rather than the town, and by the late 1940s the practice was well on the way out: but my mother, born before the First World War, had been officially offered a 'match' with a local farmer – an offer she turned down because she judged the peasant's life too hard. 'You would always be lugging around pails of water,' was her response – and indeed she would have had to wait for the **EEC intervention money** to see **mod cons** on the average small farm in western Ireland.

Yet the influence of the matchmaker lingered on in the sense that marriage was judged largely according to its suitability as a match: suitability of economic status, of family union, of religion and character.

I had a cousin who walked out with a Protestant for 15 years, and at the end the families still could not agree on a compromise where religion was concerned; so the unofficial engagement was broken off. A waste of a young woman's life, one might think, particularly since, in those times, young people generally remained virgins throughout a courtship. And yet, she says now that she had a lucky escape; she lives happily as a single woman, and the Protestant – didn't he turn out a bit of a **louche** character after all! There you are, you see, *you can't be too careful; you cannot be rushing into these things*.

Now we all marry – the provident and the improvident alike; those who have passed the character test of a ritualised courtship and those unable to sustain personal loyalty for five minutes. Romantic love and a meaningful personal relationship are the shifting sands on which modern marriage is built: economic interest, dynastic advancement, family cohesion, duty, responsibility and the very considerable shame that a marital separation would bring (not to mention the fear of eternal damnation) were the rocks on which it was constructed in the past.

In a book recently published, the journalist Maureen Green suggested that one of the problems today is that just too many of us marry, inevitably including individuals who are not suited to married life. A hundred years ago, about 20 per cent of any given European population would remain unmarried, and if you believe in theories of natural selection, that 20 per cent would probably include many folks unsuited to marriage by character or economic ability. Today, 93 per cent of the population gets married at least once: the mating game has never been more popular, though one marriage in three among first marriages ends in divorce, and more than 40 per cent of second marriages are also dissolved.

Paradoxically divorce does not dent the popularity of marriage, indeed; it releases on to the remarriage market a fresh set of potential partners each year. Thus the lonely heart adverts go on and on, the marriage bureaux flourish.

Some aspects of the matchmaking scene today are surprising: there is absolutely no demand for it in Wales, where to seek a partner through a third party is to lose face. Some aspects are depressingly unsurprising: there is *always* a demand for women under 30 and there is *always* a surplus of women over 40. And that picture is the same worldwide.

The matchmaking business, though flawed and imperfect, is actually less of a racket, too, than one might imagine; if you charge people too much you do not get the business. Computer dating can be useful in that it can deal with much greater numbers, and thus widen a client's choice, yet it is often less satisfactory in the end than a skilled and experienced marriage bureau operator. The computer dating system matches people according to interests, which is not a bad guideline; but it may omit human chemistry. 'We had everything in common – except that we didn't like each other,' said one dissatisfied customer of her computer-drawn date.

From an article in the *Daily Telegraph* by Mary Kenny

EEC intervention money: money paid to Ireland since it joined the common market
mod cons: modern conveniences, such as running water
louche: unreliable

Unfamiliar words

Decide on the most probable meaning of the following in the context, using the aid given.

1 **well on the way out** (line 7)
2 **lugging** (line 14)
3 **pails** (line 14)
4 **walked out with** (line 27) apart from its literal meaning
5 **shifting sands** (line 52) what are you reminded of in physical terms here, and how is the image appropriate?
6 **dent** (line 84) normally 'cause a hollow to appear in' e.g., in the bodywork of a car in a crash, but here?
7 **lonely hearts adverts** (line 87) what sort of people put advertisements of this kind in the newspapers, and why?
8 **a third party** (line 94) who are the first two?
9 **lose face** (line 94)
10 **a racket** (line 103)

Reading for detail

Answer the following questions, comparing each of the statements made below with the text. *Only one answer* is correct.

1 The writer's mother refused the match offered to her because
A she did not like the man who was proposed.
B she did not fancy being a farmer's wife.
C she thought matchmaking was out of date.
D her family was opposed to it.

2 The writer's cousin regarded her courtship as
A a waste of her youth.
B an unsuccesful battle to convert her boyfriend to her religion.
C the natural course of events in the circumstances.
D the cause of her alienation from her parents.

3 The writer suggests that it is a test of the couple's character for them
A to be romantically in love.
B to demonstrate their fidelity in courtship.
C to marry with the approval of their families.
D not to be ashamed of divorce.

4 The effect of divorce becoming much more easily obtainable in Europe has been that
A more people are free to get married.
B people have been put off marrying.
C people have been put off marrying again.
D second marriages have proved more successful than first marriages.

5 The writer thinks matchmakers are more reliable than computer dating agencies because they
A are more honest.
B know more suitable prospective partners.
C know more about their clients' personal interests.
D can use their own judgement to help find compatible partners for their clients.

Words often confused

characteristic, distinctive, intrinsic, peculiar, uncommon

Use each of the above *at least once* to complete the sentences below, but do not use any of them more than once in the same answer.

1 While stamps of this kind are relatively __________, they have very little __________ value.

2 It is __________ of him to want to do everything his own way but I cannot understand why he dressed the characters in the play in such a __________ way. I suppose Hamlet's father needs a __________ costume to show he is different from the rest, but this ghost looked as if he had come from Mars!

3 The customs of these tribes are of __________ interest to all anthropologists, and many have shown an __________ degree of curiosity in them. The man in this picture is wearing the __________ tribal headdress, but he also has these __________ marks on his face, indicating that he is the chief. The form of the marks is __________ to tribes living in this part of New Guinea.

Divorce

Read the passage to gain a general impression of its content, but concentrate on imagining the situations that are described and the language used to describe them.

I'm afraid the proposed **new grounds for divorce**, making the mere break-down of the marriage sufficient cause, have come a good deal too late for my wife and me. Twenty years ago, fine. We had a total breakdown of relationships on the way from the church to the reception, I remember, when I made a light-hearted comment about a seedy man on the bride's side of the aisle who looked, as I put it, like **Chester Conklin** with a hangover. How was I to know he was my wife's favourite uncle? She had a sharp comeback about my best man's socks; I compared them favourably with her mother's hat; she cried and made her nose bleed; and by the time we got to the house the situation was in ruins. Terrible. We were laughing about it only the other day.

We often wonder how we got through the honeymoon, really. Minor troubles began on the quayside at Dieppe, where she seemed to think it was her job to yell out for porters. Nothing embarrasses a young husband like the sight of his wife behaving like a man, and I told her so. She said there was no alternative, if I was under the impression that I could get a porter by sitting on the baggage looking pathetic and muttering an occasional 'Er'. I warned her not to try to run my life, she told me not to be hypersensitive, I accused her of being bossy . . . or perhaps it was the other way round, it's a long time ago now. We were trying to establish the truth of the whole infuriating business only last week, when I couldn't get a taxi outside **the Old Vic**. If these enlightened new divorce moves had come sooner we should never have been outside the Old Vic, at least not together. We should have split up in Dieppe, on the issue of whereabouts in a bed a man was entitled to put his feet. Bachelors of twenty-five years standing can't be expected to change their sleeping habits overnight, as I said at the time. It all began with her wanting to bed down, I remember, when I still needed the light to finish the latest **Eric Ambler**. Then the next morning she came storming in from the bathroom saying I'd used her oatmeal complexion soap again. This has been a constant source of friction ever since, I may say – all friction and no lather, as a matter of fact, which proves that I only pick it up by mistake, with no intention whatsoever of starting anything. 'You don't imagine,' I said to her as recently as last Thursday, 'that I *want* to use that muck?' 'Calling my cosmetics muck,' she said, 'comes well from a man with an after-shave lotion called "Skin Bracer." And why don't you come over here and do these rotten bits behind the water pipes, instead of enjoying yourself with all the easy up and down wall parts?'

We were painting the bathroom, I ought to say, and nerves were taut, as always at times of do-it-yourself. It was a typically feminine switch of targets, all the same, from oatmeal soap to a supposed cheating over work allocation. 'I notice,' I said, 'that you got up here and pinched the best brush, leaving me the one with the sticking-out bristles that paint all the bits I'm trying to miss.' 'Whose fault's that?' she said. 'You shouldn't have stayed downstairs watching ***Crossroads***.' 'It was ***Dr Kildare***,' I said.

The marriage then broke down, and wasn't in going condition again until supper time (cheese pudding and chocolate souffle to follow).

From *Pick of Punch* by Basil Boothroyd

new grounds for divorce: the Divorce Law referred to was passed in 1969
Chester Conklin: a comic actor in silent films
The Old Vic: a London theatre
Eric Ambler: a popular writer of mystery stories
Crossroads and ***Dr Kildare***: popular television programmes 15 years ago. *Crossroads* still is!

Unfamiliar words

Decide on the most probable meaning of the following in the context, using the aid given.

1 **seedy** (line 7) a favourable comment, or not? It refers to dress and general appearance.
2 **hangover** (line 9) after drinking the night before.

3 **comeback** (line 11)
4 **quayside** (line 19) Dieppe is a port in northern France.
5 **yell** (line 20)
6 **storming in** (line 41) coming in like a __________
7 **lather** (line 44) he was trying to use it for shaving.
8 **muck** (line 49)
9 **taut** (line 56)
10 **pinched** (line 60) slang for the obvious word here
11 **bristles** (line 61) which parts of the brush?

Interpretation of text

In preparation for the examination, the questions in this type of exercise are now given in multiple-choice format. Look for the explanation that coincides with what you understand the text to mean and what you imagine the author's humorous intentions were. *Only one answer* is correct.

1 The conversation the writer describes after his wedding is included to show
A that a marriage can break down for trivial reasons.
B that marriages can easily survive the little quarrels that occur.
C that the divorce laws should have been changed 20 years ago.
D how easily young couples can misunderstand each other.

2 The origin of the argument at Dieppe was that
A the writer objected to his wife shouting at him.
B the writer was embarrassed by his wife's vulgar behaviour.
C the writer's wife wanted to show she was the boss.
D the writer's wife was exasperated by his passive attitude.

3 The sentence beginning: 'If these enlightened new divorce moves . . .' in paragraph 2 means that
A the couple would never have gone to the theatre again because of this experience.
B as a result of their experience, they would have finally decided whose job it was to call for taxis.
C they would never have met again, because they would have been divorced.
D they would only have met at the theatre by chance.

4 The writer's reference to himself as 'a bachelor of twenty-five years' standing' means that
A he did not really think of himself as married.
B he was 25, and used to sleeping alone.
C he had married rather late in life.
D his wife should have shown more consideration for his feelings.

5 The writer describes his use of his wife's soap as 'all friction and no lather' because
A it caused an unnecessary row between them.
B it is not suitable for shaving.
C he picked it up by mistake.
D he thinks it is muck.

6 His wife refers to the bits behind the water pipes as 'rotten' because
A the metal work there was rusty.
B she could not reach them with such a bad brush.
C she objected to her husband telling her to paint them.
D they were the most difficult to paint.

7 The writer regards it as 'typically feminine' to
A change the subject when losing an argument.
B cheat so that he has to do all the more unpleasant jobs.
C insist on having the best brush.
D want to be the boss when they are decorating the house.

Vocabulary expansion

1 **boo, cheer, groan, scream, sob**
The writer's wife decided to **yell** out for a porter at Dieppe. In other words, she 'shouted loudly'. All the verbs listed above also describe noises that people make, in different circumstances. Use each *once only*, in the correct form, to complete the following sentences.

1 His supporters __________ the President enthusiastically at the end of his speech.
2 The girl __________ for help when the thief pulled out a knife.
3 He had been badly hurt when he fell from the horse and lay on the ground, __________, and in obvious pain.
4 The child burst into tears when she heard that her cat had been killed, and __________ uncontrollably for several minutes.
5 The crowd __________ when the captain of the home team was sent off the field.

Crime and the Law

Introductory exercise

1 **Crime:** If someone commits a crime, the following may happen to him/her. Put them in the correct order. He/She may be:
   a) convicted
   b) tried
   c) accused
   d) charged
   e) sent to prison
   f) arrested

   In what circumstances could someone accused of a crime be
   a) acquitted?
   b) allowed to appeal?
   c) granted bail?
   d) reprieved?

2 **Trials:** In most cases, the police **take legal action** against those accused of crimes, but there are also civil cases where individuals **bring an action/suit** against others. Important criminal cases **are heard before judges**, but the majority are dealt with by **magistrates**, or **Justices of the Peace**, who are not qualified lawyers, in general.
   What part do the following play in the trial?
   a) the defendant
   b) the defending counsel
   c) the judge
   d) the jury
   e) the prosecuting counsel
   f) the plaintiff
   g) the witnesses

   Which of them is/are most likely to do each of the following?
   a) prepare a case
   b) plead 'Not Guilty'
   c) give evidence
   d) instruct the jury
   e) reach a verdict
   f) pronounce sentence
   g) discharge the prisoner
   h) sum up
   At what point in the proceedings would these actions take place?

Judging

Read the following passage to gain a general impression of its content.

In theory, the job of a trial jury is to listen to all the evidence presented, form impressions of the various parties involved (including the accused), and then to reach a verdict based on an objective assessment of what they have heard and seen. It is assumed that a decision made by twelve people is preferable to one made by a single individual, since individual prejudices and biases can be exposed in discussion, thus allowing a verdict to be reached on purely rational consideration of the facts. For what actually goes on in the jury room at a real trial, we have to rely on anecdote and conjecture; since the presence of psychologists would be unlikely to make the jurors' task any easier, it is quite right that they should not be allowed to sit in on the discussions. We do, however, have indirect evidence about the way in which juries reach their verdicts, from studies in which the tape-recorded transcripts of real trials are played to 'juries' recruited from the general public (as real jurors are), who can be observed, and even exposed to experimental manipulation, while trying to arrive at a decision.

I doubt if you will be surprised to learn that the most striking finding to emerge from these studies is that **we are no more objective at judging than we are at remembering**. In one experiment, subjects were asked to re-enact the role of a jury at a civil law case, in which they had to assess the sum to be paid in damages to a farm-worker who had badly cut his hand on improperly maintained farm equipment. The task was carried out by a number of different 'juries', and it was found that the level of damages they awarded could be greatly inflated by the simple expedient of showing a picture of the damaged hand while the jurors listened to details of the accident. The pictures could have played no part in helping the jury to establish the facts of the case; indeed, the practice of allowing juries to examine murder weapons or photographs of mutilated bodies can only make it less likely that they will reach their verdict on rational grounds.

Even when they are not encouraged to react emotionally by manipulative prosecutors, juries may be less influenced by the evidence presented than by the subjective impressions they form about the protagonists, and we shall see that these impressions may be creatures of little substance. Moreover, whereas in theft trials jurors' attitudes towards the defendant are found to change as the evidence unfolds, in rape trials jurors show a worrying tendency to stick to their initial impressions – and, in these trials, it is their attitude towards the victim rather than the defendant which turns out to be the single most important factor in determining the verdict they reach at the end of the day. Trial re-enactment studies reveal that juries are particularly influenced by their assessment of character in five key areas – how friendly, warm, trustworthy, competent and intelligent a person appears. In a case of theft, if the defendant strikes them as untrustworthy and stupid, they initially see him as guilty; in discussions at the end of the trial, his intelligence becomes a less important factor, though their judgement of his trustworthiness – reasonably enough – influences their verdict. But in a rape case, if the jurors consider the *victim* untrustworthy, the defendant is likely to get off, regardless of the impression he creates or the nature of his defence.

I repeat that this evidence comes from mock trials, and that we cannot assume that real-life jurors have an equally scanty regard for the evidence they hear. But the fact that subjective impressions are so important even when the 'jurors' can't see the witnesses (they are usually just listening to a tape-recording of the court proceedings), coupled with the finding that people in groups tend to take riskier decisions than they would as individuals (probably because they feel less responsibility for any consequences their decisions may have), suggests that the effectiveness of the jury system might at least bear empirical examination.

From *Habits* by John Nicholson

we are no more objective. . . : see 'The Effect of Language on Juries (page 119)

Unfamiliar words

Decide on the most probable meaning of the following in the context.

1 **biases** (line 8)
2 **anecdote** (line 12)
3 **conjecture** (line 12)
4 **transcripts** (line 18)
5 **damages** (line 29)
6 **inflated** (line 33)
7 **creatures of little substance** (line 47)
8 **key areas** (line 58)
9 **mock trial** (line 69)
10 **scanty** (line 71)

Reading for gist

Answer the following. *Only one answer* is correct.

1 The theoretical justification for the jury system is that
A groups are more rational collectively than individuals.
B jurors are objective.
C jurors are unlikely to be prejudiced.
D the verdict depends on a majority vote.

2 In the case of the farm-worker, the juries
A awarded high damages when he showed his hand.
B awarded high damages only if they had seen pictures of the injuries.
C awarded high damages because the equipment had not been properly maintained.
D established the facts by studying pictures of the hand.

3 The principal risk of the jury system is that juries
A can be influenced by prosecutors.
B change their minds as the evidence is presented.
C disregard the evidence because of their personal impressions of defendants.
D make up their minds about cases in advance.

4 The most important difference in the attitude of juries in rape trials, as compared with theft trials, is that they
A are guided by their assessment of people's trustworthiness.
B base their verdict on their assessment of the victim.
C are governed by first impressions.
D do not take intelligence into account to the same extent.

5 The evidence obtained from mock trials
A cannot be taken seriously.
B is reliable, because it is based on tape recordings.
C is unreliable, because the jurors have no real responsibility.
D suggests that groups are less concerned by their verdict than an individual.

Words often confused

1 appoint, engage, enlist, hire, recruit

All these verbs have meanings relating to **employ**, but some have other meanings in different contexts. Use each of them *at least once* in the correct form to complete the sentences below, paying attention to the constructions used and the contexts in which they appear.

1 Tom and Sally are __________, and plan to get married next year.
2 He has been __________ manager of the sales department.
3 He __________ in the army as a volunteer.
4 As soon as they arrived on the island, they __________ a car and __________ one of the local inhabitants as their guide.
5 I tried to get in touch with her because we had not __________ a time for the committee meeting, but every time I rang her the line was __________.
6 People like him who __________ in politics know how to __________ the sympathy of an audience and as a result __________ new members for the party. When the Committee __________ him Branch Secretary, I thought that all he would have to do would be to __________ halls for visiting speakers and things like that, but now I realise that it's virtually a full-time job.

2 capable, competent, effective, efficient, qualified

Use each of the above *at least once* to complete the sentences below, paying attention to the constructions used and the contexts in which they appear.

1 The court referred the matter to Parliament because it did not consider itself __________ (or __________) to express an opinion on a political matter.
2 I much prefer my secretary to many better __________ women that I interviewed.
3 In so far as the Government is attempting to find __________ measures to solve the problem of unemployment, we are prepared to give it our __________ (partial, limited) approval, but we do not really believe it is __________ of solving

these problems unless it can set up an __________ service for recruiting young people in the areas offering them the best prospects of work and supervised by the __________ authority.

4 A __________ lawyer like yourself must know that all of us are __________ of committing crimes in certain circumstances.

The Law

Read the following passage, paying close attention to detail.

A walk up Middle Temple Lane from the Thames, and across the Strand into the Royal Courts of Justice, provides a glimpse of a large chunk of the ancient carcass of the English legal system, still crawling with life. Three quarters of the 3,800 practising barristers in England and Wales have their **chambers** at the Inns of Court, all within half a mile of the Royal Courts. The barristers walk characteristically hands in pockets and **splay-footed**, in a kind of **legal aid** waddle, maintaining an air of private gentility which belies the fact that a large proportion – perhaps the majority – now depend for their living on state-aided clients.

A peep through the glass-panelled doors of some of the 50 court rooms in the Royal Courts, at cobwebbed wigs and black gowns, barristers swaying slowly on their feet, and eyebrowed glances from judges in the stillness, evokes a picture of the English judicial system absurdly theatrical and archaic.

The truth is that most people in England and Wales are too over-awed by, or ignorant of, the law even to go to a High Street solicitor if they have a 'legal' problem other than a serious criminal charge against them, or the desire to make a will or to buy a house. The great bulk of legal disputes that arise are settled a long way from this concentration of legal **masonry** and manpower in the Strand. Well over 90 per cent of criminal cases are tried in magistrates' courts. Sixty different statutory tribunals, outside the court structure altogether, hear about 150,000 cases a year, compared with just over 2,300 actions in the High Court. And the great majority of divorce cases are now heard in the County Courts.

One of the most distinctive and pervasive aspects of the English legal system is the rigid segregation of the two branches of the profession into barristers and solicitors. The separation of the two branches is maintained by rules of practice and etiquette, as intricate and fixed as a caste system, but it is not based on any consistent functional division – say, between generalists and specialists. With only rare exceptions, a client cannot go straight to a barrister. **Referrals** have to be made by a solicitor. The principal specialism of **the bar**, it is sometimes claimed, is advocacy. Only barristers can present a case in the High Court or (again with some exceptions) the three tiers of the Crown Courts, which, in 1972, replaced the Assizes and Quarter Sessions in the provinces. Barristers, particularly those in London, may well be specialists in some aspect of the law: criminal, commercial, **conveyancing** and so on.

But, equally, firms of solicitors specialise. They can also represent their clients in magistrates' courts and in the County Courts, which handle minor civil matters. Some barristers never, or hardly ever, appear in court. Some solicitors do a great deal of advocacy, but only in the 'lower courts'. Both barristers and solicitors can be either specialists or generalists, advocates or desk-bound. The distinction between the two sides of the profession is really fixed at entry, the would-be barrister going to the Inns of Court in London and solicitors getting **'articles'** in an office. There is no easy way of transferring from one side to the other, even though most entrants now have law degrees and the division is more to do with a very silly notion of **Gentlemen and Players** than anything of conceivable value.

From an article by Gavin Weightman in *New Society*

chambers: rooms used as offices by barristers
splay-footed: with the feet turned outwards
legal aid: paid by the state to defend clients who cannot afford to pay a lawyer themselves
masonry: the implication is that the lawyers in the Strand form a kind of secret society, like the masons
referrals: the appointment of a barrister to take a case
the bar: the profession of barrister and all those who have qualified as barristers
conveyancing: that part of law dealing with the transfer of property
articles: the qualifications allowing a solicitor to practise
Gentlemen and Players: an annual cricket match that used to take place between amateurs and professionals; here, the suggestion is an artificial, largely social distinction between similar professions

Unfamiliar words

Decide on the most probable meaning of the following in the context, using the aid given.

1 **chunk** (line 4)
2 **carcass** (line 4) what sort of body?
3 **crawling with life** (line 5) what sort of life, if you defined 'carcass' correctly?
4 **waddle** (line 11) 'splay-footed' (see above) what sort of creatures walk like this?
5 **cobwebbed** (line 18) what sort of creature makes a cobweb, and in what sort of house would you find one?
6 **eyebrowed glances** (line 20) how do you imagine the judge looks at the barristers?
7 **tiers** (line 58)
8 **generalists** (line 73) as distinct from specialists
9 **desk-bound** (line 74) as distinct from being an advocate in court
10 **would-be** (line 76) at the beginning of their studies

Reading for detail

Answer the questions, comparing each of the statements made below with the text. *Only one answer* is correct.

1 The impression of the English legal system given by a visit to the Royal Courts of Justice is that it is
A a proof that only rich men can obtain justice.
B entirely centralised.
C more dead than alive.
D out of date.

2 What makes the picture of English justice seem absurd is that
A barristers speak in such a strange way.
B court actions take place behind closed doors.
C lawyers depend on state-aided clients for work.
D the costumes and gestures suggest people acting in an old play.

3 Most people in England and Wales
A are only allowed into the High Court for criminal cases.
B ignore the High Court because they trust local lawyers.
C do not usually think of consulting lawyers if they have a complaint to make.
D only consult lawyers when they are under arrest, awaiting trial.

4 The main difference between barristers and solicitors is that
A only barristers can speak in court.
B solicitors are not allowed to speak in the High Court.
C solicitors are specialists, while barristers are not.
D they have quite different functions.

5 The difference between barristers and solicitors is established by
A family background.
B free choice.
C open public examinations.
D the way the lawyer entered the profession.

Words often confused

belie, deceive, disguise, misunderstand, perjure, retract
Use each of the above *at least once* in the correct form to complete the sentences below. Pay attention to the constructions used.

1 He was forced to __________ his accusation against the defendant when it became clear that the chief witness had __________ himself in court in order to __________ the jury.
2 His cheerful expression __________ (or __________) the seriousness of the occasion.
3 There is no __________ the fact that I voted against you at the meeting, but I don't want you to __________ my motives. My intentions were honourable and I think you are __________

yourself if you imagine that my opposition to you is based on personal grounds.

4 Unfortunately, his performance as King Lear __________ our confidence in him. He managed to __________ his voice to sound like an old man, but he never convinced the audience in the part and he seemed to have __________ most of the director's advice on the interpretation of the role.

G

Vocabulary expansion

fluctuate, sway, undulate, vibrate, wave

Barristers in court are described in the passage as **swaying slowly on their feet** (moving gently from side to side). Use the most appropriate of the above verbs, in the correct form, to complete the sentences below, paying attention to the context in which they appear.

1 The house __________ every time a plane passes overhead.

2 Some people describe the south of England as flat, but it is really __________ country, rising and falling in low hills and valleys.

3 The price of gold __________ so much from one month to another that gold cannot really be regarded as a safe investment.

4 People __________ flags as the President passed by.

5 The flags of all the nations __________ in the breeze at the opening ceremony of the World Championships.

6 During the day, the temperature has __________ between 10 degrees and 20 degrees centigrade.

7 The opinion polls always __________ at this stage of an election campaign but that speech last night is bound to have __________ many people in the Senator's favour.

8 He stood on the platform at the back of the train, __________ gently as it picked up speed and he felt the floor begin to __________ beneath him, and __________ to the crowd that had gathered to see him off.

Murder in an English Country House

Read this passage, noting down any words that are unfamiliar to you and gaining a general impression of its content, and then read Passage B that follows on page 147 for comparison before examining the vocabulary and the incidents that take place in detail.

A

Ackroyd was sitting as I had left him in the arm-chair before the fire. His head had fallen sideways, and clearly visible, just below the collar of his coat, was a shining piece of twisted metalwork.

Parker and I advanced till we stood over the recumbent figure. I heard the butler draw in his breath with a sharp hiss.

'Stabbed from be'ind,' he murmured. 'Orrible!'

He wiped his moist brow with his handkerchief, then stretched out a gingerly hand towards the hilt of the dagger.

'You mustn't touch that,' I said sharply. 'Go at once to the telephone and ring up the police station. Inform them of what has happened. Then tell Mr Raymond and Major Blunt.'

'Very good, sir.'

Parker hurried away, still wiping his perspiring brow.

I did what little had to be done. I was careful not to disturb the position of the body, and not to handle the dagger at all. No object was to be attained by moving it. Ackroyd had clearly been dead some little time.

Then I heard young Raymond's voice, horror-stricken and incredulous, outside.

'What do you say? Oh! Impossible! Where's the doctor?'

He appeared impetuously in the doorway, then stopped dead, his face very white. A hand put him aside, and Hector Blunt came past him into the room.

'My God!' said Raymond from behind him; 'it's true, then.'

Blunt came straight on till he reached the chair. He bent over the body, and I thought that, like Parker, he was going to lay hold of the dagger hilt. I drew him back with one hand.

'Nothing must be moved,' I explained. 'The police must see him exactly as he is now.'

Blunt nodded in instant comprehension. His face was expressionless as ever, but I thought I detected signs of emotion beneath the stolid mask. Geoffrey Raymond had joined us now, and stood peering over Blunt's shoulder at the body.

'This is terrible,' he said in a low voice.

'Roger hadn't an enemy in the world,' said Blunt quietly. 'Must have been burglars. But what was the thief after? Nothing seems to be disarranged?'

He looked round the room. Raymond was sorting the papers on the desk.

'There seems nothing missing, and none of the drawers show signs of having been tampered with,' the secretary observed at last. 'It's very mysterious.'

Blunt made a slight motion with his head.

'There are some letters on the floor here,' he said.

I looked down. Three or four letters still lay where Ackroyd had dropped them earlier in the evening.

But the blue envelope containing Mrs Ferrars's letter had disappeared. I half opened my mouth to speak, but at that moment the sound of a bell pealed through the house. There was a confused murmur of voices in the hall, and then Parker appeared with our local inspector and a police constable.

'Good evening, gentlemen,' said the inspector. 'I'm terribly sorry for this! A good, kind gentleman like Mr Ackroyd. The butler says it is murder. No possibility of accident or suicide, doctor?'

'None whatever,' I said.

'Ah! A bad business.'

From *The Murder of Roger Ackroyd* by Agatha Christie

Murder in Los Angeles

Read this passage, comparing it to Passage A, before examining the vocabulary and the incidents that take place in detail.

B

I went downstairs, listened outside the manager's door, heard nothing, went in and crossed to put the keys on the desk. Lester B. Clausen lay on his side on the couch with his face to the wall, dead to the world. I went through the desk, found an old account book that seemed to be concerned with rent taken in and expenses paid out and nothing else. I looked at the register again. It wasn't up to date but the party on the couch seemed enough explanation for that. Orrin P. Quest had moved away. Somebody else had taken over his room. Somebody else had the room registered to Hicks. The little man counting money in the kitchen went nicely with the neighbourhood. The fact that he carried a gun and a knife was a social eccentricity that would cause no comment at all on Idaho Street.

I closed the register, glanced over at Lester B. Clausen again, wrinkled my nose at the stale air and the sickly sweetish smell of gin and of something else, and started back to the entrance door. As I reached it, something for the first time penetrated my mind. A drunk like Clausen ought to be snoring very loudly. He ought to be snoring his head off with a nice assortment of checks and gurgles and snorts. He wasn't making any sound at all. A brown Army blanket was pulled up around his shoulders and the lower part of his head. He looked very comfortable, very calm. I stood over him and looked down. Something which was not an accidental fold held the Army blanket away from the back of his neck. I moved it. A square yellow wooden handle was attached to the back of Lester B. Clausen's neck. On the side of the yellow handle were printed the words 'Compliments of Crumsen Hardware Company'.

It was the handle of an ice pick . . .

I did a nice quiet thirty-five getting away from the neighbourhood. On the edge of the city, a frog's jump from **the line**, I shut myself in an outdoor telephone booth and called the Police Department.

'Bay City Police. Moot talking,' a furry voice said.

I said: 'Number 449 Idaho Street. In the apartment of the manager. His name's Clausen.'

'Yeah?' the voice said. 'What do we do?'

'I don't know,' I said. 'It's a bit of a puzzle to me. But the man's name is Lester B. Clausen. Got that?'

'What makes it important?' the furry voice said without suspicion.

'**The coroner** will want to know,' I said, and hung up.

From *The Little Sister* by Raymond Chandler

the line: the city limit within the Police Department of Bay City have jurisdiction

The coroner: person responsible for determining the cause of death at a trial

Unfamiliar words

Decide on the most probable meaning of the following in the context.

1 **recumbent** (A, line 5)
2 **hilt** (A, line 9)
3 **perspiring** (A, line 14)
4 **stolid** (A, line 34)
5 **tampered with** (A, line 43)
6 **pealed** (A, line 51)
7 **the party** (B, line 6)
8 **gurgles** (B, line 17)
9 **snorts** (B, line 17)
10 **furry** (B, line 35)

Comparison of texts

Compare the two passages in order to find the answers to the following multiple-choice questions. Check each statement for *true* or *false* against the two texts. *Only one answer* is correct.

1 The two murder cases are similar because of
A the method of killing.
B the motive for the murder.
C the position of the dead body.
D the weapons used.

2 It appears that in both cases the narrator
A had not seen the victim before.
B had not seen the victim recently.
C had spoken to the victim on the same day.
D was personally acquainted with the victim.

3 The reactions of the narrator in Passage B are most like those of __________ in Passage A.
A the butler
B the narrator
C Raymond
D the police inspector

4 The narrator of Passage B behaved differently from the narrator of Passage A by
A disturbing the position of the body.
B handling the murder weapon.
C informing the police of the crime.
D leaving the scene of the crime.

5 In both cases,
A nothing was missing from the scene of the crime.
B the narrator noticed something was missing.
C the narrator was familiar with the contents of the room.
D there was evidence that the motive was robbery.

Reading for detail

Study each passage individually in detail, and compare the statements made below with the original, testing each for *true* or *false*. *Only one answer* is correct.

1 In Passage A, Blunt's reaction on seeing the body was one of
A horror.
B indifference.
C restraint.
D shock.

2 The police inspector's attitude towards those he found in the room was one of
A accusation.
B indifference.
C respect.
D suspicion.

3 In Passage B, the explanation the narrator found for the register being out of date was that
A the accountant was inefficient.
B the manager drank too much.
C the manager was dead.
D two guests had moved recently.

4 His suspicions were aroused by
A the fold in the blanket.
B the sight of the ice-pick.
C the silence in the room.
D the smell of alcohol.

5 The atmosphere surrounding the crime in Passage B suggests that the narrator
A was surprised to find a dead body in that neighbourhood.
B was investigating a previous crime committed there.
C realised who had committed the crime.
D thought the police might involve him in the killing.

Words often confused

1 acquaint oneself with, communicate (to/with), confide (in/to), drop a hint (to), inform (of)

Use each of the above *at least once* in the correct form to complete the sentences below, paying attention to the constructions and prepositions used.

1 The moment the police were __________ the crime, the news was __________ all the local stations.
2 Before investigating the crime himself, the Chief Inspector decided to __________ the victim's background. At first, he only encountered suspicion and no one was willing to __________ him, but eventually the victim's brother __________ him __________, implying that his brother had been involved with gangsters.
3 The police __________ the inspector that there was no way of __________ the main suspect because he had left the country, but an informer __________ (or __________) that he had been seen in Paris, and this information was immediately __________ Interpol.

2 disturb, embarrass, interfere (in) (with), overturn, trouble, upset

Use each of the above *at least once* in the correct form, paying attention to the constructions used and the contexts in which the verbs occur.

1 He was careful not to __________ the position of the body before the police arrived.
2 The young man was obviously extremely __________ when he heard the news; he broke down and sobbed uncontrollably.
3 At first, I hesitated to __________ you in your work, and I hate to __________ you with a silly question. . .
4 The cat jumped onto the table and __________ (or __________) the milk jug.
5 You needn't __________ to explain. I have no wish to __________ your personal life, and have no wish to ask you any questions that might __________ you.
6 At first, nothing but the movement of the oars __________ the calm surface of the lake, and then, without warning, the boat __________.

3 accidental, casual, incidental, random, unintentional

Use each of the above *at least once* to complete the sentences below, paying special attention to the contexts in which they appear.

1 A verdict of __________ death was returned on the victim.
2 He has composed the __________ music accompanying the modern-dress version of *Macbeth*.
3 I'm terribly sorry if you were upset by my remarks. Any reference to you was quite __________ on my part.
4 Judging from the reactions of a __________ sample of potential users in the market, the book will be a success.
5 A long time ago, people were expected to dress for dinner, but now everyone wears __________ clothes.
6 He saves money by employing __________ labourers, and paying them by the hour, together with __________ expenses, instead of having to pay National Insurance contributions for them.

4 bent, creased, folded, wrinkled

Use each of the above *at least once* to complete the examples below. Which of these words would be the most appropriate to use to describe the following?

1 someone's arms __________ across his chest
2 the face of a very old woman, with lines under the eyes and in the cheeks
3 a nail that is not straight
4 clothes that have been tightly packed in a suit case
5 a tablecloth neatly put away in a cupboard after a meal
6 a bicycle wheel after a minor accident

Lexical Progress Test 6

You must choose the word or phrase which best completes each sentence. For each question, 1 to 25, indicate the correct answer, A, B, C or D. The time for the test is 20 minutes.

1 She __________ the letter and put it in the envelope.
A bent B folded C twisted D wrinkled

2 The children had not seen the car approaching, so I __________ to them to get onto the pavement.
A cheered B cried C howled D yelled

3 The highlight of his acting career was the opportunity to play the __________ of Hamlet.
A characterisation B part C personage D play

4 You needn't have __________ to wash up. I would have done it.
A pained B troubled C wearied D worried

5 Teachers like students to be __________ to what they are saying.
A attentive B guarded C prudent D watchful

6 Most __________ tennis stars learn the game at an early age.
A hopeful B prospective C will-be D willing

7 The __________ music for the play has been taken from the works of Vivaldi.
A incidental B intervening C supplementary D passing

8 The children all __________ their flags as the procession passed by.
A flew B furled C swung D waved

9 What is usually called 'magic' is really a trick. The quickness of the hand __________ the eye.
A belies B deceives C disguises D mistakes

10 Marry in __________ and repent at leisure.
A haste B hurry C quickness D rush

11 I'm surprised they have __________. They seemed a happy couple.
A broken down B come apart C split up D turned off

12 They spent the night in a youth __________.
A home B hostel C house D inn

13 We must prevent that kind of disaster at all __________.
A chances B costs C expenses D risks

14 Before leaving the house, you should __________ that all doors and windows are locked.
A assure B ensure C insure D reassure

15 The first performance of the play was fortunately much better than the dress __________.
A practice B rehearsal C review D trial

16 He was lucky to get the house for less than the asking __________.
A amount B cost C price D value

17 He said that he would sue us, but I don't think he'll __________ his threat.
A achieve B bring about C carry out D perform

18 The painting has been __________ to Leonardo da Vinci, but it is almost certainly the work of one of his followers.
A accounted B attributed C claimed D referred

19 Trains are __________ to delay because of the fog.
A bound B likely C probable D subject

20 This diet is intended to __________ your weight.
A diminish B lose C reduce D subtract

21 These customs are __________ to certain tribes in the Pacific islands.
A characteristic B distinctive C peculiar D uncommon

22 The President made reference to the matter in his inaugural __________.
A address B debate C discussion D revision

23 He __________ in the army as a volunteer.
A engaged B enlisted C hired D recruited

24 Prices have __________ considerably over the past six months.
A fluctuated B swayed C undulated D waved

25 The Government's move is aimed at restoring confidence in the economy and discouraging __________ investment.
A hesitant B predictable C sensational D speculative

Test Papers

Test 1

This paper is in two parts, Section A and Section B. For each question you answer correctly in Section A you gain one mark; for each question you answer correctly in Section B you gain two marks. No marks are deducted for wrong answers. Answer all the questions. Indicate your choice of answer as shown below.

Section A

In this section you must choose the word or phrase which best completes each sentence. For each question, 1 to 25, indicate the correct letter, A, B, C or D.

1 This __________ of dog is very useful for hunting.
A breed B caste C clan D make

2 Now that the portrait is completed, you must choose an attractive __________ to hang it in.
A easel B frame C fringe D rim

3 The __________ of the order has already arrived. We are only waiting for a few extra copies.
A bulk B heap C majority D pile

4 We have a __________ arrangement to meet for lunch every fortnight.
A deep-seated B durable C long-lived D long-standing

5 He __________ his seat in Parliament in order to become ambassador to France.
A renounced B replaced C retracted D withdrew

6 His steering failed on the country road, and the car ended up in a __________.
A ditch B furrow C gutter D trench

7 He took off his hat and __________ politely to my mother.
A bent B bowed C crouched D knelt

8 John does not find that his new job provides him with sufficient __________ for his ability.
A capacity B opening C range D scope

9 His attitude is __________ of contempt for ordinary people.
A evident B indicative C positive D revealing

10 We have had many problems to cope with, but by now we can see light at the end of the __________.
A battle B day C road D tunnel

11 Production has been delayed because of a shortage of __________ materials.
A base B prime C raw D rough

12 The informer __________ the inspector a hint about the whereabouts of the wanted man.
A dropped B let C suggested D warned

13 The carriers __________ slowly up the mountainside, through the heavy snow.
A dawdled B leapt C strolled D trudged

14 Before making such a long journey, I must have the car thoroughly __________.
A controlled B overhauled C overruled D scanned

15 It is extraordinary that such an insignificant little man should __________ so much power.
A draw B manage C sway D wield

16 In the __________ of my not being there to meet you, our representative will take you to your hotel.
A event B occasion C occurrence D possibility

17 He has a little __________ next to his garage where he makes things for the house.
A housework B mill C workhouse D workshop

18 He __________ speeches, like most politicians.
A is accustomed to make
B is accustomed to making
C is used to make
D is usually making

19 He was set free yesterday after being __________ of the crime.
A acquitted B discharged C excused D exempted

20 His aunt died, leaving him a small __________ in her will.
A dowry B grant C heritage D legacy

21 I expect all of you to be here five minutes before the examination begins, without __________.
A fail B failure C fault D miss

22 They withheld the news of the defeats suffered elsewhere on the front, because it would have undermined the soldiers' __________.
A mood B moral C morale D temper

23 Put some oil on the door hinges to stop them __________.
A screeching B shrieking C squeaking D squealing

24 He never __________ his early promise as a musician.
A carried out B discharged C fulfilled D performed

25 Few governments __________ up to the expectations of those who voted for them.
A hold B keep C live D reach

Section B

In this section you will find after each of the passages a number of questions or unfinished statements about the passage, each with four suggested answers or ways of finishing. You must choose the one which you think fits best. For each question, 26 to 40, indicate the letter A, B, C or D as the correct answer.

First Passage

The modern sitting-room is no longer the space round the hearth. It has become a miniature theatre, based upon the television set. Chairs are grouped as in a cinema, thrust aside only when guests appear, and a general lighting has been replaced by standard lamps for the odd eccentric who may want to read. But the sad facts of life are not reflected in the architecture. There is seldom an alcove into which the flickering screen can be built. The television set, like the radio, remains an excrescence, an intrusion upon a family life still theoretically centred upon the hearth. No sitting-room is planned with the television set, or alternative screen, in open possession of what would once have been the fireplace. Realising this, we look round to see what other features reflect, or fail to reflect, the life we actually live. We thus notice the absence of a picture rail, a Victorian fitting which assumed, and rightly, that wall decorations are likely to be hung. This assumption is still correct but the gyproc or plaster has now to be drilled and plugged, damaging the surface and offering the interesting possibility that the drill will make contact with an electric cable hidden in the plasterwork. No builder ever obviates this inconvenience by inserting a wooden rail, flush with the surface, at a standard distance from the ceiling. In rather the same way the window pelmets are no part of the room's design but an inevitable afterthought, an occasion for more hammering and drilling, intrusion and mess. While the architect has failed to foresee the need for curtains, the electrician has anticipated the need for standard lamps, vacuum cleaners and television, spoiling the effect by placing his wildly unstandardised plugs at floor level where they are most likely to be damaged. Defects such as these are repeated throughout the house but will not be the subject of further comment.

26 The writer blames architects for
A failing to build sitting-rooms with television sets already installed.
B failing to provide an appropriate place for the television set.
C intruding on family life.
D planning the design of sitting-rooms to make television viewing more comfortable.

27 The lack of a picture rail in the modern sitting-room
A is due to the fact that people no longer need to hang pictures.
B is practically certain to result in damage to the pictures.
C is the cause of frequent accidents in the home.
D makes it necessary to drill holes in the wall.

28 The writer suggests that the risk of drilling into an electric cable could be avoided if the builder
A copied the Victorian idea of picture rails.
B gave the householder a plan of cables installed.
C made a space for a wooden rail in the surface of the wall.
D provided a wooden rail plugged to the wall.

29 With regard to window pelmets, the writer criticises architects for
A intruding on the occupiers in order to put them up.
B overlooking the fact that curtains cannot be hung without them.
C putting them up at the last minute to support rails.
D waiting for the occupiers to choose their curtains before installing them.

30 The electrician, according to the writer,
A apparently installs whatever plugs he happens to have to hand.
B causes damage by failing to insulate the wires and cables.
C does his job much more efficiently than the architects.
D fails to foresee the number of connections that will be required.

Second Passage

There was some curious riddle about Uncle Charlie's early life which not even our Mother could explain. When the Boer War ended he had worked for a time in a Rand diamond town as a barman. Those were wide open days when a barman's duties included an ability to knock drunks cold. Uncle Charlie was obviously suited to this, for he was a lion of a man in his youth. The miners would descend from their sweating camps, pockets heavy with diamond dust, buy up barrels of whisky, drink themselves crazy, then start to burn down the saloon.

. . . This was where Uncle Charlie came in, the king-fish of those swilling bars, whose muscled bottle-swinging arm would then lay them out in rows. But even he was no superman and suffered his share of damage. The men used him one night as a battering-ram to break open a liquor store. He lay for two days with a broken skull, and still had a fine bump to prove it.

Then for two or three years he disappeared completely and went underground in the Johannesburg stews. No letters or news were received during that time, and what happened was never explained. Then suddenly, without warning, he turned up in Stroud, pale and thin and penniless. He wouldn't say where he'd been, or discuss what he'd done, but he'd finished his wanderings, he said. So a girl from our district, handsome Fanny Causon, took him and married him.

He settled then in the local forests and became one of the best woodsmen in the Cotswolds. His employers flattered, cherished, and underpaid him; but he was content among his trees. He raised his family on labourer's pay, fed them on game from the woods, gave his daughters no discipline other than his humour, and taught his sons the skill of his heart.

31 The riddle of Uncle Charlie's early life was that he had
A been employed to knock people out.
B been injured himself, although a good fighter.
C disappeared for some time, leaving no trace.
D worked as a barman in South Africa.

32 Uncle Charlie's job in the Rand diamond town was
A simply to serve drinks.
B to keep drunken miners out of the bar.
C to knock out the customers.
D to serve drinks and prevent trouble.

33 Uncle Charlie was eventually injured when
A he realised that he was no superman.
B he was recovering from a broken skull.
C he was no longer strong enough for the job.
D some men smashed a door open with his head.

34 Fanny Causon married Uncle Charlie because
A he had lived such an adventurous life.
B he said his adventures were over.
C she felt sorry for him.
D she had not heard from him for a long time.

35 The only criticism Uncle Charlie could have made of his employers, once he became a forester, was that they
A did not respect him.
B expected him to feed his children on what he caught.
C ought to have given him more money.
D treated him unkindly.

Third Passage

A For small, quiet firm in luxury offices near Fleet Street. Must be numerate, methodical worker, educated 'A' level standard with 120 w.p.m. shorthand. Cheerful, well-spoken and of good appearance. Age 25–35. Salary reviewed after six months. No agencies. Please ring me at my office. 303 2000. £11,000

B Prestige financial company with elegant offices requires a secretary for one of their Directors. Fluent spoken and written Arabic and speeds of 80 w.p.m. shorthand and 60 w.p.m. typing are a necessity. You will be required to prepare complicated itineraries as well as carrying out PA duties for the Director, who travels 50% of the time. Age 25–35. 01-388-9981 Secretary Recruitment Agency. £9000 plus

C If you are active, intelligent, attractive and capable of working on your own, the Director of a small consultancy business in West London needs you to help run the show. You should be 23 with three years' experience and hold a current driver's licence. Salary *c* £7500 p.a. + car. 01-616-5363

D Mature, competent secretary seeking fulfilment in a challenging environment is sought by a top American bank to organise executive offices. Good secretarial skills and relevant experience, preferably gained in a financial environment, are essential. Additional benefits include help with mortgage.
01-477-7050
Bank Consultants Ltd.
£8500 plus

E A major restaurant group catering for the young and trendy seeks a bright, extrovert PA/Secretary to dynamic Managing Director. You should be able to project a first-class image in terms of grooming and personality. A good sense of humour is essential. Solid senior level background needed. Age 28–35. 01-388-7969 Jane Wallis Consultants *c* £10,000

36 The need to take responsibility for other employees is stressed in
A Advertisement B.
B Advertisement C.
C Advertisement D.
D Advertisement E.

37 The ability to represent the firm on one's initiative is emphasised in
A Advertisements A and B.
B Advertisements B and C.
C Advertisements C and D.
D Advertisements D and E.

38 A lively personality to reflect that of the boss is required for the job advertised in
A Advertisement A.
B Advertisement B.
C Advertisement C.
D Advertisement E.

39 Accuracy and attention to detail is the most essential requirement for the job advertised in
A Advertisement A.
B Advertisement B.
C Advertisement D.
D Advertisement E.

40 All the advertisements offer some additional advantages in terms of financial prospects or working conditions except
A Advertisement A.
B Advertisement B.
C Advertisement D.
D Advertisement E.

Test 2

Section A

In this section you must choose the word or phrase which best completes each sentence. For each question, 1 to 25, indicate the correct letter, A, B, C or D.

1 Before the nine o'clock news, here is an official __________.
A advertisement B advice C announcement D threat

2 The statue of the town's most distinguished citizen was __________ by the Mayor at an official ceremony yesterday.
A opened B unpacked C unveiled D unwrapped

3 He __________ his shoulders and walked off without a word.
A knitted B scratched C shook D shrugged

4 It is the responsibility of the police to __________ the law.
A compel B enforce C force D urge

5 You can't expect people to be perfect. We're all __________.
A defective B fallacious C fallible D faulty

6 He was a bitter opponent of ours at one time, but now he has been __________ to our ideas.
A ensured B converted C convinced D overcome

7 The conflicting statements issued by the Government are bound to encourage __________ investors.
A hesitant B predictable C sensational D speculative

8 He's the __________ image of his father. They're so alike!
A alive B identical C lively D living

9 The house is part of his __________ from his aunt.
A heritage B inheritance C testament D will

10 The sound of the horses' __________ could be heard in the distance.
A claws B hooves C pads D paws

11 The Youth __________ Association exists to provide accommodation for young people when they are travelling.
A Homes B Hostels C Houses D Inns

12 Guests are requested to __________ their hotel rooms before noon.
A abandon B discharge C displace D vacate

13 While I cannot promise that the car will be ready by tomorrow I __________ you that we are doing our best to complete the job.
A assure B ensure C insure D reassure

14 What would you like for the first __________? There are quite a lot of interesting things on the menu.
A course B dish C cover D plate

15 The storm began so suddenly that I hardly had time to __________ to the children to take cover.
A cheer B cry C howl D yell

16 Students wishing to re-enrol are __________ to come to the office before the end of the month.
A advised B commanded C notified D suggested

17 You shouldn't talk about him failing. You'll __________ his confidence.
A underestimate B undergo C undermine D worry

18 I doubt if the amount of food I have ordered will be __________ for so many people.
A adaptable B adequate C fitted D suitable

19 More __________, less speed.
A haste B hurry C quickness D rush

20 The lorry overturned in the middle of the road and brought the traffic to a __________.
A closure B conclusion C standstill D stoppage

21 I'm glad to say that the advantages of the plan __________ the disadvantages.
A overbalance B overlook C outweigh D prevail

22 She has such a beautiful __________. She must look after her skin.
A aspect B complexion C outline D visage

23 You are not __________ to join this club unless you are 18 or over.
A available B eligible C legitimate D permissible

24 After the accident, the car was so badly smashed up that it was __________ by the insurance company.
A discarded B laid off C put down D written off

25 The car __________ its way slowly up the twisting mountain road.
A bent B did C turned D wound

Section B

Choose the answer which you think fits best. For each question, 26 to 40, indicate the letter A, B, C or D as the correct answer.

First Passage

One of the strangest things about controversy over advertising is that the greater the fuss, the more of a mystery the industry itself seems to become. Advertising is a passionate area. It seems to affect those who attack it and those who defend it in remarkably similar ways. Before long both are exhibiting the same compulsive urge to overstate their case so that it is difficult to believe that the critics and the defenders of advertising are even arguing over the same thing.

But just as it seemed sensible to us to regard advertising without going to either extreme, so it also seemed logical to try and find out, as cold-bloodedly as we could, what advertising in the Britain of the 'sixties really was.

We knew that it consumed around £500 million a year, or roughly 2 per cent of the national income. We knew that it employed something over 200,000 individuals, the majority of whom were paid salaries considerably above the national average. And we knew that it was supposedly run in accordance with certain rather vague and often complex rules and 'professional' taboos.

But once we tried finding out exactly what all this money went on, what all these highly paid individuals did for it (and with it), and how the rules and taboos influenced them, a curious thing happened. This strange animal called advertising, so loathed by its critics and so beloved by its defenders, began to disappear. In its place were advertising men and advertising agencies – all working in different ways and to different rules and all showing quite startling differences of competence, taste and effectiveness.

We started by expecting to find a conspiracy of case-hardened persuaders. We ended by discovering groups of well paid, highly anxious individuals all trying, in their various ways, to accommodate a number of opposed and often contradictory forces within their work. Their success or failure in reconciling these forces results in the advertising we all must endure.

All this seemed of considerable importance. For unless society is willing to give advertising a complete *carte blanche* (which strikes us as lunacy) or to ban all advertising totally (which strikes us as absurdity) any future move to reform advertising will have to make the mental effort to understand what it is about and why its practitioners behave as they do. To understand this the first necessity will be to understand these forces that shape their working lives.

26 The advertising industry is a mystery to most people because
A everyone makes such a fuss about it.
B it is such a controversial subject.
C its critics and defenders are not really talking about the same thing.
D no one seems able to discuss it calmly and rationally.

27 The writers began their investigation of advertising
A in an analytical, unprejudiced frame of mind.
B in an attempt to discover its professional secrets.
C in order to expose its faults to the general public.
D to find out the basic facts and figures connected with its organisation.

28 What surprised the writers most, once they had begun their investigation, was that
A advertising executives were so highly paid.
B it was impossible to find out where all the money went.
C the rules and taboos they had heard about did not exist.
D there was so little consistency that it was impossible to generalise.

29 The average advertising executive, in the writers' opinion, is
A incapable of coping with so many conflicting forces.
B more sensitive and concerned about his work than is generally believed.
C overpaid and overworked.
D so cynical because of his experience that he inflicts his cynicism on the public.

30 The writers believe that society should
A let advertisers go on more or less as they like.
B impose strict controls on all advertising immediately.
C reform advertising on the lines they themselves have proposed.
D study advertising and its problems before making changes.

Second Passage

Speke was 30, some six years younger than Burton, and although a story was put about at one time that he was an Anglo-Indian with mixed blood there was no truth in it; he came from a West Country family that dated back to Saxon times. He was tall and slender and his blue eyes and fair hair gave him rather a Scandinavian appearance. Moreover he looked after himself; he ate a great deal but drank very little and never smoked.

Like Burton, Speke had entered the Indian Army, though at an earlier age and as a cadet, and had fought in the Punjab. Like Burton, he had a taste for solitary expeditions in India, though of a very different kind; he used to go shooting in the distant Himalayas. Speke had a mania for shooting – few specimens in India and Tibet, he says, did not fall to his gun – and his various journeys on local leave took him into very remote places where, possibly, no other European had been before. This was part of the toughening-up process, and Speke was not unconscious of his own virtue in this matter. He was not like his brother officers in India, he wrote later, somewhat smugly. He never 'idled away his time or got into debt': he was away in the mountains collecting specimens and opening up the unexplored country; and the authorities approved of this.

Already in India, long before he met Burton, Speke had a great object in view; he had decided that as soon as his long leave fell due he would make a journey through unexplored Africa, travelling from the east coast to the headwaters of the Nile, and then sail downstream to Egypt. On the way he would gather specimens of rare birds and animals, and eventually he would build up a natural history museum in his father's country house in England. Of his three years' leave from the army, two were to be spent on the journey and the third year he was to recuperate at home. He saved his money, he planned, and when his ten years' service in India was up in 1854 he sailed for Aden, carrying with him £390 worth of beads and other barter goods with which he proposed to enlist the help of the natives when he crossed to the African mainland.

31 Speke's ancestry was
A mixed.
B ultimately Scandinavian.
C uncertain.
D wholly English.

32 Speke's experience differed from Burton's because
A Burton was not an army officer.
B he had visited places where no European had been before.
C he liked hunting.
D he preferred to make expeditions in the company of other people.

33 Speke's attitude towards other officers in the army was based on
A a desire to please senior officers.
B a self-satisfied feeling of moral superiority.
C a snobbish consciousness of his military rank.
D the realisation that he was stronger and braver than the rest.

34 Speke planned to
A join Burton in order to explore Africa.
B reach the highest rank in the Indian Army.
C retire from the army after three years to look after a museum.
D return to the army after he had spent some time in Africa and England.

35 Speke took large quantities of goods to Aden in order to
A exchange them for supplies there.
B finance his African expedition.
C gain the good-will and assistance of African people.
D pay for his journey once he arrived in Africa.

Third Passage

Tom Fleming is not my favourite royal event commentator, being given to pomp and much circumstantial detail. He knows the State Coach weighs 4½ tons and was delivered at five in the morning, and the names of all the horses: Budapest, Beaufort, Rio, Santiago, and so forth. So forth not being a horse, of course.

They are greys because it shows the red and gold harness so well and that must be one reason why London, grey in style and stone, lends itself so well to pageantry. When most truly moved Fleming is barely rational: 'One wonders what the conversation will be in the stable tonight when these horses get home.'

However, let joy be unconfined and criticism minimal. The walkabout was a genuinely gay and pretty business with the Queen being handed a painting here, a posy there. I watched with close attention and fed my findings into a computer. The conclusion is that the Queen is likeliest to stop and talk to you if you are a young, male foreigner in a funny hat sitting in a wheel-chair near a Boy Scout; the Duke if you are a nun with a periscope.

Bearskins do not count as funny hats, though Prince Charles was committed to wearing one which rendered him unrecognizable.

The best way to see St Paul's is to be a bat. The remarkable aerial shots from the dome were as round as a gunsight with the crimson carpet crossing exactly where the Queen knelt. Her vulnerability throughout the procession was both worrying and yet a defence in itself. Her face in church and perhaps off-guard seems to fall into lines for which grief would hardly be too strong a word.

The drive back was a relaxed affair with boys in jeans running to keep up with the landau, pigeons surprised by the joy and not a car in sight except on sufferance. The whole heart of London was what planners are pleased to call a pedestrian precinct. Just people, how pleasant.

36 The point of the phrase 'So forth not being a horse, of course,' is to
A show what silly remarks the commentator made.
B emphasise the irrelevance of the details in the commentary.
C contrast the name with those of the horses.
D draw readers' attention to the use of capital letters for names elsewhere.

37 The commentator became 'barely rational' when he
A explained that the horses were chosen for their colour.
B suggested that the horses would be the main topic of conversation that evening.
C implied that the horses would discuss the procession.
D got so excited about the beauty of the horses.

38 The procedure of the walkabout is apparently intended to give the royal family an opportunity to
A receive presents.
B talk to the public.
C pick out funny people in the crowd.
D wear strange uniforms.

39 The Queen's vulnerability was 'both worrying and yet a defence in itself' because she
A was not guarded from would-be assassins.
B was off-guard and not expecting an attack.
C looked sad, which upset the writer.
D looked so sad that no one would have had the heart to kill her.

40 The pleasantest thing about the drive back from St Paul's from the writer's point of view was that
A boys ran after the coach.
B the pigeons seemed to share the occasion.
C there was no traffic in the centre of London.
D the people in the crowd were so nice.

Test 3

Section A

In this section you must choose the word or phrase which best completes each sentence. For each question, 1 to 25, indicate the correct letter, A, B, C or D.

1 He's always __________ of his success. I'm tired of hearing about it.
A boasting B exulting C glorying D proclaiming

2 The students were interested in what the teacher was saying and listened __________.
A attentively B guardedly C prudently D watchful

3 My secretary has typed out the first __________ of the lecture, but I must revise it before I give it at the conference.
A attempt B design C draft D trial

4 As the minutes ticked by, and we held on to our narrow lead, our hopes of victory __________ steadily.
A arose B aroused C raised D rose

5 He __________ to take us to court if we did not pay the rent immediately.
A advised B menaced C threatened D warned

6 __________ from old wounds disfigured the old soldier's face.
A Blots B Scars C Scrapes D Scratches

7 The author insisted on making changes in the play as late as the dress __________.
A practice B rehearsal C review D trial

8 I doubt if I will be __________ enough to play tomorrow.
A fit B healthy C recovered D sound

9 He opposed the marriage at first, but eventually gave __________ to his daughter's entreaties.
A opening B place C position D way

10 You are __________ yourself if you imagine that I care about what you said or the way you behaved.
A belying B deceiving C disguising D mistaking

11 The thief __________ her handbag and ran away.
A gripped B hugged C snatched D wrenched

12 We've just received the first consignment of radios. The next __________ will be delivered in June.
A batch B collection C shoal D squad

13 In his closing __________, the Chairman thanked all those who had contributed to the success of the occasion.
A address B debate C discussion D revision

14 It's not surprising that he bitterly __________ being overlooked by the party when a new leader was chosen.
A disregards B grudges C objects D resents

15 The shares are likely to rise in value following the recent take-over __________.
A attempt B bid C challenge D investment

16 It was obvious that he had been affected by the blow from the way he __________ across the ring.
A hobbled B limped C loped D staggered

17 He was __________ of murder.
A charged B condemned C convicted D judged

18 He hurt his knee early in the game, and __________ off the field.
A carried B left C limped D trod

19 The shopping bag broke and everything I had bought was scattered all over the pavement, but no one __________ to help me.
A pained B troubled C wearied D worried

20 In this part of the country, the fields are separated by stone __________.
A fences B hedges C barriers D walls

21 If the dispute cannot be resolved, the Government has insisted that it should go to independent __________.
A arbitration B election C referee D trial

22 What __________ of car do you drive?
A brand B fabrication C make D mark

23 The police believe that the robbers could only have known when the money was to be withdrawn as a result of __________ information.
A confident B inside C interior D paying

24 I just have a few household __________ to cope with, and then I'll be ready to go out.
A charges B chores C errands D works

25 The police managed to __________ down the owner of the car by broadcasting a message on the radio.
A catch B search C trace D track

Section B

Choose the answer which you think fits best. For each question, 26 to 40, indicate the letter A, B, C or D as the correct answer.

First Passage

Everything was the wrong way about. Midwinter fell in July, and in January summer was at its height; in the bush there were giant birds that never flew, and queer, antediluvian animals that hopped instead of walked or sat munching mutely in the trees. Even the constellations in the sky were upside down and seemed to belong to another system of the sun. As for the naked aborigines, they were caught in a timeless apathy in which nothing ever changed or progressed; they built no villages, they planted no crops, and except for a few flea-bitten dogs possessed no domestic animals of any kind. They hunted, they slept, just occasionally they decked themselves out for a tribal ceremony, but all the rest was a listless dreaming.

A kind of trance was in the air, a sense of awakening infinitely delayed. In the midsummer heat the land scarcely breathed, but the alien white man, walking through the grey and silent trees, would have the feeling that someone or something was waiting and listening. The smaller birds did not fly away as they did in Europe. The kookaburra approached, uttered its raucous guffaw, then cocked its head, waiting for a response. The kangaroo stood poised and watching. The earth itself had this same air of expectancy, as though it were willing the rain to fall, as though it was waiting for fertilization so that it could come to life again.

And in fact an awakening did occur in the south-eastern corner of the continent when the first white settlers arrived in 1788. Somehow European crops were made to grow in land that had never been tilled before, and imported cattle, horses and sheep managed to survive in a country where the farmer had no precedents to guide him. Every man was a Robinson Crusoe. A flood could and did wipe out a year's labour in a single day, and when a drought began there was no knowing when it would ever end. Everything was new and had to be begun from the beginning.

But it was a healthy country. Along the coast at least there was a sparkle in the air, a sense of vigour, of light and space, that the colonists had never known in Europe. On the whole it was a mild climate by the sea – they had about as much rain as England and the sun had no more than a Mediterranean warmth – and by 1860, places like Sydney, Melbourne and Adelaide were flourishing settlements.

26 What distinguished the attitude to life of the aborigines from Europeans was that they
- A had no interest in altering their existence.
- B lacked the natural resources to build and cultivate.
- C preferred to lead a free, open-air life.
- D spent most of the day asleep.

27 The writer suggests that the first white men in Australia would have sensed from the behaviour of the natural life he encountered an atmosphere of
- A anticipation.
- B hostility.
- C renewal.
- D suspicion.

28 The first white settlers in Australia established themselves by
- A adapting what they brought with them to local conditions.
- B relying on frequent shipments of everything they needed from Europe.
- C rescuing what they could from shipwrecked vessels.
- D turning the natural resources of the country to advantage.

29 The writer says that 'every man was a Robinson Crusoe' because
- A the conditions were so arduous that the settlers' survival was often threatened.
- B they had to learn to live entirely from the resources of the new country.
- C they had to proceed on their own initiative by a system of trial and error.
- D they were exiles from their own country.

30 The climate in the places where the first settlers established themselves
- A was very similar to that of England.
- B was suitable for their purposes.
- C was typical of Australia as a whole.
- D went from one extreme to another.

Second Passage

On a February morning in 1966 Cleve Backster made a discovery that changed his life and could have far-reaching effects on ours. Backster was at that time an interrogation specialist who left the CIA to operate a New York school for training policemen in the techniques of using the polygraph, or 'lie detector'. This instrument normally measures the electrical resistance of the human skin, but on that morning he extended its possibilities. Immediately after watering an office plant, he wondered if it would be possible to measure the rate at which water rose in the plant from the root to the leaf by recording the increase in leaf-moisture content on a polygraph tape. Backster placed the two psychogalvanic-reflex (PGR) electrodes on either side of a leaf of *Dracaena massangeana*, a potted rubber plant, and balanced the leaf into the circuitry before watering the plant again. There was no marked reaction to this stimulus, so Backster decided to try what he calls 'the threat-to-well-being principle, a well-established method of triggering emotionality in humans'. In other words he decided to torture the plant. First of all he dipped one of its leaves into a cup of hot coffee, but there was no reaction, so he decided to get a match and burn the leaf properly. 'At the instant of this decision, at 13 minutes and 55 seconds of chart time, there was a dramatic change in the PGR tracing pattern in the form on an abrupt and prolonged upward sweep of the recording pen. I had not moved, or touched the plant, so the timing of the PGR pen activity suggested to me that the tracing might have been triggered by the mere thought of the harm I intended to inflict on the plant'.

Backster went on to explore the possibility of such perception in the plant by bringing some live brine shrimp into his office and dropping them one by one into boiling water. Every time he killed a shrimp, the polygraph recording needle attached to the plant jumped violently. To eliminate the possibility of his own emotions producing this reaction, he completely automated the whole experiment so that an electronic randomizer chose odd moments to dump the shrimp into hot water when no human was in the laboratory at all. The plant continued to respond in sympathy to the death of every shrimp and failed to register any change when the machine dropped already dead shrimp into the water.

31 At the time when he made his discovery, Backster was
- A a secret agent with the CIA.
- B an employee of a company manufacturing lie detectors.
- C doing research work on interrogation techniques.
- D teaching policemen.

32 Backster's experiment was designed to find out
- A how the plant would react to ill-treatment.
- B if the polygraph was capable of working with vegetable organisms.
- C if the polygraph would indicate the effect of the plant being watered.
- D whether there were parallels between the electrical resistance of human skin and leaves.

33 Backster's procedure in torturing the plant was suggested to him by his
- A irritation at the plant's failure to respond.
- B knowledge of plant behaviour.
- C previous experience with human subjects.
- D purely sadistic impulses.

34 The plant reacted to Backster's stimulus when he
- A burned one of its leaves.
- B decided to try the 'threat-to-well-being' principle.
- C dipped one of its leaves into a cup of hot coffee.
- D made up his mind to burn the leaf.

35 When the shrimp experiment had been automated, the plant
- A displayed the same reactions as before.
- B failed to respond unless human beings were present.
- C only occasionally responded to a shrimp being killed.
- D responded whenever shrimp were dropped into the water.

Third Passage

A

Civil Service pensions

SIR—You carried a report (May 22) that 'nine out of 10 retired civil servants live on a pension of less than £5,000 a year, and thousands have to "grub along" on £46 a week or less.'

After more than 40 years in industry, as a professional engineer, working at home and abroad for the same company or its successors, my company pension now, five years after retirement, amounts to £2,640 a year or £50.77 per week.

Those in industry must be bewildered by the way civil servants live in a world apart, where their employer does not pay corporation and other taxes; a world where all pensions must be equal, but those of civil servants must, as of right, be more equal than others.

It is not as though they were grateful!

A. L. BODE
C. ENG. F.I.E.E.
Swinford, Leics

B

Service to industry

SIR—I was interested to read Mr Gerald Bartlett's report on low civil servants' pensions.

I worked for a famous British electrical company for 45 years and have just retired. My salary on leaving was over £9,000.

My pension is £35 a week and is not index-linked. By my standards the civil servants do very well.

J. SMITH
Brighton, Sussex

C

Double booked

SIR—One solution to the problem experienced by Dr J E White (May 18) would be to educate hospital clerical staff to refrain from the practice of booking all out-patients for their appointments at precisely the same time.

I am sure readers have experienced having to wait in draughty, crowded hospital corridors, because the waiting rooms are also full, for anything up to three hours for out-patient appointments. It is no wonder that there is reluctance to attend future appointments.

E. MULLINS
Thorpe Audlin, W. Yorks.

D

Double booked

SIR—Mr E Mullins really should be more aware of his facts before castigating hospital clerical staff for 'booking all out-patient appointments at precisely the same time.'

In the majority of cases it is not the clerical staff who determine the booking times but the consultant or registrar and occasionally the nursing staff.

Most medical records officers have frequent reviews of the waiting time for patients and if this is excessive try to get the appointment times changed. Sometimes the consultant agrees, sometimes not.

Unfortunately patients themselves do not always help when they arrive late for appointments and occasionally not at all.

Most clerical staff are extremely conscientious and feel grieved when patients have to wait for long periods.

J. V. MITCHELL
Okehampton, Devon

36 In Mr Bode's letter, his tone is
A angry.
B astonished.
C amused.
D ironic.

37 Mr Bode and Mr Smith
A have retired recently.
B previously worked in industry.
C have pensions below the Civil Service minimum.
D are referring to different reports.

38 In their attitude towards civil service pensions, they
A agree in thinking those pensions are excessive.
B agree that civil servants are ungrateful.
C agree that civil servants have little cause for complaint.
D do not agree over the fundamental issue involved.

39 From Mr Mullins' letter, we can deduce that the problem Dr White originally raised was that
A hospital clerical staff are uneducated.
B hospital clerical staff make too many appointments for the same time.
C patients do not always keep appointments.
D patients are often kept waiting too long.

40 Mr Mitchell defends hospital clerical staff on the grounds that they
A do not book more than one patient at the same time.
B are not responsible for deciding the times of appointments.
C always change appointment times in cases of hardship.
D cannot be blamed if patients do not turn up on time.

Answers

Chapter 6: Introductory exercise

1 Marlon Brando
2 Dustin Hoffman
3 Jacques Tati
4 Orson Welles
5 Humphrey Bogart
6 Warren Beatty and Faye Dunaway
7 Paul Newman and Robert Redford
8 Gene Kelly
9 Lisa Minnelli
10 Anthony Perkins, Janet Leigh
11 Anthony Quinn
12 Humphrey Bogart and Ingrid Bergman
13 Bing Crosby and Bob Hope
14 Alec Guinness
15 Gene Hackman
16 a train, Buster Keaton
17 a boat, Humphrey Bogart
18 a sledge, Orson Welles in *Citizen Kane*
19 a shark, Roy Scheider in *Jaws*
20 King Kong

Chapter 10: Introductory exercise

1903 The first flight of the Wright brothers
1911 Roald Amundsen reaches the South Pole
1917 The Russian Revolution
1929 The Wall Street Crash
1933 Hitler takes power in Germany
1945 The end of the Second World War
1953 Mount Everest climbed for the first time
1963 The assassination of President Kennedy
1969 The first landing on the Moon
1974 Nixon resigns because of Watergate

Chapter 13: Introductory exercise

1 Cars: 5, 9, 10, 12, 14
Computers: 2, 3, 8, 13, 15
Insurance policies: 1, 4, 6, 7, 11

Chapter 14: Introductory exercise

the North Pole: Peary in 1909
the South Pole: Amundsen in 1911
the source of the Nile: Speke in 1858
the top of Mount Everest: Hillary and Tenzing in 1953
the Moon: Armstrong and Aldrin in 1969

Index

The index includes new vocabulary which has occurred in **Words often confused** and **Vocabulary expansion** exercises.